ANTI-PORN

About the Author

Julia Long holds a PhD on feminist anti-pornography activism from London South Bank University. She has a professional background in gender equality policy, education and HIV prevention and support, and she currently works for an organisation combating male violence against women. Julia is a longstanding radical feminist activist and has been an active member of the London Feminist Network and OBJECT.

ANTI-PORN

THE RESURGENCE OF ANTI-PORNOGRAPHY FEMINISM

Julia Long

ZED BOOKS
London

Anti-Porn: The Resurgence of Anti-Pornography Feminism
was first published in 2012 by Zed Books Ltd, 7 Cynthia Street, London N1 9JF, UK

www.zedbooks.co.uk

Designed and set by Kate Kirkwood
Index by John Barker
Cover designed by Stuart Tolley

A catalogue record for this book is available from the British Library
Library of Congress Cataloging in Publication Data available

ISBN 978-1-78032-026-7 hb
ISBN 978-1-78032-025-0 pb

*Dedicated with love
to the memory of my mother, Stella Maria Long,
and my sister, Catherine Maria Long*

CONTENTS

ACKNOWLEDGEMENTS

I would like to thank all at Zed Books for their help and support in ensuring that this book made it through to completion. My very grateful thanks to Tamsine O'Riordan, senior commissioning editor, for her constructive feedback, gentle encouragement, persistence and endless patience. Thanks also to Jakob Horstmann for helpful comments in the early stages of writing. I thank Dr Shaminder Takhar and Professor Rosalind Edwards at London South Bank University, who supervised the doctoral research that has informed a substantial part of this book.

I thank my family for their love and support, especially my father John Long and sister Loretta Pearce. Special thanks to my niece Natasha Pearce for an informative conversation about music videos, and to Francesca and Dominic. My love and thanks always to Rosh and Kevin Latham, and Silvana and Saverio Di Donna: *vi tengo sempre nel mio cuore e vi ringrazio per tutto.* I thank Julie Ashton, Louise Cannon, Penny French and Jude Lobley for the innumerable joys and pleasures of their friendship over many years, and for unfailingly providing a warm and sustaining Yorkshire welcome whenever I have needed it.

I thank all the activists I interviewed as part of my doctoral research. It is a privilege to work with my sister-activists in the London Feminist Network and OBJECT, and in particular

ACKNOWLEDGEMENTS

I thank Katie Toms, Laurie Oliva, Anna van Heeswijk and Sareyeh Hadian for their love and friendship throughout the writing of this book. My thanks to Finn Mackay for her loyalty, steadfastness, intellectual generosity and generally futile efforts to keep me on task. Heartfelt thanks and gratitude to Sara McHaffie, who miraculously swooped in at the final stages of writing, offering invaluable help with compiling the bibliography, sharing ideas and commenting on draft chapters. At a time when I was particularly isolated and struggling, Sara's friendship provided much-needed light and laughter, and I am blessed to count her as a friend.

I thank the many radical feminists from whose work I have benefited immeasurably over many years. I had the good fortune to be taught by a radical feminist in the days when it was not quite the rarity that it is now; I was even more fortunate that that teacher was Susanne Kappeler. I am especially grateful to Gail Dines for her generosity and kindness, and for her vision in building an international network of activists. I thank Lierre Keith, Liane Timmerman, Angela Gbemisola Was Soudjoukjian, Lisa-Marie Taylor, Naomi Stevens and Silvia Murray Wakefield for showing me the meaning of the word 'solidarity'. And I thank the wonderful online community of radical feminist bloggers, whose work is a revelation.

Finally, as a lesbian feminist, I wish to acknowledge the huge debt of gratitude I and many others owe to Sheila Jeffreys. It is no exaggeration to say that her courageous and visionary work has been, for many of us, life-changing.

In these bleak times, to feel part of a radical feminist movement is the most incredible joy and source of sustenance. To all those who have brought me to this place, my debts and thanks are boundless.

To find blasphemy offensive,
you would have to believe in God.
To find pornography offensive,
you would have to believe in women.
SUSANNE KAPPELER, *The Pornography
of Representation*

If you're lying in a ditch with a truck on your ankle,
you don't send somebody to the library to find out
how much the truck weighs. You get the truck *off*.
FLORYNCE KENNEDY

INTRODUCTION

On a warm summer evening in June 2010, a group of around 30 pyjama-clad OBJECT activists gather outside a Tesco's store in central London. The pyjamas were a reference to a notice that the supermarket chain had sent out, requesting customers not to wear pyjamas when visiting the store, as some customers found them offensive. Finding a hook via which to convey their message of the harms of pornography – 'porn is more offensive than pyjamas' – the activists had donned nightwear and congregated for a protest against the sale of lads' mags at eye-level in the store. On entering the store, a group of activists set about covering individual lads' mags with brown paper bags on which had been written feminist messages, such as 'This is hate speech' and 'This promotes rape culture'. As the display of magazines was quickly transformed into a wall of DIY feminist critique, other activists milled around the store, depositing small cards subverting Tesco marketing slogans between the cereal packets and cans of beans: 'Tesco's (de)values women'; 'Get rid of lads' mags – every little helps'. At the signal of a whistle, all 30 activists formed a human chain, whipped out some tambourines, and proceeded to dance a conga in and out of the store aisles, chanting 'Let's get rid of lads' mags!' When the activists finally left, after much exuberant chanting and dancing around the store, they continued to protest outside the

1

store for a further two hours, chanting, singing, leafletting and talking to passers-by.[1]

What is motivating a new generation of feminists to get involved in anti-porn campaigns? A glance around mainstream culture in my own city tells a story of the banality of women's sexual objectification in Western culture in the twenty-first century. Over the past two decades, the mainstreaming of pornography and the expansion of the global sex industry have become increasingly apparent in the UK. Lap-dancing clubs doubled in number between 2004 and 2008, from an estimated 150 to 310 (OBJECT, 2008). In 2007, a Playboy store opened in London's Oxford Street, selling Playboy-branded clothing and accessories; Playboy-branded products were already widely available in high street stores such as Superdrug and Argos. A new Playboy Club, complete with women dressed in 'bunny' outfits, opened in London in 2011, some thirty years after the original one closed. Pole-dancing classes are promoted as a fitness and leisure activity for women and girls across the UK, and burlesque striptease has undergone a revival, with clubs and performances an increasingly common feature of nightlife leisure. Mainstream films released in 2008 include titles such as *Zac and Miri make a Porno* and *Donkey Punch*.[2] 'Lads' mags',[3] displayed at eye level, are widely available in supermarkets, newsagents and garages; a study published in 2011 found that the general public cannot differentiate between the language used in such magazines to talk about women and that used by convicted rapists (Horvath *et al.*, 2011). A music video titled 'Monster' by Kanye West features semi-naked women hanging from chains; another by Nicki Minaj, titled 'Stupid Hoe', refers to women as 'bitches', 'stupid hoes' and 'nappy headed hoes', and features images of the singer sexualised to resemble a wild animal in a cage. The number of labiaplasties carried out under the British National Health Service almost tripled between 2006 and 2008 (Davis, 2011).

In January 2012, news broke that around 40,000 women in the UK who had undergone breast enlargement surgery were fitted with implants filled with industrial-grade silicon. In a bar in the House of Commons, a beer branded 'Top Totty', complete with pump clip featuring a cartoon image of a semi-naked woman wearing bunny ears, is served to the nation's politicians and their guests. When a female Labour MP protested, she was met with general derision for being 'humourless' and 'puritanical' (Ross, 2012). Every morning, the newspaper with the largest circulation in the UK continues to serve up a Page 3 picture of a topless woman for its 7 million readers, as it has done for the past forty years.

Alongside its influence on mainstream culture, the pornography industry itself has expanded to unprecedented levels. In 2006, it was estimated to be worth around $96 billion globally, with over 13,000 films released each year, 420 million internet porn pages and 68 million search engine requests for porn daily (Dines, 2010: 47). In addition to its ubiquity, evidence suggests that the content of pornography is also changing. Content analysis of pornographic films suggests that 'physical and verbal aggression are the norm rather than the exception' and that 94 per cent of all acts of aggression were directed towards women (Bridges, 2010: 46). Increasingly, debates take place within media and policy arenas around the effects of pornography on young people, and the 'sexualisation' of girls in particular.

In the light of what is now widely acknowledged as the increasingly normalised presence of the sex industry within mainstream society, what evidence is there of feminist dissent? Are women embracing the invitation to present themselves as sexualised objects, in the name of liberation and empowerment? It would appear that the mainstreaming of pornography has taken place in the context of a relative silence from the feminist movement: certainly, since the mid-1990s there has been little evidence of the protests and actions carried out over the prior decade in the USA and UK by groups such as Women Against Pornography (WAP), Women Against Violence Against Women (WAVAW), 'Angry Women' and the Campaign Against Pornography (CAP). 'Third wave' feminist writing of the 1990s, such as *The Bust Guide to the New World Order* (Karp and Stoller, 1999), took a liberal stance towards pornography and the sex industry, viewing earlier anti-pornography campaigns as prudish and puritanical, and framing women's relationship to pornography in the neoliberal language of choice, agency and empowerment. Third wave feminism had little to offer women who had been exploited and abused in pornography or who felt unhappy with the increasing presence of pornography in the culture and the effects that it was having on their lives. The powerful critiques of pornography that had informed second wave campaigns were off the menu as Women's Studies gave way to Gender Studies. Anti-porn feminists Catharine MacKinnon and Andrea Dworkin were held up as spectres of a censorious and dreary past, accused of pursuing 'an unappealing politics of exclusion' through 'depriv[ing] women who produce or consume pornography of the right to their sexuality' (Waters, 2007: 255). Instead, women were exhorted to explore pornography in pursuit of their own sexual pleasure, with Debbie Stoller enthusiastically leading by example, declaring that she would leave 'no sexual avenue unexplored' in her 'quest for sexual satisfaction' (quoted in Waters, 2007: 258). For those who did not like what they found in the course of such an exploration, the answer was to subvert, reappropriate, re-signify or create more images: Judith Butler, luminary of the new Gender Studies programmes, advocated the 'production of a chaotic multiplicity of representations' (Butler, 2000: 504), advice which has been eagerly taken up by producers of 'feminist' porn to no noticeable effect in terms of counteracting the misogynist content of mainstream pornography. The very ubiquity of pornography was offered as evidence both of its legitimacy and of the redundancy of anti-porn feminist arguments (Waters, 2007: 259; Williams, 2004: 1). With a feminist agenda of sexual politics usurped by an agenda of sexual pleasure (Jeffreys, 1996), the porn industry continued to expand unabated.

However, the first decade of the twenty-first century saw the first murmurings of dissent, growing to what has become a new wave of feminist anti-porn activism. While, importantly, some anti-porn feminist writing had continued in the 1990s (see for example Dines *et al.*, 1998; Russell, 1998), the new decade saw a proliferation of such texts, produced from diverse locations and incorporating a new generation of voices alongside those of longstanding anti-porn feminist academics (Stark and Whisnant, 2004; Levy, 2005; Jensen, 2007; Jeffreys, 2009; Boyle, 2010; Dines, 2010; Tankard Reist and Bray, 2011; Tyler, 2011a). In the USA, the campaign group Stop Porn Culture!, set up in 2007 by Gail Dines and colleagues, produces anti-porn slideshows and runs training sessions and conferences; in Australia, grassroots campaigns movement Collective Shout 'mobilis[es] and equip[s] individuals and groups to target corporations, advertisers, marketers and media which objectify women and sexualise girls to sell products and services';[4] in Norway, The Feminist Group Ottar holds monthly protests outside strip clubs in Bergen and Oslo. In Iceland in 2010, strip clubs were made illegal by a government 43 per cent of whose members are women, and which is led by the world's first openly lesbian head of state. In the UK, stickers saying 'Hate Sexism' and 'Misogyny: Hard to Spell, Easy to Practice' have started appearing on lads' mag displays; anti-porn blogs and groups have emerged; women have begun taking to the streets to protest new Playboy stores and clubs; and national campaigns have been established, calling for stricter licensing laws around lap-dancing clubs and restrictions on the sales of lads' mags. Feminists once again are mobilising around an anti-porn agenda. This book sets out to investigate this new wave of activism and to examine the perspectives on pornography that inform it.

I shall try to understand the significance and salience of anti-porn feminism in the twenty-first century, in the context of the pornification of Western culture. The emergence of the new activism is worth investigating for a number of reasons. First, in debates around the concept of 'postfeminism' there is a recognition of the common (mis)perception that gender equality has been achieved, and a concern that many women, especially young women, do not identify with the term 'feminist' (Whelehan, 2000; Gill, 2007b; Tasker and Negra, 2007; McRobbie, 2009; Woodward and Woodward, 2009). The emergence of anti-porn feminist groups seems to offer important new information with regard to these questions. Second, it is apparent that until recently there has been a marginalisation of feminist voices resisting pornography, with discourses of individual 'empowerment' and 'pleasure' becoming dominant in relation to female participation in and consumption of pornography and the sex industry. The emergence of feminist anti-porn groups seems to indicate a marked departure from these dominant discourses, and I shall demonstrate that issues of violence against women, inequality and sexual exploitation are once again taking centre stage in feminist analyses of pornography.

The book draws on my doctoral research, which involved carrying out ethnographies with two UK-based anti-porn feminist groups, OBJECT and Anti-Porn London, alongside interviews with twenty-four anti-porn feminist activists from across the UK. In the course of writing the book, I carried out a number of additional interviews, in order to capture some of the developments I was witnessing in the activist scene in

London.[5] The dynamic and sometimes transient nature of grassroots activism means that any study can only hope to offer a snapshot of patterns, issues and trends as they are configured in a particular moment, and the remarkable resurgence of grassroots feminism in the UK in the first decade of the twenty-first century formed a vibrant and constantly changing context for my research. Since the time of my original fieldwork (2007–10), one of my case study groups, Anti-Porn London, is no longer active in campaigning and mainly exists as an online resource; the other, OBJECT, has gone on to develop new projects. New groups have emerged, others have split; groups with different membership bases and modes of organising come together to work on specific issues or to coordinate protests, and new women activists and supporters are constantly seeking out and discovering feminist groups.

Whilst solidarity, shared convictions and support are much in evidence, tensions, conflicting ideologies and disputed agendas make the broader grassroots movement a place of contention as groups disagree on issues of organisation, approach and the very meaning of the term 'feminism'. Importantly, the beginnings of an international feminist anti-porn network is emerging, as activists from different countries create opportunities to meet, strategise and organise, facilitated and supported in no small part by the work of Gail Dines and the Boston-based Stop Porn Culture! and by the Australian feminist publisher Spinifex Press, whose collection *Big Porn Inc.* (Tankard Reist and Bray, 2011) brought together writings by academics and activists from a range of locations.

Given the main location of my research, the major focus of this book is UK-based activism. In the earlier chapters, however, my discussion of second wave anti-porn activism and the debates on pornography that dominated 1980s feminism includes reference to the United States. From my discussions with anti-porn feminists in other countries, it would appear that many of the issues that my case study groups are dealing with, and the strategic approaches they adopt, are common to anti-porn struggles in a range of contexts. I hope that this book will form part of a wider conversation on anti-porn feminism to which feminists in a range of locations will add their stories, experiences and understandings.

As I shall explain in Chapter 2, references to pornography in this book generally refer to mainstream pornography that is targeted at and viewed by heterosexual men. Since the focus of the book is anti-porn feminism, I refer specifically to the 'hegemonic' pornography (Chancer, 1998: 77) or 'everyday' pornography (Caputi, 2003; Boyle, 2010) which dominates the market and is the concern of the groups that I studied. Although I make reference to 'feminist' porn, the book does not address porn aimed at gay male consumers or women. The book also covers an anti-lap dancing campaign, since the activism I was researching focused on the issue of sexual objectification, and therefore saw clear links between lap dancing, pornography and other aspects of the sex industry. Both groups and individual activists saw pornography and lap dancing – 'dancing pornography' ('Stella', in Tankard Reist and Bray, 2011) – as part of the same wider issue of the sexual objectification of women and commodification of women's bodies.

I conducted my research and write this book as a radical lesbian feminist who is engaged in anti-porn feminist activism, alongside other feminist campaigns and struggles. I conducted my ethnographies as a participant observer with both Anti-Porn London and OBJECT, located very much as an 'insider' on the insider–outsider spectrum (Long, 2011). Those seeking a dispassionate, neutral account of the various feminist perspectives on pornography will be disappointed; then again, it is unlikely that the cover of this book would have attracted such a reader. Such readers, should they exist, would of course be disappointed with any account of the topic, including that provided by a supposedly 'neutral' researcher, since it is doubtful whether such an account is possible. Feminist challenges over many decades to positivist notions of objectivity and impartiality have established the understanding that all knowledge production is historically and socially contingent, situated within sets of power relationships, particularly that of its relationship to the subject(s) of its research, and is inevitably informed by underlying values, assumptions and investments. Like any researcher, I write from a specific, situated position, in a particular relationship to my research topic and research participants, influenced by numerous factors, including personal politics, experience, 'race', ethnicity, age, class and sexuality. Throughout my doctoral studies, I aimed to ensure self-reflexivity in my research through developing 'reflective practice' (Naples, 2003), an approach which involves finding practical ways to incorporate questions of positionality at all stages of the research process (Long, 2011).

The book examines key moments in the trajectory of second wave anti-porn feminism as well as providing an in-depth account of two British groups active in the re-emergent movement. In Chapter 1, I provide a context for the resurgence of anti-porn feminism through a brief account of the development of anti-porn feminism in relation to the wider women's liberation movement in the USA and the UK, charting its emergence through the feminist politicisation of male violence against women, and following its trajectory through the era of backlash and conservatism of the 1980s, to its decline – in terms of prominence and visibility at least – in the 1990s. In Chapter 2, I examine definitions of pornography and the ideological perspectives that underlie feminist debates on pornography. The chapter offers an account of anti-porn perspectives on the main issues of contention within the debates, including questions of male violence against women, free speech, censorship, choice and consent. Chapter 3 engages with the mainstreaming of pornography, considering what is meant by the terms 'sexualisation' and 'pornification' and examining the implications of processes of pornification for women's freedom and equality. Chapter 4 maps the re-emergence of anti-porn feminism in the wider context of a resurgence of grassroots feminist activism in twenty-first-century Britain, examining the ways in which new groups organise themselves and how they develop and execute their campaigns. Focusing on two groups, Anti-Porn London and OBJECT, I examine their key campaign messages and provide an in-depth analysis of their modes of organising, tactical repertoires, impact and significance in relation to the current context and in the light of earlier, second wave campaigns. The book concludes by reflecting on current feminist anti-porn approaches and offering thoughts on the directions that future activism needs to take.

In her address to the conference on 'Pornography and Pop Culture: Re-framing Theory, Re-thinking Activism', held in Boston in 2007, Rebecca Whisnant offers some thoughts on the kind of feminism necessary to meet the challenges of the globalised pornography industry and the pornification of culture. Whisnant's compelling analysis exposes the inadequacy of liberal approaches in dealing with these challenges, and she advocates for a radical feminist critique that can theorise the structures of inequality on which pornography depends, and which it perpetuates and maintains. Whisnant reflects on what kind of feminist strategies might be necessary to provide activists with a robust roadmap to be effective in challenging, and ultimately dismantling, both the pornography industry and the male demand for pornography.

In her presentation, Whisnant puts forward a number of proposals as to what an effective feminism might look like and what it might need to do in order to confront the realities of pornography and pornification. First, she suggests that the movement simply needs more people articulating a feminist critique in the public realm. Such a critique must involve a clear radical feminist analysis that offers an alternative to both pro-porn and religious conservative positions. Second, she argues that this critique of porn culture must be connected to a broader critique of the commodification of everyday life and must champion a non-marketised conception of freedom. Finally, anti-porn feminists must strive to imagine, create and support visions of alternative realities – to encourage people to think 'deeply and creatively' about what sexual freedom is; to 'richly imagine' a world without sexual violence, and to 'use the power of our desire' to help bring this world into being (Whisnant, 2007). With these proposals in mind, I invite you to engage with the struggles, visions and creativity of anti-porn feminists over four decades and to join me in reflecting on what is currently happening and what might need to happen next.

Notes

1 A video of the protest is available at <http://www.youtube.com/watch?v=iA7aAi zybG8> (accessed 1 May 2012).

2 The title *Donkey Punch* refers to a form of life-threatening sexual assault originating in violent pornography.

3 'Lads' mags' are magazines aimed at men which mainly feature images of semi-naked women along with articles about sport, cars and other 'men's lifestyle' topics.

4 <http://collectiveshout.org/about/> (accessed 1 May 2012).

5 All interviewees have been given pseudonyms, except in some cases where an individual activist is particularly associated with a specific group, in which case the full name of the activist has been given, with her permission.

CHAPTER 1
Anti-Porn Feminism and
the Women's Liberation Movement

The history of anti-pornography feminism is a brave, turbulent and deeply instructive one. Emerging in the late 1970s, in the context of the anger and energy of the women's liberation movement (WLM), anti-porn perspectives were engendered through processes of consciousness raising and through the development of important theoretical insights into the relationship between cultural practices, representations and women's subordination. Whilst not initially a central concern within second wave feminism, pornography was increasingly foregrounded by the late 1970s. During the 1980s, the fierce and passionate battles of anti-porn feminists were contested from within the movement itself, in what were regrettably to become known as the 'feminist sex wars'.[1]

This chapter will trace the trajectory of anti-porn politics and activism within second wave feminism,[2] looking at how they emerged, why they were contested, and how the voices of anti-porn feminists were increasingly silenced from the early 1990s. Focusing on the US and UK movements, where anti-porn feminism was particularly prominent, the chapter does not aim to provide a comprehensive historical account;[3] rather, its purpose is to offer a context and background from which to examine the resurgence of anti-porn feminism that is the main subject of this book.

The birth of the women's liberation movement

In order to make sense of the emergence of anti-porn feminism, it is necessary to understand something of the beginnings of second wave feminism, which in the USA was shaped by women coming from different locations and movements, including middle-class, educated women and women active within the civil rights and radical/leftist, anti-Vietnam war movements. In the early years of the second wave, liberal or reformist feminism constituted the dominant strand of the movement in the USA; the publication of liberal feminist Betty Friedan's *The Feminine Mystique* (1963) is frequently identified with the 'birth' of US second wave feminism. Friedan's highly influential analysis of the 'problem with no name' – the condition of educated, middle-class white American women confined to domestic roles as housewives and mothers – provided an empirical and theoretical basis for the promotion of a liberal feminist agenda, which she pursued through founding, along with others, the National Organisation of Women (NOW) in 1966. From its origins as a response to the lack of political will in the USA to introduce and implement effective laws against sex discrimination in the workplace, NOW championed a reformist approach, lobbying for legislative change and equality of opportunity in areas such as education and employment. Its stated purpose was to 'take action to bring women into full participation in the mainstream of American society now, exercising all the privileges and responsibilities thereof in truly equal partnership with men' (Friedan, 1966).

However, even from these early days, hints of what was to develop into anti-porn feminism are discernible. Although NOW focused on legislative change, it nonetheless recognised the significance and impact of the kinds of media images that were to become a focus for the more radical activism that was to follow:

IN THE INTERESTS OF THE HUMAN DIGNITY OF WOMEN, we will protest, and endeavor to change, *the false image of women now prevalent in the mass media*, and in the texts, ceremonies, laws, and practices of our major social institutions. *Such images perpetuate contempt for women* by society and by women for themselves. (NOW Statement of Purpose, Friedan, 1966; my emphasis)

Alongside NOW, other more identifiably radical feminist groups emerged during the 1960s, growing out of the frustration experienced by women active in the civil rights, new left and anti-Vietnam war movements. Women involved in such movements had found themselves sidelined, expected to take on subordinate roles and treated as sex objects – as epitomised by the notorious reputed comment from Stokely Carmichael, the leader of the Student Non-Violent Coordinating Committee, that 'The only position for women in the SNCC is prone' (King, 1987). Initially, such experiences led women to take action within the movements in which they were involved (Byrne, 1996; Jones and Brown, 1968; Evans, 2007), but soon they began leaving to create their own movement, along with those who wanted to move beyond the liberal feminist agenda of NOW in pursuit of more radical goals. Florynce Kennedy is an important figure in these struggles, bringing the politics of the black power and civil rights movements to bear on a predominantly white feminist agenda. Having joined the New York chapter of NOW in 1967, alongside other African-American feminists (such as Shirley Chisholm and Pauli Murray) and white feminists (such as Kate Millett), she was to leave the following year in view of what she found to be a regressive and racist politics on the part of the national leadership of NOW, which marginalised radical feminism and failed to support black liberation and anti-war movements (Randolph, 2011).

In the UK, the WLM emerged predominantly from radical and

new left politics (Gelb, 1986; Weir and Wilson, 1984). Socialism and Marxism were particularly influential in the early days of UK feminism (Gelb, 1986: 108), with the 1966 publication of Juliet Mitchell's socialist feminist analysis of women's position under capitalism, *Women: the Longest Revolution*, providing a landmark for the new movement. Early second wave British feminism mobilised around class more than race (Bouchier, 1983: 56); key moments included the Hull fishermen's wives' protest, the strike held by the Ford motor company machinists at Dagenham (Gelb, 1986: 107; Rowbotham, 1972), and efforts to form alliances with and shape trade unions (Weir and Wilson, 1984).

Particularly significant in relation to the development of anti-porn feminism was the impact of the sexual revolution. The 1960s saw an era of decensorship in both the UK and the USA, along with the relaxation of attitudes and laws around divorce, the emergence of the contraceptive pill and changing attitudes to family, sexuality and reproduction. Important legislative changes in the UK included the partial decriminalisation of homosexuality in 1967 and the legalisation of abortion[4] in the same year. However, despite the potential and real benefits for women's liberation of some of these developments, the sexual revolution was characterised by a profoundly male supremacist counter-culture which lionised misogynist writers, such as Norman Mailer and William Burroughs, and created innumerable new cultural arenas for the aggressive sexual objectification and exchange of women in the form of magazines such as *Oz* and 'liberated' practices such as swinging (Jeffreys, 1990). In this way, the sexual revolution and its masculinist heroes framed male sexual use of women as revolutionary, opening up the gateway for the expansion of pornography in the 1970s (Jeffreys, 1990; Dines, 2010; Bronstein 2011).

'We are a class': consciousness raising and women on the march

Consciousness raising (CR) played a critical role in the emergence of anti-porn feminism. CR groups were the hallmark of the second wave (Rowbotham, 1989; Arnold, 2000; Gornick, 2000); they were a key means of women's politicisation through 'the feminist practice of examining one's personal experience in the light of sexism' (Gornick, 2000: 288). Sharing and discussing experiences broke women's sense of isolation and revealed the commonalities of women's condition under patriarchy. One important result of this process was the bringing to light of the prevalence of male violence and child sexual abuse within the private context of the family and personal relationships. As we shall see, this painful process of sharing was the first crucial step leading to women's mobilisation around male violence. Consciousness raising transformed the sharing of personal experience into political analysis and, in turn, to action, highlighting the collective nature of the problem of women's oppression and generating the vital understanding that such a problem could only be addressed through collective struggle:

> We are a class, we are oppressed as a class, and we each respond within the limits allowed us as members of that oppressed class. Purposely divided from each other, each of us is ruled by one or more men for the benefit of all men. There is no personal escape, no personal salvation, no personal solution. (Jones and Brown, 1968)

By the late 1960s, hundreds of women's liberation groups had emerged in the USA, including the Furies in Washington DC; the Redstockings and the New York Radical Women in New York; Bread and Roses and Female Liberation in Boston; and the Chicago Women's Liberation Union. A similar proliferation of groups followed in the UK, and the late 1960s and early 1970s were to prove an extraordinarily creative and fertile time for the

WLM, with women's liberation groups generating an explosion of feminist actions, ideas and theory.

Whilst pornography had yet to become prominent as an issue, women's politicisation around objectification was evident from the late 1960s, in the form of high-profile beauty pageant protests. Protesters outside the 1968 Miss America beauty pageant provided a 'freedom trash can', into which women threw symbols of their oppression, such as high-heeled shoes, eyelash curlers and girdles. At the 1970 Miss World contest in London, feminists hurled smoke bombs, stink bombs and flour bombs, causing chaos and bringing proceedings to a temporary halt. The televised action was witnessed by millions, and is widely credited with mobilising a generation of women to join the women's liberation movement in Britain. Of course, such protests took place alongside other mass actions on other issues such as abortion, equal pay and the need for equality legislation. In the USA, for example, the 'Women's Strike for Equality' – with its slogan, 'Don't Iron While the Strike is Hot!' – was organised by NOW in August 1970, mobilising thousands of women across the country to stage various creative actions, including a march of fifty thousand down New York's Fifth Avenue (*Time*, 1970). Women were also beginning to make important inroads into bastions of male power, with Shirley Chisholm becoming the first black woman elected to Congress in 1968. In 1971 Florynce Kennedy founded the Feminist Party, from which platform Chisholm was launched as a presidential candidate the following year, becoming the first woman to run for the Democratic presidential nomination.

Nourishing this ferment of activism was the development of radical feminist ideas and theory. Alongside a proliferation of women's liberation pamphlets, magazines and newsletters, a rich literature was emerging in the form of publications such as *The Myth of the Vaginal Orgasm* (Koedt, 1968); 'The personal is political' (Hanisch, [1969] 2006); *The Dialectic of Sex* (Firestone, 1970); *The Female Eunuch* (Greer, [1970] 1993); *Sisterhood is Powerful* (Morgan, 1970); and *Sexual Politics* (Millett, 1970). Covering a broad terrain of language, literature, culture, religion, sexuality, personal relationships, science and politics, these foundational texts articulated and theorised the nature of women's oppression under patriarchy, challenging the assumed naturalness and inevitability of women's subordinate position. In turn, alongside these theoretical works, feminist creativity flowered in different realms, as critical understandings were complemented by the creation of a women's culture in the form of fiction, street theatre, art, music, publishing companies, cafes, resource centres and bookshops.

During the 1970s, male violence became a central focus of second wave feminism. In response to new knowledge about the prevalence of male violence, feminists set up support services for victims such as refuges and rape crisis centres, and lobbied for changes in police and criminal justice approaches to domestic violence and rape. The focus on male violence was emblematised by collective demonstrations and the assertion of women's right to enjoy public space freely and safely. 'Take Back the Night' and 'Reclaim the Night' marches, rallies and vigils were organised by feminists in numerous countries and cities. It was from this focus on male violence that pornography became a topic of feminist concern.

The development of anti-porn feminism in the USA

Radical feminist literature emerging in the USA in the 1970s developed analyses locating pornography and the sex industry within a context of patriarchal male violence against women. As early as 1974, Andrea Dworkin analysed the role of pornography, alongside other influences like myths and fairy tales, as instrumental in the social construction of women's oppression:

> Pornography, like fairy tale, tells us who we are. It is the structure of male and female mind, the content of our shared erotic identity, the map of each inch and mile of our oppression and despair.... Here we are compelled to ask the real questions: why are we defined in these ways, and how can we bear it? (Dworkin, 1974: 54)

Susan Brownmiller's *Against Our Will* argued that pornography is an enabling and instrumental element of rape culture, a culture wherein sexual violence, specifically rape and the threat of rape, enables men to control women, and where rape is consequently tolerated and normalised. For Brownmiller pornography constitutes 'the undiluted essence of anti-female propaganda' and 'the case against pornography and the case against toleration of prostitution are central to the fight against rape' (Brownmiller 1975: 394, 390), an argument memorably encapsulated in Robin Morgan's slogan, 'pornography is the theory, rape is the practice' (Morgan, 1974).

In her history of US anti-porn feminism, Carolyn Bronstein identifies three factors that motivated women to identify sexually violent media as a major cause of female oppression: the failure of the sexual revolution to deliver sexual liberation for women; new knowledge about the extent and prevalence of male sexual violence, generated within consciousness-raising groups; and the radical feminist critique of heterosexuality. These three factors 'created a volatile mix of conditions that supported the growth of the anti-porn analysis' (Bronstein 2011: 7). As Bronstein elucidates, initial campaigns in the mid-1970s were directed at media images that conflated violence and sexuality, with a specific focus on pornography coming later, and not universally endorsed by the feminist groups active in this area. Initially, groups embraced a tactical repertoire of consumer actions, public education, performance art, marches, demonstrations and conferences. They aimed to challenge media representations of male violence against women and sexist portrayals of women; to improve media standards; and to reduce violence against women. Media reform activity, such as pickets and boycotts, therefore preceded the legislative interventions that were to follow in the early 1980s.

The three key groups involved in US media and anti-porn campaigns from the mid-1970s onwards were Women Against Violence Against Women (WAVAW) in Los Angeles, Women Against Violence in Pornography and Media (WAVPM) in San Francisco and Women Against Pornography (WAP) in New York. Consumer actions and boycotts run by the groups included the lobbying of Warner Communications by WAVAW Los Angeles, in protest at the glamorisation of sexual violence depicted in an advertising campaign for the Rolling Stones' album *Black and Blue* (Bronstein, 2011). WAVPM led a similar campaign against the cosmetics company Max Factor in relation to the advertising of its *Self-Defense* brand of face cream, and also demonstrated against *Hustler* for its notorious cover illustration of a naked woman being fed through a meat grinder (Bronstein, 2011). The development of specifically anti-porn sentiment and theory was supported by the first national feminist anti-porn conference, 'Feminist Perspectives on Pornography', organised by WAVPM in San Francisco in November 1978, which concluded with a Take Back the Night march through the porn district, attended by about three thousand women. The conference led to the publication of the anti-porn anthology *Take Back the Night: Women on Pornography* (Lederer, [1979] 1980) in the following year (Brownmiller, 1999).

The move to a focus on pornography was advanced by the publication of Andrea Dworkin's foundational polemic *Pornography: Men Possessing Women* ([1979] 1981), a text that was to inspire and inform the next decade of anti-porn activism.

For Dworkin, pornography is not merely a representation of violence against women; the production and existence of pornography in itself constitutes violence against women. It must be understood in the context of, and as instrumental in the exercise and maintenance of, male power:

> The major theme of pornography as a genre is male power, its nature, its magnitude, its use, its meaning.... The valuation of women in pornography is a secondary theme in that the degradation of women exists in order to postulate, exercise, and celebrate male power. (Dworkin, [1979] 1981: 24–5)

Dworkin was based in New York and, of the three groups mentioned, it was the New York-based Women Against Pornography that foregrounded pornography as an issue, moving away from the broader 'media representations' agenda of WAVAW and WAVPM (Bronstein, 2011). WAP's activist repertoire included developing and leading guided public tours of the adult entertainment district of Times Square, enabling women outside the industry to witness first hand the images and practices of the sex industry. In 1980, WAP initiated a national boycott of the film *Deep Throat*, following Linda Lovelace's revelations of the abuse that she had endured from her husband in the making of the film (Bronstein, 2011). WAP also developed anti-porn slideshows, which they used to educate women about the realities of the porn industry and porn content.

The development of anti-porn feminism in the UK

As I have mentioned, pornography was not a central issue in the early years of the UK WLM (Rowbotham, 1989; Lovenduski and Randall, 1993; Rees, 2007), perhaps unsurprisingly, given the influence of Marxism and the focus on class. Pornography was not addressed in the original four demands produced as a result of the first WLM conference at Ruskin College, 1970:

equal pay for equal work; equal education and job opportunities; free contraception; and free 24-hour community-controlled childcare. At annual WLM conferences up to and including 1978, three more demands were formulated: legal and financial independence for women; an end to discrimination against lesbians and a woman's right to define her sexuality; and freedom for all women from intimidation by the threat or use of male violence – together with an end to the laws, assumptions and institutions that perpetuate male dominance and men's aggression towards women. The last two – particularly the final demand regarding an end to male violence, which passed after much heated debate at the final WLM conference in Birmingham in 1978 (Rees, 2007: 103–4) – have obvious implications for the development of anti-pornography feminism.

Radical and revolutionary feminists within the UK women's movement were instrumental in putting male violence against women emphatically on the WLM agenda, from which two different strands of feminist politics developed. The first was issue-based, developing in response to domestic violence, rape and sexual harassment, focusing on 'the practical work of institution building, resource allocation, and networking as solutions to important problems' (Lovenduski and Randall 1993: 304). The second – that which developed around pornography – was far more contentious, with feminists 'compet[ing] with each other and with other established political actors to determine the nature of the issue' (*ibid.*: 304).

As we shall see in Chapter 2, second wave feminist interventions in the area of pornography were entering an arena where other discourses had prevailed in terms of both legislative approaches and public opinion: discourses categorised by Jesska Rees as 'moral bloc' and 'left liberal' approaches (Rees, 2007: 204–5). The 'moral bloc' approach, exemplified by the fervid contemporary campaigner Mary Whitehouse and her National

Viewers and Listeners Association (NVALA), saw pornography – along with drugs, alcohol, homosexuality and abortion – as a product of the permissive society: a socially malign influence that undermined traditional values. Whitehouse and the NVALA 'campaigned hard to restrict media representations of permissiveness, arguing that such representations on television, in films, and on radio were both signs and causes of moral degeneration' (*ibid.*: 202). A landmark moment for the moral bloc was a high-profile rally held in Trafalgar Square in September 1971 by the Festival of Light evangelical Christian movement, supported by Whitehouse and the NVALA, as well as public figures such as singer Cliff Richard. The stance of the Festival of Light epitomised the moral bloc perspective on pornography, framing it as symptomatic of the permissive 'filth' that was leading to moral degeneracy (*ibid.*: 202–3). This conservative perspective was the dominant anti-porn position of the early 1970s, counterposing the views of left-liberals, who saw pornography as a liberatory and revolutionary force. The battle-lines of pornography were thus drawn up as the 'heroic progressives versus the reactionary prudes' (Jeffreys, 1990: 59), and for left-liberals, Mary Whitehouse represented a figure of ridicule and contempt. As Kappeler notes, 'For the cultured liberal the highest source of embarrassment is the suggestion, or perception, that he might be accused of Mary Whitehouse-ism, and he shares this with the leftist' (Kappeler, 1986: 33).

For left-liberals, pornography represented two fundamental freedoms: freedom of expression and the freedom of the individual within the private realm. The deep-rooted nature of these values is strikingly illustrated by the recommendations of the Williams Committee on Obscenity and Film Censorship, set up in the mid-1970s. The committee, chaired by moral philosopher Professor Bernard Williams, viewed a wide range of pornography, from soft-core to hard-core, as detailed by committee member Polly Toynbee, who recounts a gruesome list of scenes, featuring:

> women engaged in sexual intercourse with pigs and dogs ... castration, cannibalism, flaying, the crushing of breasts in vices, exploding vaginas packed with hand grenades, eyes gouged out, beatings, dismemberings, burnings, multiple rape, and any and every other horror that could ever befall the human body.
> (Toynbee, 1981, cited in Itzin, 1988: 39)

As Catherine Itzin suggests, the substitution of the word 'female' for 'human' would enhance the accuracy of Toynbee's account (Itzin, 1988: 39). It is indicative of the supreme social value accorded to the two freedoms mentioned above, that, after watching such scenes, the committee nonetheless recommended 'the greatest possible freedom from censorship combined with rather stringent restrictions on the open display of material' (Report of the Williams Committee, 1979, cited in Itzin, 1988: 41). The first half of this recommendation clearly represents an eagerness to protect the pornographer's freedom of expression alongside the viewer's freedom of consumption (Kappeler, 1986: 29), consistent with left-liberal values. The second half of the recommendation, focusing on the 'open display' of material, protects the inadvertent viewer, the 'involuntary audience', in a manner entirely consistent with the freedoms mentioned above: as long as nobody is 'forced to consume anything unless they choose to' (*ibid*.: 30), the freedoms of the pornographer and the voluntary consumer remain protected. Questions of the freedom of the women involved in the production of the pornography, and of the implications of such material in relation to women's social and cultural inequality, remain unaddressed.

As the campaigns of the NVALA and the recommendations of the Williams Committee indicate, neither moral bloc nor left-liberal approaches were concerned with issues of inequality or sexual politics. As Rees notes, feminists entering pornography debates had to negotiate these established discourses, as well as formulating their own theories and asserting feminist priorities, concerns and objections (Rees, 2007: 207). Feminists campaigning against pornography were aware that they would be accused of aligning themselves too closely with conservative anti-porn campaigners:

> Right from our inception in the summer of 1977, we encountered hostility and opposition from within the WLM. 'We can't be seen to be against porn, we'll be associated with Mary Whitehouse.' 'Let men have their porn; it's their right; I just don't want to see it or know about it.' These were things we had felt also – but wanted to work through and get beyond. (McNeill, 1985: 18)

The courage of such a stance should not be underestimated, given that many of these women had come to feminism from the left, and were acutely aware of the stigma – the 'highest source of embarrassment' – of being perceived in leftist circles as in any way akin to Whitehouse. They were emphatic, however, that such perceptions should not deter them:

> The fear of being associated with Mary Whitehouse and her ilk just because they attack porn, though we reject and are actively struggling against everything else that they stand for, must not hold us back. (Katyachild et al., 1985: 15)

The feminist anti-porn perspective that was being developed was, as we shall see in Chapter 2, entirely distinct from both moral and liberal perspectives on pornography. In 1977, the first British feminist anti-pornography group – the London Revolutionary Feminist Anti-Pornography Consciousness-Raising Group – was set up (Jeffreys, interview in Rees, 2007: 207). The group's name is cumbersome – unsurprisingly, it became shortened to the 'Porn Group' – but its component elements are important. First, it highlights the role of revolutionary feminists in pioneering anti-porn feminism in the UK. Revolutionary feminism,[5] prominent in the UK from 1977 to 1983, embraced and built on radical feminist understandings of patriarchy, and was forthright in naming men as the problem, rather than capitalism or some other oppressive force. Revolutionary feminists particularly focused on male violence and heterosexuality as means of the patriarchal control of women (Rees, 2007: 1). The group's name also highlights the importance of consciousness raising in developing theory and understandings of the nature of pornography. The group emerged from the ordinary experiences of its members – the witnessing of explicit pornography featuring double-page spreads of women's genitals 'being perused by young boys in corner newsagents' shops' (Jeffreys, 1990: 251). From this starting point, group members set about studying pornography in order to understand its content, meaning and function in respect of patriarchal society. As Sheila Jeffreys explains, the consciousness-raising element was crucial, since '[a]s daughters of the sexual revolution', group members 'had to overcome some powerful conditioning through consciousness-raising sessions before we could articulate our rage' (*ibid.*).

During its first year, the group held weekly consciousness-raising sessions, working on the themes of porn and sexuality, as well as giving talks, running workshops and participating in and initiating a number of actions (McNeill, 1985: 18). The group framed porn within a broader understanding of male violence: they participated on the first London Reclaim the Night march, which went through the sex industry district in Soho, and with a sister organisation, the Rape Action Group, organised the first ever picket of a shop for selling porn (*ibid.*). In February 1978, the group emphatically placed pornography on the agenda at the London Revolutionary Feminist Conference (*ibid.*). Presenting a paper titled 'Pornography', they identified four specific ways in which pornography undermines women's status and power: as a form of social control of women; as a backlash to gains made by women, through the growth in its availability; as 'male-defined sexuality'; and as linked to sexual violence, through its validation of men 'not seeing women as people, whilst it facilitates and justifies rape, violence and physical abuse' (Katyachild *et al.*, 1985: 13–14). These arguments were to inform the anti-porn activism that became a prominent feature of British feminist protest in the 1980s. The paper was a call to arms, asserting the 'revolutionary potential of an attack on porn' and exhorting women to take direct action:

> A main object of action around porn would be to mobilise the anger and hate of all women in the fight against male supremacy. [...] If all women decided that porn should not exist and smashed and destroyed it on news-stands, billboards, in the windows of sex shops ... then at least it would be driven underground. This would be a beginning, since the end of the struggle could only be the destruction of male supremacy itself. (Katyachild *et al.*, 1985: 14–15)

The call was taken up with conviction by a number of feminists, who, at another London Reclaim the Night march later that year, covered pornographic magazines in a Soho shop with stickers and were met with physical violence from the proprietor 'brandishing first a stool and then a hammer to ward the women off' (Rees, 2007: 213). As Rees recounts, 'when the women retaliated, the police stepped in', using truncheons indiscriminately and arresting sixteen of the women, who 'were later charged with offences including obstruction, threatening and insulting behaviour, assault, and actual bodily harm'. A defence campaign was launched for the 'Soho Sixteen', and the subsequent trials were used by the group 'for publicity purposes, staging demonstrations and arguing in court that the police had misled the court in accounts of their own acts of violence'.

As a new decade dawned, British feminist campaigns against pornography became militant, galvanised by the theoretical critique of pornography developed by revolutionary feminists and by US works such as Dworkin's *Pornography: Men Possessing Women*. From 1980, around forty WAVAW groups were established across the country, carrying out days of action, protests and pickets outside sex shops. WAVAW developed a reputation as the more 'extreme' wing of the feminist movement (Engle, 2007) due to its adoption of direct action techniques, although the broad tactical repertoire embraced by groups also included leafletting and lobbying local authorities to refuse licences to sex shops (Rees, 2007: 219–22). The Oxford WAVAW group's conference on 'Pornography Is Violence against Women' attracted four hundred women.

A second group, Angry Women, were the most militant offshoot of women's anti-porn activism at the time. Angry Women, organised as small, autonomous groups in cities such as London and Brighton, broke windows, sprayed graffiti, fly-posted and leafletted in the fight against pornography. They poured cement down the toilets and threw eggs and red paint at the screens of cinemas showing films that glamorised sexual violence, such as Brian de Palma's *Dressed to Kill*. Some glued the locks of sex shops and stole pornographic magazines, burning them and sending the ashes to the press (*ibid.*: 233–4). The most notorious, however, was the Leeds group, who became known as the 'sex shop arsonists', 'the most underground and militant story of the English WLM' (*ibid.*: 224). Angry Women carried out nineteen arson attacks on Leeds sex shops and sex cinemas, with results ranging from minimal damage to shops being completely gutted, though none of the attacks resulted in injury to life. Only one woman was ever charged in relation to the attacks; the charges were subsequently dismissed and no one was ever convicted.

Rees argues that during the events of 1981–2, through the combination of various forms of activism and debate, 'revolutionary feminists claimed, and were ceded, a hegemonic position within feminism regarding anti-pornography politics' (*ibid.*: 227). It was not to go unchallenged for long.

The backlash and the 'sex wars'

The 1980s saw a shift to a far more conservative climate on both sides of the Atlantic, with the Reagan-Thatcher era bringing in a programme of financial deregulation and privatisation of nationalised industries; the escalation of the Cold War; a return to 'family values'; and a serious backlash against the gains of feminism. In the USA, Ronald Reagan removed the Equal Rights Amendment from the Republican agenda even before he was elected; backed a Human Life Amendment that would have banned abortion; and, in 1981, attempted to introduce the Family Protection Act, which, had it passed, would have seriously eroded equal opportunities for girls in schools, enforced the teaching of marriage and motherhood for girls, and banned legal aid for women seeking a divorce. Meanwhile, in the UK, the Thatcher government pursued its 'Victorian values' agenda through legislation such as Section 28 of the Local Government Act 1988. This law banned the 'promotion' of homosexuality by local authorities and the teaching in schools of the acceptability of homosexuality as a 'pretended' family relationship, thus creating a culture of fear that effectively silenced teachers from speaking honestly about lesbian and gay sexualities in sex education classes, and from offering support to lesbian and gay students. A severe programme of public sector spending cuts meant the loss of jobs and vital services for women. In both the US and the UK, social inequalities increased, single mothers were particularly demonised and economically marginalised, and a general climate of homophobia prevailed in the context of the AIDS crisis.

Whilst the conservative backlash was clearly in evidence from the political powers of the day, a legacy of the sexual revolution could also be seen as contributing to the backlash against feminism, as the 1980s witnessed a rapidly increasing circulation of pornography, which was becoming far more readily available through video technology and the expansion of cable television.

It was against this backdrop that 'US feminism fractured along political fault-lines defined by conflicting views of prostitution and pornography and related conceptions of power, agency, and sexuality' (Miriam, 2005: 1). Such conflicting views were not confined to the USA; the 'sex wars' – as such debates became known – were also very much in evidence in both feminist academic debates and activist initiatives in Britain.

The appropriateness of the term 'sex wars' to describe these highly contested debates within feminism in the 1980s is questionable, not only because of its unfortunate sensationalist qualities, but also because, for radical feminists with a critique of pornography as a form of violence against women, the 'wars' did not take place *within* feminism, but rather were an attack *on* feminism (Jeffreys, 1990). The debates were characterised by polarisation between radical feminist and libertarian positions, broadly representing 'anti-pornography' and 'sex-positive' perspectives, although the latter term in particular is problematic, since it implies that being anti-porn equates to being anti-sex, which – unless one is working with an extremely limited and specific definition of sex – is clearly not necessarily the case. A more accurate term would, presumably, be 'pro-pornography'. In any case, neither term fully reflects the complexity of the debates, since some feminists might be critical of porn, but in disagreement regarding what should be done about it. So-called 'sex-positive' perspectives emerged as a reaction to anti-porn feminism, and are typified by a collection (Vance, 1984) resulting from a controversial conference, 'Towards a Politics of Sexuality', held at Barnard College in the USA, which had focused on questions of sexual pleasure and desire from a libertarian perspective, largely evacuated of any structural analysis of women's oppression. The fundamental assumption of 'sex positivity' is the right to sexual pleasure – which is seen as inherently good – and to the exploration and expression of sexual desire, with little concern for any questioning or critique of these desires. Sex positivity thus diverged from established practices of consciousness raising, which had sought not to take personal experience at face value, but to scrutinise it in the light of understandings of patriarchy.

The Barnard conference was picketed by anti-pornography feminists for giving a platform to proponents of sado-masochism, a practice which they understandably perceived as antithetical to feminist politics. In turn, feminists associated with the 'sex-positive' perspective were critical of what they perceived as anti-porn feminists' monolithic view of pornography as a central determinant of women's oppression, and were similarly critical of potential attempts to utilise the state in attempts to deal with pornography, particularly through censorship. Lisa Duggan and Nan Hunter, founding members of the Feminist Anti-Censorship Taskforce (FACT), assert the sex-positive position to be one of 'sexual dissent', a concept that they claim 'forges a connection among sexual expressions, oppositional politics and claims to public space'. From this position, they envisage any potential feminist attempts at censorship or regulation of pornography as having dangerous consequences for women and other marginalised groups, claiming that 'restriction and regulation of sexual expression is a form of political repression aimed at sexual minorities and gender nonconformists' (Duggan and Hunter, 1995: 5).

Whilst we will look at these arguments in greater depth in Chapter 2, it is worth attending to the shift in register executed by Duggan and Hunter in their framing of these debates. No longer a terrain of sexual politics, analysed in terms of structural relations of inequality between women and men – as in the work of Andrea Dworkin, for example – pornography has now become the site of struggle between 'sexual minorities and gender nonconformists' and oppressive forces that would stifle 'sexual dissent' and 'sexual expression'. Any relationship to patriarchal social structures is magically erased. As we shall see in Chapter 2, an influential essay by Gayle Rubin (1984) laid the groundwork for this shift, and helped to marginalise the specifically *feminist* critique of porn, which continued to focus attention on power relations between women and men. This move was a crucial step in bringing about the decline of anti-porn feminism.

Given the conservative climate and attempts by both the Thatcher government and the Reagan administration to limit freedoms for women and freedoms around sexuality, it is understandable that many feminists, who otherwise may have been critical of pornography, were wary of campaigns that they feared might result in increased state powers to pursue a retrograde and oppressive agenda. New groups that emerged in opposition to anti-porn campaigns focused on the issue of censorship, as indicated by their names: the Feminist Anti-Censorship Taskforce (FACT) in the USA and Feminists Against Censorship (FAC) in the UK. The implication that anti-porn feminists were thus *pro*-censorship was misleading. As early as 1978, the UK Anti-Porn Group had stated explicitly:

> We do not seek to change the law towards increased censorship. We could not advocate any increase in the repressive activities of the institution (the state) which males use to legitimise their control of us. (Katyachild *et al.*, 1985: 16)

The persistent mischaracterisation of the anti-porn position as 'pro-censorship' is noticeable in much pro-porn literature of the time (Chester and Dickey, 1988; Vance, 1984; Segal, 1993a). Significantly, there is little evidence that pro-porn arguments engaged with the complexities and inherent problems with the notion of censorship, which anti-porn campaigners addressed in powerful and sophisticated critiques (see Dworkin, 1985; Itzin, 1992a). Nowhere is this mischaracterisation more striking than in anti-censorship responses to what was to be the most important and ground-breaking anti-porn intervention to date: the ordinances[6] proposed in Minneapolis and Indianapolis by Andrea Dworkin and feminist legal scholar Catharine MacKinnon.

'Our day in court': the Dworkin-MacKinnon ordinance

While Dworkin and MacKinnon were teaching a course on pornography in Minneapolis, they were approached by a number of community groups concerned at proposed zoning legislation that would have restricted public availability of pornography to certain geographical areas, disproportionately affecting poorer neighbourhoods (Kelly, 1988b: 52). Faced with this injustice, and in view of the inadequacy of available legislative approaches to address the harm pornography does to women, Dworkin and MacKinnon drafted an ordinance that marked a radical departure in how pornography was framed: they defined pornography as a violation of women's civil rights and made it actionable under the law (Keith, 2011a).

Starting from the premise that pornography harms women, the ordinance put forward a radical feminist definition of pornography as material that sexually subordinates women:

We define pornography as the graphic, sexually explicit sub-ordination of women through pictures or words, that also includes women dehumanised as sexual objects, things or commodities, enjoying pain or humiliation or rape, being tied up, cut up, mutilated, bruised or physically hurt, in postures of sexual submission or servility or display, reduced to body parts, penetrated by objects or animals, or presented in scenarios of degradation, injury, torture, shown as filthy or inferior, bleeding, bruised, or hurt in a context that makes these conditions sexual.

Erotica, defined by distinction as not this, might be sexually explicit materials premised on equality.

We also propose that the use of men, children or transsexuals in the place of women is pornography. (Everywoman, 1988: 2)

The ordinance offered an individual woman – or group of women – who had been harmed by pornography the opportunity to seek redress from the relevant producers and distributors. Importantly, the ordinance was drafted as a civil rather than criminal law; it did not propose the 'prior restraint' of material, and therefore would not increase state powers of censorship; rather, it would give women 'our day in court, to try to prove that we were hurt, either in the making or in the consuming of the material. If a woman can prove harm to a jury of her peers, which would not be easy, then she can get monetary damages from the makers and distributors of that pornography, and that specific piece of pornography would be removed from the marketplace' (Keith, 2011a). In order to take a case, a woman would have to show that the material in question functioned to subordinate women, and was covered by the above definition. She would also have to make one of three possible charges, in order to show harm: 'that she was coerced into participating in the production of pornography; that she was forced to view pornography; that she was assaulted as a direct result of pornography' (Kelly, 1988b: 55).

A fourth charge could be brought by a group of women, and would involve demonstrating that the public availability of pornography constitutes a violation of women's civil rights. As Keith notes:

> The real brilliance in this approach is that pornography is what pornography does. It has to meet the definition but beyond that if no one is hurt – forced into it, assaulted because of it – if there is no victim – then there's no lawsuit. So if pornography doesn't create harm, then pornographers have nothing to fear. (Keith, 2011a)

Following the drafting of the ordinance hearings were held over two days in December 1983, at which evidence of the links between pornography and sexual violence was provided by women who had been abused either in the production of pornography or through its use, along with that of researchers, women's groups and practitioners working to prevent and combat sexual violence. The ordinance was passed twice in Minneapolis, but subsequently vetoed by the mayor in both instances. A similar version of the ordinance was also passed in Indianapolis, but ruled unconstitutional by the District Court (Kelly, 1988b). Further attempts to introduce versions of the ordinance also took place in other US cities and states.

In Indianapolis, the ruling of the District Court was appealed by the Mayor, and was again judged to be unconstitutional by the Court of Appeal. Significantly, however, the judge had been persuaded by the evidence presented in support of the ordinance, and agreed with the fundamental argument that pornography functions to subordinate women. Ironically, it was the very recognition of its subordinating power that led the judge to draw the conclusion that pornography therefore constitutes a form of political speech, the freedom of which is protected under the First Amendment of the US Constitution. Finally, the case went to the Supreme Court where it was 'summarily affirmed' – an unusual and extremely significant move, which meant that no similar legislation could be introduced in the USA (Kelly, 1988b; Keith, 2011a).

While Dworkin and MacKinnon were battling to get their ordinance passed, a group was set up by feminists in opposition to their endeavours. The Feminist Anti-Censorship Task force (FACT) joined a coalition of industry representatives and civil liberties pressure groups to fight the ordinance. FACT produced a brief setting out a number of arguments against the ordinance, which can be summarised as follows: pornography is not central in maintaining gender equality; key terms in the ordinance remained undefined and are therefore open to definition by judges; the ordinance represents women as fundamentally weak, helpless victims and men as sexual aggressors; and the ordinance assumes a simple link between words, images and behaviour. Finally, the brief argues that pornography has multiple meanings and, that some women enjoy it and it warns that there are serious dangers in restricting sexually explicit speech (Kelly, 1988b: 56). The arguments contained in the brief will be discussed in Chapter 2; for now, it is worth attending to the fundamental misrepresentation of the ordinance inherent in the brief and implied by the name adopted by FACT. The key position of FACT and the brief is clearly one of anti-censorship and consequently it ignores what is probably the most important thing about the ordinance: the fact that it does *not* call for prior restraint, but rather offers women the chance of legal redress if they can prove that they have been harmed through the production, distribution or use of pornography. Liz Kelly reflects on the brief's curious lack of engagement with the most original and innovative aspects of the ordinance:

> What I still find extraordinary is that the feminist opposition totally failed to address what is most interesting about the

ordinance. First, that it attempts to embody feminist and women-centred definitions in a legislative format, and second, that it seeks to empower women rather than the police or the state. It almost seems a deliberate misreading to stir up fear of state censorship. (Kelly, 1988b: 59)

The claim of the FACT brief that the ordinance was attempting to restrict sexually explicit speech is quite simply inaccurate: the definition of pornography in the ordinance makes clear reference to the 'sexually explicit *subordination of women*' (my emphasis), so claims that other kinds of sexually explicit material – such as sexual health or education materials – might be subject to censorship seem unfounded. And given the three elements that would comprise the necessary grounds for a case – the subordinating and pornographic nature of the material in line with the ordinance definition, combined with the demonstration of harm in relation to its production, distribution or use – the claims of the FACT brief seem even more redundant. No state censorship would be involved: as Kelly states, '[t]here is quite simply no case unless a woman takes one and feels she can demonstrate each of the three stages of proof required by the ordinance' (*ibid.*: 59).

In any event, the decision of the Supreme Court ensured that the potential of the ordinance was never to be tested in US cities and states. However, the approach developed by Dworkin and MacKinnon provided inspiration to anti-porn feminists on the other side of the Atlantic, where similar 'sex war' battles were being fought.

Campaigns against pornography in the UK

In the UK, as WAVAW activities declined in the mid-1980s, new campaigns against pornography were championed by strategically located individuals and new groups. In 1986,

Labour Member of Parliament Clare Short introduced a Ten Minute Rule Bill in the House of Commons, to outlaw 'the display of pictures of naked or partially naked women in sexually provocative poses in newspapers', which became known as the Page 3 Bill (Benn, 1988; Itzin, 1992a: 590), with reference to *The Sun* and other tabloid newspapers where such pictures are published daily. In Parliament, Short's speech presenting the Bill drew jeers, laughter and crude personal remarks from male Conservative MPs; significantly, members of the same party that *favoured* restrictions in terms of the availability of material they saw as 'promoting' homosexuality. Only one Conservative female MP supported the Bill, and the Conservative Edwina Currie positively attacked it, telling the press that her husband wished that she looked like a Page 3 model (Short, 1991: 4). In the UK in the 1980s, it was Labour women on the left of the party who took up anti-porn initiatives – including Clare Short, Jo Richardson and Dawn Primarolo, all of whom were champions of women's rights. This support from Labour women politicians, evident also in the first decade of the new century, tends to be overlooked in accounts which hold that anti-porn initiatives involve feminists in alliance with conservative moralists.

While Short's Bill drew contemptuous jeers from male Conservative MPs and a campaign of ridicule and vilification from *The Sun* (Short, 1991: 6–7), it also drew a huge response from women, who wrote to tell her how much they hated and felt undermined by Page 3:

> [T]he most urgent message was that they were shaking with rage at how I was treated. I was deeply touched by this enormous affection from women I had never met. The strength and loveliness of it far outweighed the humiliation and nastiness I had experienced before.
>
> As the days went by, the letter continued to flow in. They came in their thousands.... Not only was I deeply moved by the letters, but I was educated too. They said so much, so eloquently.

Women of all ages, backgrounds, politics and experiences wrote about their feelings. Some brought me to tears.... . There were letters from women who had had breasts removed in cancer operations, who said how much it hurt them that their husbands brought such papers into their house. I remember one who asked me not to write back because her husband would be angry if he knew she had written to me. (*Ibid.*: 5)

The strength of feeling conveyed by Short's correspondents is indicative of the level of distress and anger that was fuelling campaigns and initiatives from a number of different quarters. Several trade unions and pressure groups were taking action, with the Women's Media Action Group (WMAG) addressing pornography as part of their wider campaigning around the representation of women in the media (Itzin, 1992a: 589) and the Association of Cinematograph Television and Allied Technicians (ACTT) and National Union of Journalists (NUJ) formulating policies and adopting resolutions to support campaigns against pornography (*ibid.*: 590, 592–3). Significantly, given the nature of the organisation, the National Council for Civil Liberties resolved at its annual general meeting in April 1989 to 'consider the kinds of specific legislation (both civil and criminal) which could be enacted to curb the production and distribution of pornographic material; material which should be narrowly defined as that which sexualises violence and the subordination of women' (*ibid.*: 593). The influence of the Dworkin-MacKinnon ordinance is clearly visible in the wording and approach of the resolution. Feminists were also beginning to explore and debate the potential and implications of extending pre-existing legislation that prohibited incitement to racial hatred to cover material that incites hatred on the basis of sex (Moore, 1988), as part of a range of possible legislative approaches that included adapting the Dworkin-MacKinnon ordinance and building on sex discrimination legislation (Itzin, 1992b).

Following her earlier Ten Minute Rule Bill, in March 1989 Clare Short presented a Private Members' Bill to 'remove pornography from the press and the workplace' (Indecent Displays Newspapers and Workplace Bill 1989), supported by many Labour women MPs, including Jo Richardson, Dawn Primarolo, Margaret Beckett, Alice Mahon, Joan Ruddock, Diane Abbott, Audrey Wise, Mo Mowlam and Ann Taylor (Itzin, 1992a: 592). In July of the same year, Dawn Primarolo presented a Private Members' Bill which sought to limit the sale of soft-core pornographic magazines, such as *Mayfair* and *Penthouse*, to licensed vendors, removing such publications from the top shelves of local newsagents and chains such as W. H. Smith. The Primarolo Bill defined pornography in terms of its depiction of women or women's body parts as 'objects, things or commodities, or in sexually humiliating or degrading poses, or being subjected to violence' (*ibid.*: 594). In 1989, Clare Short, along with Barbara Rogers, editor of *Everywoman* magazine, formally launched the Campaign Against Pornography (CAP) at the House of Commons. At the same event, they simultaneously launched the publication of the complete transcript of the Minneapolis hearings (Everywoman, 1988). Again, the influence of the ordinance on UK campaigning is evident in relation to these campaigns and legislative initiatives.

CAP established a high profile: it held a number of national conferences; established a widespread national campaigning network; secured funding for paid staff; and organised a number of campaigns, one of the most notable being 'Off the Shelf', which sought to mobilise women at the grassroots to lobby both local newsagents not to stock porn and national chain W. H. Smith to stop distributing it (Itzin, 1992a: 595). A second, smaller group, the Campaign Against Pornography and Censorship (CPC), was also launched in 1989, basing its name and campaigns on the premise that pornography itself constitutes a form of censorship of women, through a number of silencing effects.[7] CPC was particularly interested in adapting the Dworkin-MacKinnon ordinance to the British context. In opposition to these groups, Feminists Against Censorship (FAC) was set up. A key argument of this group was that censorship is used to suppress dissent and to victimise minorities, and thus could be used against the interests of women. While to some extent concerns regarding the implications of censorship for disadvantaged and minority groups were understandable in the context of 1980s Britain, the ideological basis and interests of FAC are significant. Its politics are indicated by the constituent groups involved in setting it up: 'lesbians who had been active in the pro-s-m lobby joined forces with heterosexual academic feminists to form Feminists Against Censorship (FAC) – specifically created to fight feminist campaigns around pornography within the lesbian and women's movements' (Reeves and Wingfield, 1996: 63–4). The leaders of FAC were largely 'intellectuals and artists, some of whom [were] themselves directly involved in the production of feminist erotica' (Lovenduski and Randall, 1993: 129) – apparently not merely 'feminist erotica' either, since FAC membership included Isobel Kaprowski, editor of the UK *Penthouse* magazine (Reeves and Wingfield, 1996: 69). FAC members, therefore, were more likely to take a libertarian approach, being concerned with issues of freedom of expression and possibly their own vested interests in cultural production that might include pornography. Further, as Reeves and Wingfield point out, women in FAC and other pro-porn lobbies often have a 'material interest' alongside financial or ideological ones. For pro-porn heterosexual feminists, a stake in heterosexuality as an institution 'means that they are willing to employ the most circular and reactionary of arguments in order to lead them not to question what is one of the most central bases of their lives and identities'. Similarly, for some lesbians 'sexualising inequality is also critically central to their identities. For them, there is just as strong a need not to question pornography, or sado-masochism, or even heterosexuality' (*ibid.*).

Of the three groups, it appears that the stance of anti-porn groups CAP and CPC was closer to the sentiment of large numbers of British women. Clare Short's Bill had drawn a passionate and heartfelt response from thousands of women, and a subsequent survey carried out in the summer of 1986 by the mainstream weekly magazine *Woman* found that 90 per cent of readers were in favour of banning Page 3 (Benn, 1988: 32). Again, women sent in responses in their thousands, objecting to the pressure such images put on women to conform to certain stereotypes of feminine attractiveness; angry at the hypocrisy of Page 3 in the face of the social disapproval regarding breastfeeding in public; and angry at the sexist attitudes that Page 3 encouraged, particularly with regard to workplace sexual harassment. A group of women working in a Midlands factory voiced their resentment at the way that Page 3 sanctioned sexual harassment among their male colleagues: 'We're sick of all the crude and disgusting things men say to us at breakfast time while they are looking at Page 3s' (quoted in Benn, 1988: 32). As Benn notes, a surprising feature of the letters was the prevalence of specifically feminist arguments and vocabulary – 'exploitation/denigration/commodity/ stereotype/passivity/availability/object' – from a constituency of women who did not necessarily identify as feminist. Benn notes that this language is in contrast to 'the cooler, more sophisticated, more technical vocabulary of self-referring feminists writing or politicking in the 1980s' (*ibid.*: 33), which, in some feminist circles, had superceded the language of objectification and exploitation. It seems likely that the shared language and shared perspectives expressed by 'non-feminist' women and CAP and CPC can partly be explained by the fact that these campaign groups were led by women coming from a sexual violence perspective (Lovenduski and Randall, 1993: 129), with direct knowledge and understanding of the ways in which pornographic images functioned to subordinate women in everyday situations, whether on the factory floor or in situations of domestic violence. Perhaps unsurprisingly given its membership, it seems that FAC was unwilling to engage with the realities of pornography as it played out in the lives of thousands of women.

One effect of the polarisation of the debate was a resulting paralysis for many feminists in terms of making political progress on the issue. Writing at the time, Benn observes that:

> Questions around style, diverse sexualities and erotic imagery are now hotly debated among feminists, so that no-one is quite sure any more which images are degrading, which progressive, which subversive. Who dares say? Nothing is so simple, and a simplicity of perspective can fuel a more dynamic politics, while awareness of complexity can paralyse. (Benn, 1988: 34)

In view of the distress voiced by thousands of women in relation to Page 3, one might wonder at the effectiveness and usefulness of a feminism paralysed by the apparent 'complexity' of such imagery and the way that it functions in society. Benn uses the term 'awareness' in relation to this supposed complexity; 'assertion' might be a more appropriate word, since the presence and function of such images is not necessarily that complex in the light of feminist understandings of patriarchal power (it was notable that similar handwringing about 'complexity' was not much in evidence in relation to issues like equal pay and abortion rights). It is interesting to review these debates in the light of subsequent developments, over twenty-five years on:

not only are Page 3 and 'top shelf' pornography still very much in evidence in British culture, but the top shelf has moved down to the middle shelf in the form of 'lads' mags', and the influence of pornography is clearly evident across mainstream culture, as we shall see in Chapter 3. What is striking is how little the anti-censorship position takes account of the consequences of the creation of social norms and processes of normalisation: legislation, such as that proposed by Short and Primarolo, has *normative* effects, in that it helps to shape what is considered normal, acceptable and desirable in the culture. In the absence of any effective regulation or means of challenge to the industry, it has been profit-motivated porn producers and distributors – rather than feminist activists and feminist politicians – that have had a relatively free rein in shaping the norms of mainstream culture.

The decline of anti-porn feminism

> I went through a period, this would have been in the 90s, where the feminist movement were blockading just about everything, and I remember going into the offices where I worked and it being picketed by the feminists and things. Now, that's all gone…. I think everybody accepts now that women will always be thought of as sex objects by men, but the thing about 'well, don't treat me as a sex object' – well, I'm sorry love, everybody is going to – that is life. (Botham, 2008)

Both CAP and CPC ceased activities in the mid-1990s, from which point it is generally acknowledged that feminist anti-porn activism and the feminist debates around pornography fell into a relative silence (McRobbie, 2009; Walter, 2010). Any conclusions regarding this 'silence' need to be qualified, however, since it is not the case that there were no vigorously contested debates around sexual violence and the sex industry after the early 1990s. As Kathy Miriam points out, in many ways the 'sex wars' of the 1980s reconfigured themselves into the no less fiercely contested debates around 'sex trafficking' in the 1990s, particularly in the Vienna debates leading up to the production of the Palermo protocol on trafficking in 2000 (Miriam, 2005: 1). However, pornography *per se* was not such a central debate at this time, and the development of neoliberal-inflected versions of feminism and the concept of 'postfeminism' in the 1990s tends to support the conclusion expressed by Miriam that the '"sex wars" ... were apparently settled by the end of the decade, with "pro-sex" advocates declared the winners'. To the undoubted satisfaction of pornographers like Deric Botham, and the devastation of radical feminists who had struggled so courageously against the porn industry, the 'radical feminist anti-pornography and anti-prostitution position ha[d] been effectively marginalised' (*ibid*.: 1), ensuring that 'the transformation of pornography into a hugely profitable and mainstream industry sector in the 1990s was able to take place with little interruption from the pickets and protests that characterised the previous two decades' (Jeffreys, 2009: 63).

The demise of feminist anti-pornography activism in the 1990s needs to be seen in a number of contexts, primarily the context of the decline of the visible women's liberation movement (Lovenduski and Randall, 1993: 359–60; Epstein, 2001) and changes within British feminism at that time. Historically, social movements have tended to emerge and decline according to 'cycles of protest' (Pizzorno, 1978), and the decline of the women's movement as it was originally configured in the USA and UK is perhaps unsurprising. Moments of disruption are followed by routinisation (Tarrow, 1998); intense activity, by 'latent' periods (Melucci, 1989). Tarrow offers four reasons as to why specific cycles come to an end: activists' exhaustion and disillusionment ('burnout'); institutionalisation of radical ideas; factionalism within the movement; and the role of the state and agencies of control in shaping the trajectory of the movement, through rewarding moderate aspirations and penalising or repressing more radical goals and activities (Tarrow, 1998). Each of these elements played a part in the decline of 1980s anti-porn activism.

For some activists, 'burnout' no doubt played a role in the decline of the women's movement (Epstein, 2001); activists talk of the intensity of their involvement in radical feminist activities of the 1970s and 1980s (Engle, 2007), which entailed a high degree of personal investment that for some proved difficult to sustain within an increasingly neoliberal, socially conservative climate. Lack of funding undoubtedly took its toll (Whittier, 1995: 85–91), as did the nature of the campaign work, which included engagement with hardcore and often violent pornographic content. The ongoing caricaturing and vilification of feminist anti-porn perspectives in the popular press is also likely to have contributed to burnout.

It was, however, the lack of a unified position on pornography amongst feminists that perhaps most contributed to burnout, since fighting external enemies is incalculably more difficult and exhausting without a shared vision and strong baseline of solidarity. Precious time and energy that could have been spent fighting the porn industry was diverted by the need constantly to reassert and defend an anti-porn position in the face of an onslaught from pro-porn, libertarian elements within the movement itself. These bitter divisions on the subject of pornography inevitably reduced capacity and energy, with identity politics and a more general fragmentation of the movement also perhaps playing a part.

In relation to the development of identity politics, it is notable that anti-porn feminism had been to some extent, though certainly not universally, a movement of white women. This in part reflects the fact that white, middle-class women formed the majority of movement participants in the early days of second wave feminism, perhaps inevitably, given that these women were more likely to have the time and resources necessary to participate, compounded by the fact that black women's energy was split between fighting black liberation struggles alongside women's liberation. While in the late 1960s and early 1970s African-American feminists played a key role in the cross-fertilisation of ideas, politics and strategies across the two movements, the struggle of fighting oppression on two fronts was obviously a double burden on the energy and resources of black feminists, and one that was not always taken up and shared by white feminists. In terms of the presence of specifically black feminist voices within anti-porn feminism, the context of the development of a broader black feminist politics is significant. Where many of the key feminist texts of the early 1970s were produced by white women, a wealth of black feminist writing followed in the 1980s. Work by Angela Davis (1982), bell hooks (1982), Alice Walker (1983), Audre Lorde (1984a) and Patricia Hill Collins (1990) contributed to a body of black feminist theory and critique, along with the powerful and influential collection *This Bridge Called My Back* (Anzaldúa and Moraga, 1984), which brought together voices of black, Latina, Native American and Asian American feminists. Powerful critiques of the racism in pornography and the sexual commodification of black women have been produced by both black and white feminists (Dworkin, 1981; Forna, 1992; hooks, 1998; Dines, 2010), and some black feminists writing during the 'sex wars' were generally critical of pornography and practices such as sado-masochism (Lorde, 1984c, 1988). Yet, given the intersection of oppressions of sex, race and class in pornography, far more work remained to be done in order to address the specific oppression of black women in pornography. Unfortunately, the 'sex wars', ascendancy of pro-porn sentiment and fragmentation of the movement meant that the context was not conducive to the development of such work in the 1990s.

The aftermath of second wave feminist activism was characterised by the professionalisation and institutionalisation of feminist concerns, which became incorporated into local government structures, state bodies and universities. This process can be seen as both beneficial and detrimental to feminist goals: beneficial in bringing about key changes in institutional practices, but detrimental in that such gains tended to involve a more compromised position, and were thus won at the expense of more radical aims (Griffin, 1995: 4–5). In the UK, institutionalisation tended to favour liberal feminist approaches, and while organisations such as the Greater London Council developed policies around sexist advertising, radical feminist critiques of pornography were generally not high on the agenda. Whilst the development of Women's Studies within the academy had initially created opportunities for radical feminist ideas to be disseminated, the subsequent move to Gender Studies and the emergence of postmodernist feminism contested terms such as 'woman' and 'patriarchy', making debates around pornography more difficult, since the very terms of the anti-porn position were thrown into question. The ascendancy of queer theory within Gender Studies departments shifted attention from male oppression of women under patriarchy to a focus on concepts such as gender performativity, the binary gender system and heteronormativity. Given its preoccupation with the 'transgressive' practices of sexual minorities, queer theory left little space to address questions of the structural oppression of women and the role of pornography in maintaining and perpetuating male domination.

The role of the state also played a part in promoting a version of institutionalised feminism that to some extent served state purposes. In the 1990s, governmental priorities shaped the priorities of state bodies responsible for equality, utilising the language of gender equality to serve other agendas such as the neoliberal imperative of economic growth and competitiveness. Simultaneously, new UK legislation curtailing rights to assemble and protest could be seen as acting as a suppressing factor in terms of more radical direct action protests. Also in the UK, the Labour Party's courtship of powerful media moguls, such as Rupert Murdoch, owner of Page 3 tabloids *The Sun* and *The News of the World*, and Richard Desmond, porn magnate and owner of the Express newspaper group, helped to create an unfavourable political climate for feminist dissent around issues of the pornographic representation of women. Prime Minister Tony Blair's project of the modernisation of the Labour Party involved the silencing of feminism (Whelehan, 2000; McRobbie, 2009): in spite of the greatly increased number of women MPs in the New Labour government of 1997, the political culture promoted by Blair and his immediate (male) coterie was highly masculinised (McRobbie, 2009: 5).

This inhospitable political climate and 'resurgent patriarchalism' (McRobbie, 2009: 5) formed a continuation of the backlash against feminism documented from the early 1990s (Faludi, 1991; French, 1992; Oakley and Mitchell, 1997). Alongside this backlash, a new generation of feminists posited neoliberal versions of feminism – 'new', 'power' and 'third wave' – that placed an emphasis on individual agency and self-empowerment, marking a move away from collective action to a more individualistic brand of feminism (Wolf, 1993; Roiphe, 1994; Denfield, 1996; Walter, 1998, Karp and Stoller, 1999; Baumgardner and Richards, 2000). The new wave of feminist voices, and their enthusiastic reception by the media, helped to create a generational division amongst feminists, with Katie Roiphe, Christine Hoff Somers and Rene Denfield in particular harshly critical of what they saw as the failings of the second wave: chiefly a tendency, in their view, towards a puritanical, prescriptive, anti-sex stance and 'victim feminism' (a term which confuses the naming of male sexual violence with the construction of women as victims, thus removing responsibility from male perpetrators and placing it onto second wave feminists). It was during this period – when feminism was preoccupied with fighting 'fire with fire' (Wolf, 1993) on an individual basis – that the global sex industry grew unchecked and we 'sleepwalked' into a culture where pornography and the sex industry were increasingly normalised and mainstream (Rake, 2008). As mentioned in the Introduction, for some theorists the unprecedented expansion of the industry constituted its own legitimisation. Karen Boyle draws attention to the rhetorical strategy via which porn theorist Linda Williams closes off feminist debate by simply referencing the mainstreaming of pornography as evidence of its legitimacy: '[f]eminist debates about whether pornography should exist at all have paled before the simple fact that still and moving-image pornographies have become fully recognizable fixtures of popular culture' (Williams, 2004: 2, cited in Boyle, 2010: 1). This kind of rhetorical manoeuvre is indicative of the silencing strategies that accompanied the normalisation of porn, making it difficult for feminist critiques of pornography to gain ground during the 1990s.

The re-emergence of anti-porn activism

Following this latent period, in the early years of the new millennium, a new wave of feminist anti-porn activism emerged in response to the phenomenon of pornification. The first decade of the twenty-first century saw a growing unease with notions of 'postfeminism' and with a popular culture where retro-sexist stereotyping and increasingly aggressive and ubiquitous forms of objectification of women were proliferating, through vehicles such as lads' mags and mainstream television, music videos and stand-up comedy, often accompanied by a knowing, ironic tone which made them particularly difficult to combat (Whelehan, 2000: 67–70).

This 'overloaded' culture (Whelehan, 2000) which facilitates and promotes new forms of sexism under the banner of irony corresponds with the simultaneous immobilisation of feminism within mainstream culture and politics (McRobbie, 2009). McRobbie puts forward a persuasive analysis of what she calls the 'disarticulation' of feminism: a variety of cultural, social and political processes via which feminism is seen as being 'taken into account' in order that it can be dispensed with as no longer necessary (see also Kinser, 2004: 132–3). According to McRobbie, the 'new female subject' is offered the freedoms and opportunities of the neoliberal social order, but she is 'called upon to be silent, to withhold critique in order to count as a modern, sophisticated girl. Indeed, this withholding of critique is a condition of her freedom' (McRobbie, 2009: 18). A key part of this process involves the construction of second wave feminism as a spectre – that which is ugly, hideous and monstrous, and which must be disavowed in order for young women successfully to occupy the new subject positions offered to them. There is certainly a wealth of research which attests to young women's reluctance to embrace the term 'feminist' (Budgeon, 2001; Woodward and Woodward, 2009; Baker, 2010; Scharff, 2010). However, the women I interviewed whilst researching this book were emphatic with regard to their feminist identities and politics, and, for many of them, pornography and pornification were mobilising issues. How and why has this re-emergence of anti-porn feminism come about? Given the fallout from the 'sex wars' of the 1980s, the backlash against feminism and ascendancy of neoliberalism in the 1990s, attendant processes of pornification and the disarticulation of feminism at the beginning of the twenty-first century, why are we now seeing a re-emergence of anti-porn feminist voices? How do such voices emerge in a society where, as McRobbie suggests, to embrace a politicised, radical feminist stance is to render oneself either culturally unintelligible or stigmatised as monstrous? What opportunities exist for women to develop critiques of pornography and to get involved in activism? What are the priorities and concerns of women who embrace a feminist anti-porn position, and how do they develop a feminist consciousness in the context of a society that tells them that only certain versions of personal freedom are possible and that feminism is no longer necessary?

These questions will be addressed in Chapter 4. But first, we will engage a little more deeply with the key questions that lie at the heart of feminist debates around pornography.

Notes

1 'Sex wars' is the term that has been coined for the highly contested debates within feminism throughout the 1980s that centred on issues such as sexuality, pornography, sado-masochism and sexual representation. The debates were polarised between radical and libertarian feminists, broadly representing 'anti-pornography' and 'sex-positive' perspectives, although such terms fail to reflect the complexity of the debates. Key texts representing the 'sex-positive' perspective include Vance, 1984; Duggan and Hunter, 1995; key texts representing the 'anti-pornography' perspective include Leidholt and Raymond, 1990; Jeffreys, 1990.

2 Whilst there are numerous problems with 'wave' terminology as a means of documenting feminist movements across diverse historical and geographical locations, the term 'second wave' is used here specifically to refer to the flourishing of feminist theory and activism in the USA and the UK from the mid-1960s to the late 1980s.

3 There are numerous accounts of second wave feminism from a variety of feminist perspectives. See, for example, Coote and Campbell, 1982; Rowbotham, 1989; Ryan, 1992; Whittier, 1995; Crow, 2000; Rees, 2007; Bronstein, 2011.

4 In Great Britain only; the 1967 Abortion Act did not apply in Northern Ireland.

5 For a fascinating historical account of the theories and activities of the revolutionary feminists, including their anti-pornography work, see Rees, 2007. See also Engle, 2007.

6 An ordinance is a piece of legislation that city councils in the USA can pass in relation to their own area of jurisdiction. If there are grounds to believe any such law is unconstitutional, it can be challenged at the level of the District Court, right up to the Supreme Court.

7 The ways in which pornography functions to silence women is discussed in Chapter 2.

CHAPTER 2
Pornography and
the Feminist Divide

As we saw in Chapter 1, feminists challenging pornography in the late 1970s were entering an arena where prevailing discourses had already established understandings of pornography either with reference to a conservative, moralising agenda, or through liberal notions of the right to freedom of expression and the 'liberation' of sexuality. In the following decade, debates around pornography intensified within the feminist movement itself, as feminists fiercely contested the meaning, nature and significance of pornography – and what, if anything, should be done about it. This chapter explores some of the questions and arguments that lay at the heart of these debates, and that have subsequently received renewed attention from a new generation of anti-porn activists. Whilst the chapter integrates some of the new anti-porn writing that has emerged more recently (Tyler, 2011b), critical work focusing specifically on the 'mainstreaming' of pornography will be explored in greater depth in Chapter 3.

It should be borne in mind when considering these debates that pornography itself is, of course, not a 'given'. It is the nature of intellectual debate that the debate itself contributes to a reification of its object, so that the object becomes seen as a fixed and immutable entity that exists universally and inevitably across different historical and geographical contexts. It is important to remember that this is not the case: while sexually explicit depictions have existed across different cultures from ancient times, the modern concept of pornography developed as a term and a genre within the minority world in the nineteenth century (Kendrick, 1997). Pornography in its current form can be traced from the *Playboy* era of the 1950s through to the globalised and highly technologised industry of the 1990s and 2000s (Dines, 1998a, 2010; Boyle, 2010). Studying the development of pornography as a genre reveals both patterns and variations regarding content, distribution and consumption. Many majority-world cultures have no equivalent tradition to current minority-world pornography (although the porn industry is increasingly and aggressively targeting emerging markets in the majority world and developing economies, as we shall see in Chapter 3). It is important to keep this short history in mind; to remember that it was not always thus, is not everywhere thus, and need not be thus in the future. Similarly, it is vital to be mindful of the absences that pornography engenders: the forms of expression rendered invisible, the modes of relationship rendered unimaginable and the language rendered unspeakable when pornography dominates the culture and the marketplace.

Defining pornography

There is no commonly accepted definition of pornography; the term has variously been defined with reference to moral, aesthetic or political frameworks. Dictionaries commonly define pornography in terms of its genre as a mode of representation, and its understood purpose. For example:

> *n.* 1 the explicit description or exhibition of sexual activity in literature, films, etc., intended to stimulate erotic rather than aesthetic or emotional feelings [Gk *pornographos* writing of harlots f. *Pornē* prostitute + *graphō* write] (Allen, [1964] 1991)

Noun: obscene writings, drawings, photographs, or the like, especially those having little or no artistic merit. (Dictionary.com)

Both definitions introduce a consideration of aesthetics, respectively emphasising either the understood purpose of pornography, 'to stimulate erotic ... feelings', or its lack of 'artistic merit'. Whilst these dictionary definitions therefore frame pornography in terms of 'explicit' sexual content and aesthetic value, the etymology of the word is illuminating regarding the sexual politics that inhere in the term, since the term refers to writing about prostituted women.[1] This etymology introduces the possibility of a more political definition, as it derives from a specific and unequal social and economic situation between the respective subject and object positions of writer and prostitute.

Anti-pornography feminists have emphasised the significance of this etymology in their analyses of pornography. Andrea Dworkin interprets the ancient Greek *pornē* and *graphos* as 'writing about whores', arguing that *pornē* refers specifically to

> the lowest class of whore, which in ancient Greece was the brothel slut available to all male citizens. The *pornē* was the cheapest (in the literal sense), least regarded, least protected of all women, including slaves. She was, simply and clearly and absolutely, a sexual slave. (Dworkin, 1981: 199–200).

Susanne Kappeler cites the following definition:

> Description of the life, manners, etc. of prostitutes and their patrons; hence, the expression or suggestions of obscene or unchaste subjects in literature and art. (Shorter Oxford English Dictionary, quoted in Kappeler, 1986: 155)

She points out that the economic relationship of prostitute and patron is at the heart of the definition. This emphasis on relationships of economic power and inequality between women and men is central to radical feminist critiques of pornography. For radical feminists, the etymology of the word 'pornography' is a useful reminder that pornography as a concept does not originate in notions of individual expression or erotic fantasy, but in relation to representations produced within specific, material conditions of inequality between women and men.

There was no legal definition of pornography in the UK until 2009, when a law prohibiting the possession of 'extreme pornography' defined 'a pornographic image as one which must reasonably be assumed to have been produced solely or principally for the purpose of sexual arousal' (UK Ministry of Justice, 2009). Prior to this, legal approaches to pornography rested on notions of obscenity, indecency and the tendency to 'corrupt or deprave' the persons viewing it, as in the 1959 Obscene Publications Act. Within legal arenas, questions of morality and aesthetic value vied for ascendancy in defining a contested cultural product: in the trial of Penguin Books, under the 1959 Obscene Publications Act, for its publication of *Lady Chatterley's Lover* (Lawrence, [1928] 1960), the defence of the publishers against the charge of obscenity lay in establishing that the novel was a work of literary merit and therefore served a 'public good' under Section 4 of the Act (HMSO, 1959). Similarly, the two reviews on pornography conducted in the 1970s within the UK, the Longford Inquiry and Report on Pornography (1971) and the Williams Inquiry into Obscenity and Film Censorship (1977), also constructed ideas of 'the pornographic' in relation to notions of obscenity and decency, though to very different ends (Rees, 2007: 203–7).

In the USA, the Dworkin-MacKinnon Ordinance, discussed in Chapter 1, provided an important departure from previous discursive constructions of pornography within legislative frameworks. As we have seen, Dworkin and MacKinnon's definition is overtly political, incorporating understandings of what pornography *does*: for Dworkin and MacKinnon, pornography constitutes the subordination of women through specific kinds of representations. Importantly, this definition therefore brings in a new understanding of the *function* of pornography, in addition to the traditionally understood function of sexual arousal. The ordinance distinguishes pornography from erotica, which might be 'premised on equality', emphasising the political function of pornography in perpetuating women's subordination.

Pro-porn or anti-censorship feminists contest definitions of pornography that frame it as inherently harmful and oppressive to women. Gayle Rubin, for example, takes issue with the Dworkin-MacKinnon definition of pornography, arguing that anti-porn feminists redefine pornography 'so that it is sexist and violent *by definition'* (1993: 26, emphasis in the original) whereas she sees the defining feature of pornography as its level of sexual explicitness (1993: 26) and argues that this encompasses diverse representations, not all of which fit into the Dworkin-MacKinnon conceptualisation. Of course, such arguments and counter-arguments can easily descend into circularity: if material does not fit Dworkin-MacKinnon's definition then they would obviously not categorise it as pornography; however, presumably for Rubin a more diverse range of representations and cultural products count as 'pornography' according to her categorisation.

Whilst the implications and complexities of definitions are an important part of political struggles around pornography, it is useful to remember that most people in a culture where pornography is available are able to recognise it without a consensus on a definition. Those seeking to access pornography know where to go, and they recognise pornography when they find it. It is not helpful if arguments around definitions are used as a 'dodge' (Jensen, 1998: 2): a means of avoiding serious debate around the issue of pornography. Difficulties with definitions should not be used to silence debate around pornography, and a useful working definition might combine political integrity around meaning with pragmatism. Robert Jensen thus advocates a 'dual definition', using the term pornography in two ways: first, to refer to the material sold in sex shops 'for the purpose of producing sexual arousal for mostly male consumers'; and second, concurring with Dworkin and MacKinnon's view of pornography, as 'a specific kind of sexual material that mediates and helps maintain the sexual subordination of women' (*ibid.*: 3). To the twenty-first century reader, the first part of this definition seems somewhat outdated, since most pornography is currently accessed through a variety of technological means rather than purchased in sex shops; also, 'lads' mags' and top shelf pornography are widely available in non-specialist shops including supermarkets, grocers, petrol stations and newsagents. Nonetheless, with certain modifications, the definition sets out the purpose and nature of pornography in a way that enables rather than hinders debate.

Another means of avoiding unnecessarily circular arguments around definitions is to grant that ideas about what constitutes pornography may differ, but to be clear about what is being referred to in a given context. Given the global scale of the porn industry, and clearly discernible patterns regarding who owns, produces, performs in, distributes and consumes pornography, it is useful to distinguish a dominant form of pornography (such as that produced and consumed by men). This might be referred to as 'everyday' pornography (Caputi, 2003; Boyle, 2010) or 'hegemonic' pornography: the kinds of sexual representations 'likely to become ideologically predominant over others' in a society largely controlled by men (Chancer, 1998: 77). Hegemonic pornography might be considered to be 'characterised by repetitive themes often interwoven in formulaic fashion'. Thus Chancer, like Jensen, provides a workable and pragmatic definition; one which in fact is quite consonant with that of Dworkin and MacKinnon, given the content of most mainstream pornography (Bridges, 2010). With 'gonzo'[2] porn identified as currently the 'overwhelmingly dominant porn genre' (AVN 2005, cited in Dines, 2010), the nature of the repetitious themes and formulae can be further elucidated: gonzo is characterised by 'hard-core, body-punishing sex in which women are demeaned and debased' (Dines, 2010: xi). These dominant and endlessly repeated themes reveal the connection between porn content and the preoccupations, anxieties and obsessions of hegemonic masculinity (Dines *et al.*, 1998; Jensen 2007; Kimmel, 2008; Dines, 2010), indicative of an intended and assumed male consumer. Research into the demographics of porn use identifies that, indeed, most porn users are male (Cooper *et al.*, 2002; Stack *et al.*, 2004), a finding strikingly reflected at the international porn summit *Xbiz EU 2011*,[3] where, with one notable exception (discussed in Chapter 3), porn consumers were universally assumed to be male and referred to exclusively using male pronouns. Finally, research into how porn production, marketing and distribution operates within the context of a complex, highly sophisticated and technologised capitalist industry further helps to set out the parameters of hegemonic pornography (Johnson, 2010; 2011).

The porn debates: ideological frameworks

Pro-porn and anti-porn perspectives are informed by very different ideas about the nature of social reality and social relations. Whilst nuances and complexities are evident across the spectrum from pro-porn to anti-porn positions, it is none-theless helpful to identify the key ideological concepts and assumptions that inform the different theoretical perspectives articulated within the debates.

Conservative frameworks
Conservative views on pornography are rooted in notions of public morality, decency and 'traditional' values. Sex is seen as an impulse to be contained and controlled, with the appropriate context for sexual relations being heterosexual marriage, primarily for purposes of procreation: other kinds of sexual relations or expression are seen as unnatural and threatening to public morality and decency. In particular, sexual behaviour and expression is to be kept away from children and others who might be vulnerable to corruption. Conservative views on sexuality inform the conservative position on pornography, since porn is seen as an expression of sexuality. The conservative position also brings in questions of 'taste': the idea that par-ticular forms of sex or sexual expression might be distasteful or disgusting; offensive to moral decency. The conservative ideal of marriage as the most appropriate and desirable context for sexual relations locates women within the private sphere, historically under the ownership and control of one man. The anti-feminist Madonna/whore view of women thus emanates from a conservative position, since conservative attitudes to sex are based on absolutist framings of what constitutes 'good' and 'bad' morality. Women who fulfil the traditional role of wife and mother are therefore considered good, whereas women whose sexual behaviour is located outside such boundaries are considered bad. Unsurprisingly, then, conservative views are not much in evidence within feminist debates on pornography. What *is* striking, however, is the consistency with which a *feminist* anti-porn position is misrepresented as a conservative

position. As we shall see, the feminist critique of pornography is entirely distinct from the conservative view, based on radically different sets of assumptions, understandings and values. Indeed, the radical feminist position that informs anti-porn feminism has produced equally thoroughgoing critiques of compulsory heterosexuality, marriage, the nuclear family and the sexual double standard, from the same set of assumptions and premises.

It is extremely significant, therefore, that anti-porn feminists have been characterised repeatedly as constituting a 'new moral purity movement' (Wilson, 1993: 28) – as 'anti-porn crusaders' (McIntosh, 1993: 160), responsible for stirring up a 'moral panic' (Rubin, 1984) around pornography and perpetuating myths of 'good' and 'bad' women. This misrepresentation of anti-porn feminism is so prevalent within feminist debates that it seems to indicate an almost wilful refusal to engage with their arguments, in a way that could be interpreted as ideologically motivated.

Left-liberal frameworks
Core beliefs and assumptions of anti-censorship or pro-porn positions originate from a left-liberal framework, as exemplified by the 1960s culture of the sexual revolution (Jeffreys, 1990). As in the conservative view, sex is seen as an impulse, although unlike conservatives left-liberals see this as good and natural, something to be liberated rather than constrained and controlled.

According to liberal social theory, the basic unit of society is the individual, seen as autonomous, self-willed and pre-social, rather than shaped by society (Cameron and Frazer, [1985] 2010; Keith, 2011a). Society, therefore, is made up of distinct, autonomous and unitary subjects, and the major political conflict for liberals is the tension between the respective freedoms of diverse individuals, and the role of the state in balancing these. A key principle of liberal social theory is that an individual has certain inalienable rights, independent of any social arrangements, which must be protected from state interference; at the same time, some element of state protection is needed to guarantee these individual rights from other individuals who might impinge on them. The liberal solution to these tensions is to assert a clear distinction between the public and the private, with the public domain seen as an appropriate arena for state authority, whilst the private remains a realm of individual freedom beyond state interference (Cameron and Frazer, [1985] 2010: 137). It is not difficult to see how these assumptions lead to an anti-censorship stance. For the liberal, porn reflects the individual's (historically, men's) basic 'need' for the sexual acts depicted in it; such a need is good and should be liberated; subjects should therefore have the freedom to enjoy porn within the private realm, beyond state interference. Whilst the freedom to enjoy porn is valued as part of the sacrosanct liberal notion of the private freedom of the individual, the left-liberal approach also allows for what is, in fact, the public accessibility of women to men. Unlike the conservative model of sex as an impulse to be controlled and limited to the context of monogamous, heterosexual marriage, the left-liberal model sees sex as a good impulse to be liberated, and according to the champions of the sexual revolution discussed in Chapter 1, such liberation involves women being accessed, shared and exchanged by men. Historically, this has not been seen as harmful to women, because the liberal human subject is constructed as male – therefore pornography does not impinge on others' freedoms, since women are not actually seen as individual subjects within this model.

Another aspect of liberal thinking – idealism – is also evident within debates on pornography. Idealism posits *attitudes* as both the source and solution for oppression; thinking as the prime mover of social life; and rational argument/education as the engine of social change (Keith, 2011b: 66). On this view, changing attitudes through education, awareness raising or the production of diverse sexual representations would be considered appropriate and effective solutions to any problematic or undesirable aspects of pornography.

Whilst individual freedom is a key principle for liberals, most versions of liberalism balance this principle alongside other social values such as equality and justice (Langton, 1999). For libertarians, however, individual liberty is paramount. Whilst a libertarian stance is evident in more aggressively pro-porn positions, a liberal viewpoint might endorse a broadly anti-censorship position whilst allowing that some aspects of pornography may be undesirable and that some restrictions on individual liberty may be appropriate in view of other, competing social values.

The centrality of the individual within liberal theory takes little account of power differentials between different social groups. Socialist or Marxist theory offers a view of society that sees class conflict as the major political conflict, and therefore foregrounds structurally unequal economic relationships between social groups. Anti-censorship feminists coming from a socialist or Marxist feminist perspective therefore incorporate an acknowledgement of pornography as reflective of unequal social power relations, between social classes and between women and men. For some anti-censorship feminists, this leads to a focus on the idea of porn as a capitalist industry and on the labour aspects of participation in pornography; the issue then becomes one of campaigning for improved working conditions for porn performers, and championing non-capitalist forms of porn production. Socialist feminists broadly support the belief that sex and sexual expression are fundamentally good, seeing sexism within porn as reflective of inequalities in the wider society, and considering that a feminist focus on pornography is a distraction from the fight against such inequalities (Segal, 1993a; Rubin, 1993). For socialist feminists, patriarchal capitalist power relations have deprived women of access to sexual expression, and pornography should therefore be claimed and embraced by women as a source of potential liberation and empowerment.

Post-modernist and queer theory frameworks
Subsequent to the porn debates of the 1980s, new theoretical directions have also influenced pro-porn and anti-censorship feminist positions. Post-modern feminism and queer theory have been influential in shifting the terrain of the porn debates away from a focus on sexual politics between women and men, in favour of attention to the relationship between institutions that promote and regulate 'normative' sexual practices and the practices and rights of 'sexual minorities' (Rubin, 1984). Gayle Rubin paves the way for this development through an explicit rejection of feminism as 'the privileged site of a theory of sexuality', claiming that '[f]eminism is the theory of gender oppression' and that 'an autonomous theory and politics specific to sexuality must be developed' (*ibid*.: 307–9). Within this framework, pornography tends to be conflated with sexual expression, and valorised as a potential site of transgression of normative understandings of sexuality, and the assertion of sexual minority identities and rights to sexual expression.

The predominance of post-modernist feminism and queer theory since the early 1990s is paralleled by the rise of the concept of 'post-feminism' and the ascendancy of neoliberalism as a hegemonic political and economic ideology. Influences of these developments are also much in evidence in pro-porn writings from the 1990s onwards, with concepts of individual choice, agency and empowerment increasingly foregrounded in accounts of women's relationship to pornography.

Radical feminist frameworks

Radical feminism rejects the liberal assumption that societies are made up of equal, distinct individuals. Radical feminism, like other radical social theory, argues from the premise that the basic social unit is the group, and the individual is a social being; groups are situated within structurally unequal power relationships; and finally that the personal is political (Cameron and Frazer, [1985] 2010: 139). For radical feminists, the human subject is not simply endowed with inherent natural qualities, but rather produced and constituted through and in relationship with social processes. Social practices and institutions play a role in constructing and shaping our identities and desires; therefore, identities are not static and 'achieved' but in a constant state of production, within the context of structural inequalities between women and men. Radical feminists argue that the liberal human subject is in fact a male subject, constructed by male-dominated social institutions in a context where men have social and economic power over women. Finally, radical feminism problematises the liberal division between the public and private realms, since for radical feminists there is no realm outside of the social or where social conditions are absent. Since a key insight of feminism has been to assert the political implications of what was previously considered personal, pornography is not to be allocated a privileged place in the private realm, but is available for political analysis. For radical feminists, sex is neither inherently good nor bad, since sexual meanings and practices are socially constructed. However, within patriarchal power relations male sexuality and its associated institutions such as marriage and the nuclear family, pornography and prostitution function as key instruments of women's oppression. Rejecting liberal idealism, radical feminists offer a materialist analysis that identifies concrete systems of power as sources and solutions of oppression, with organised, collective resistance as the engine of social change (Keith, 2011b: 66).

Oppression and violence against women

The production, distribution and consumption of pornography take place within the context of male-dominated societies and women's ongoing social, political and economic inequality across the globe (UN, 2010; Banyard, 2010). Over two thirds of the world's poor and illiterate populations are women (UN, 2010). As this statistic suggests, for many of the world's women, oppression on the basis of sex intersects with further oppressions on the basis of race, class, sexuality, age and disability.

Male violence against women is a global pandemic, with up to 70 per cent of women experiencing male violence in their lifetime, usually from a partner or someone they know.[4] In the UK, three million women each year experience male violence,[5] and research indicates worrying levels of intimate partner violence experienced by teenage girls (Barter *et al.*, 2009, 2011). In the first two weeks of 2012, ten women in the UK were killed by a male partner or ex-partner:[6] a victim-blaming mentality which is in some cases inscribed in the law means that perpetrators can generally expect low sentences for such crimes. In a period of less than a month at the time of writing this chapter, national news stories featured in the British press included three separate instances of men killing their female partners and children; the trial of a man for burying his girlfriend alive; the discovery of a missing young woman's body; the conviction of a serial rapist in London.

Across the world in the same period, many millions more instances of femicide, female infanticide, rape, sexual assault, intimate partner violence, female genital mutilation, crimes in the name of honour, trafficking and sexual exploitation will have occurred, and gone largely unreported. Such crimes are seldom viewed as crimes of dominion, committed by members of a dominant class on members of a subordinate class. Very often, the gendered nature of the crime is erased: as in the phrase 'sexual grooming and trafficking of young people', commonly used by children's charities and criminal justice agencies, even though the overwhelming majority of victims are young women.[7] This context of inequality and violence against women is crucial when considering questions of the meaning and function of pornography within the culture.

Liberal perspectives frame the individual's relationship to pornography as divorced from social implications or consequences, since pornography is understood to belong to a private realm, removed from the social world where inequalities and violence are experienced. Liberal views of pornography therefore tend to have little to say about questions of oppression, since such questions rely on understandings of the unequal relationships between different social groups or classes, which are not foregrounded in liberal ideology. A liberal feminist perspective, viewing all sexual expression as fundamentally good, would argue that pornography is an important cultural form for women to embrace and enjoy, given the history of suppression and shaming of women's sexuality. Emphasising the expressive nature of pornography, liberal pro-porn feminists generally do not foreground the context of male violence against women, and where such violence is discussed in the literature, it is seen as entirely separate and distinct (Segal, 1993a; Rubin, 1993). For pro-porn feminists with an analysis of women's inequality, pornography is not identified as a single or central cause of women's oppression (Parmar, 1988: 123; Rubin, 1993). This position also tends to see pornography as separate, and considers a feminist focus on porn a distraction from issues of discrimination (George, 1988; Strossen, 1995: 267; Rubin, 1993:

24–5). The model of porn in liberal accounts is fundamentally *expressivist*, a mode of representation having little relationship with or influence over social reality.

Anti-censorship feminists might also take up the poststructuralist view that there is 'no intrinsic meaning in language' (Coward, 1987: 310) in order to argue that there is no intrinsic meaning in pornographic texts, since meaning is fluid, contingent, contextual, and based on how various elements are combined. On this view, codes of female submission, fragmentation and availability found within the pornographic regime of representation are not intrinsically harmful, but must be viewed in context and set against other forms of cultural representation. The difficulty with this view is that it fails to take into account the cumulative effect of such images (Papadopoulos, 2010; Dines, 2010) within a culture where pornography is increasingly prevalent. What happens when pornography becomes a dominant mode of cultural representation, a commonplace feature of the public realm?

Such questions notwithstanding, for anti-censorship feminists porn is fundamentally a representation: even if such representations are violent, they are nonetheless *only* representations, and to focus on them is to distract from the real instances of violence that women face (Hollibaugh *et al.* 1987; Rubin 1993: 25). To focus on pornography is to detract from the 'real' feminist business of providing and lobbying for services for victims of male violence (Strossen, 1995: 274) – a not wholly convincing argument, given that radical feminists who put pornography on the feminist agenda were also instrumental in setting up rape crisis centres and women's refuges (see Chapter 1).

To the extent that anti-censorship feminists recognise the misogynist nature of much mainstream pornography (Segal, 1993b: 5; Hollibaugh *et al.*, 1987: 78), this sexism is seen as a reflection of the sexist nature of the wider society, rather than pornography itself functioning as an instrument of oppression. There is also a tendency to minimise levels of violence within porn, arguing that anti-porn campaigns overstate the presence of violent imagery in pornography (Rubin, 1993), and claiming that depictions of violence are decreasing (Segal, 1993b: 6), which runs counter to what is known about the trajectory of the porn industry from the early 1990s into the twenty-first century (Dines, 2010; Boyle, 2010; Tankard Reist and Bray, 2011). In fact, some pro-porn feminists claim that levels of pornography in the culture have a positive correlation with gender equality (Segal, 1993b) and warn that anti-porn arguments are actually dangerous for women's equality in two ways: first by positioning women as victims, and second by risking the progress of women's equality through appealing to a sexist state to exercise censorship, which they fear would militate against the freedoms of women and other oppressed groups.

Pro-porn feminists are unconvinced by research findings that indicate links between exposure to pornography and violence against women, calling into question the validity of 'effects' research conducted under laboratory conditions and pointing to other research that does not support these findings (Segal, 1993a; Strossen, 1995). Strossen considers that such an argument is in fact dangerous and anti-feminist, since it dilutes the accountability of the perpetrator of the violence (Strossen, 1995: 268–9). Pro-porn feminists argue that rape and male violence against women 'have been present throughout most of human history' (Rubin, 1993: 25; Strossen, 1995) and claim that the understanding of pornography as violence against women 'insults the many women who experience actual, brutal three dimensional violence in their real lives' (Strossen, 1995: 276). Such a view, of course, takes no account of the experiences of women involved in the production of pornography. Segal concludes that:

It is time for feminists, and their supporters, who want to act against men's greater use of violence and sexual coercion, and their continuing social dominance, to abandon the search for some spurious causal link with 'pornography' since 'anti-pornography campaigns ... can only enlist today, as they invariably enlisted before, guilt and anxiety around sex, as well as lifetimes of confusion in our personal experiences of sexual arousal and activity. (Segal, 1993a: 19)

The substitution of 'sex' for 'pornography' in Segal's argument is significant. Corresponding to a rejection of the idea that pornography plays a role in maintaining women's oppression, some pro-porn feminists were also instrumental in shifting the debate away from the oppression of women to the oppression of 'sexual minorities' (Rubin, 1984).

Radical feminist analyses of pornography take power relations into account through the theory of patriarchy: 'a system of social structures and practices in which men dominate, oppress and exploit women' (Walby, 1990: 20). Such an understanding, far from suggesting that all women's experiences under patriarchy are the same, is perfectly consistent with a recognition that women are positioned differently according to race, economic status, sexuality, and so on. Nonetheless, patriarchal social structures and practices result in a relationship of male domination and female subordination, with ongoing inequalities evident between women and men in every aspect of life (Millett, 1970). In the context of this overarching structure of male domination, pornography is understood as one method by which men as a group assert and maintain control over women. The key anti-porn feminist argument is that pornography constitutes the eroticised subordination of women; it sexualises and naturalises male domination and female subordination. From this insight, it is evident that for anti-porn feminists, pornography does not simply 'reflect' a male-dominated society; it plays a crucial role in perpetuating and maintaining that domination. Of course, many other institutions, systems and practices also play a role in maintaining patriarchal control; as mentioned in Chapter 1, Andrea Dworkin, perhaps the best known and most influential anti-porn radical feminist, cites fairy tales alongside pornography as contributing to the subordination of women through the construction of dominant meanings of masculinity and femininity (1974). For radical feminists, pornography is part of the 'network of forces and barriers which are systematically related and which conspire to the immobilization, reduction and moulding of women and the lives we live' (Frye, 1983b: 7).

Radical feminist analyses of pornography identify its major theme as male power: 'its nature, its magnitude, its use, its meaning' (Dworkin, 1981: 24). Radical feminists see pornography as playing a cultural and social role in maintaining 'rape culture' (Brownmiller, 1975; Buchwald *et al.*, 1993); as not simply representing violence against women but actually constituting violence (Dworkin, 1981; Everywoman, 1988; MacKinnon, 1994). For Dworkin, pornography constitutes the sexual subordination of women, involving the four components of social subordination – hierarchy, objectification, submission and violence. It executes and performs this subordination through the medium of sex: 'Sex is the material means through which the subordination is accomplished' (Dworkin, 1988c: 266–7). For radical lesbian feminists, pornography is 'an institution with a key role in legitimising both heterosexuality, and violence against women' (Reeves and Wingfield, 1996: 61). It is not surprising, then, that lesbians were central to the feminist anti-pornography movement in the second wave.

Anti-porn feminists point to scholarship over several decades that has established the prevalence of violent and misogynist content in mainstream porn (Malamuth and Spinner, 1980; Cowan *et al.*, 1988; Jensen and Dines, 1998; Russell, 1998; Barron and Kimmel, 2000; Jensen, 2004b; Dines, 2010; Tyler, 2010). A comparison of two separate studies carried out in 2000 and 2007 demonstrated 'a notable increase in many aggressive behaviours in the decade between the studies' (Bridges, 2010: 47), with the 2007 study finding that 'physical and verbal aggression are the norm rather than the exception in popular pornographic films', occurring in 88 per cent of scenes. Acts of aggression included verbal abuse, choking, gagging, slapping, kicking, hitting, biting, pinching, hair pulling, whipping and physical restraint, and using weapons, and were overwhelmingly (94 per cent) directed at women; 41 per cent of scenes included 'ass-to-mouth' penetration of the woman (*ibid.*: 46). As will be discussed in the following chapter, it is freely acknowledged by those involved in the porn industry that porn has become increasingly violent and 'extreme' over the last couple of decades (Jensen, 2007; Samuels, 2009; Dines, 2010; Tyler, 2010). Summarising the results of such scholarship, Jensen identifies three key themes of pornography as follows:

(1) All women at all times want sex from all men; (2) women enjoy all the sexual acts that men perform or demand, and; (3) any woman who does not at first realise this can be easily turned with a little force, though force is rarely necessary because most of the women in pornography are the imagined 'nymphomaniacs' about whom many men fantasise. (Jensen, 2004b: 3)

Anti-porn feminists assert a number of relationships between pornography and violence against women. First, the production of porn obviously involves the participation of real women, and the repeated sexual use, abuse and penetration of their bodies in various ways: in this sense, as Dworkin argues (1981), pornography *is* violence. Citing testimonies and accounts of female performers' experiences in the industry (McGrady and Lovelace, 1980; Everywoman, 1988; Jensen, 2007; Picker and Sun, 2008; Samuels, 2009; Boyle, 2011), anti-porn feminists understand the 'body-punishing' (Dines, 2010) acts to which women performers are routinely subjected as violence, arguing that experiences of harm and violence are not necessarily dependent on whether or not someone chooses or consents to the acts which result in such harm (Whisnant, 2004).

Second, anti-porn feminists argue that there is a relationship between pornography and further acts of male violence (Russell, 1998). Women testify to men's use of pornography in perpetrating acts of sexual violence (Everywoman, 1988). This includes the use of porn in perpetrating coercive or aggressive sexual behaviour towards female partners (Paul, 2005; Dines, 2010; Rothman, 2011), and the acting out of pornographic scenarios on prostituted women (Mott, 2012). The influence of violent pornography has been implicated in high-profile cases of sexual murder (Press Association, 2004; Bindel, 2011).

A considerable body of research provides evidence of effects in relation to exposure to pornography (discussed in Jensen, 2004b). There are, of course, obvious limits to laboratory-based 'effects' experiments, and complexities of trying to attribute direct causal factors for human behaviour. However, given the content of mainstream pornography as outlined above, and the use and abuse of real women's bodies in producing it, the words of Florynce Kennedy that preface this book seem particularly apt. As Dworkin memorably articulates, given the practices involved in porn production, there seems something extraneous in looking for specific 'effects' outside of the pornography itself:

> I am very grateful to the research community, which has taken feminist theory seriously enough to try to see if in fact pornography does harm to women. I say that because I am entirely outraged that someone has to study whether hanging a woman from a meat hook causes harm or not. (Dworkin, 1988: 247)

Other anti-porn feminists advocate moving 'beyond cause and effects' in order to open up other ways of thinking about how pornography works (Cameron and Frazer, 1992; Boyle, 2000). This approach – alongside the crucial recognition of porn production as a practice involving the abuse of real women – offers particularly fruitful ways of understanding the relationship between pornography and sexual violence. It is incontrovertible that pornography puts certain representations into circulation; representations which are produced and used in specific ways. The key question is, what is the social meaning and function of these representations?

If we accept that gender and sexuality are socially constructed through social institutions and practices as diverse as children's toys and literature, education, systems of law and medicine and so forth, it seems reasonable to accept that pornography as a discourse and practice plays a similar role in the social construction of sexual and gendered identity. Given the content of hegemonic pornography, which we have already established has dominant patterns of male aggression and violence directed at women, and its purpose as a cultural product for the sexual arousal of men, it again seems reasonable to believe that pornography plays a role in shaping normative ideas of male dominance and female subordination.

Hegemonic porn is a practice, a homosocial means by which men share stories – stories that provide ways of thinking about the nature of men, women and sex. Pornography functions as 'a significant source of ideas and narratives' within culture (Cameron and Frazer, 1992: 381) and provides men 'with a vehicle through which they can enact, relive and anticipate the demands of hegemonic masculinity ... the particular power of pornography lies in linking this process to sexual arousal and pleasure' (Johnson, 2010).

In the context of the global pandemic of violence against women acknowledged at the beginning of this chapter, such narratives might be considered to constitute a form of cultural violence – an aspect of the symbolic sphere that can be used to justify or legitimise direct or structural violence (Galtung, 1990: 291). This understanding of pornography as a form of cultural violence is important, for it renders the harm of pornography intelligible, independently of attempts to demonstrate 'cause and effect'-type harms. Such an understanding is crucial, and has precedents that have been established in relation to other societal groups and cultural forms. For example, when I was a child a particular brand of jam had the image of a 'golliwog' on the jar; in primary school, the teacher read the all-white class stories from a book called *Little Black Sambo*. Such images and narratives were considered perfectly innocuous by the white majority population in 1970s Britain. However, through the struggles of anti-racist activists, over time the society reached a consensus that such cultural forms were unacceptable, since they contribute to a culture of racism. This consensus was reached without the need to prove a direct causal link between the cultural products and specific acts of violence: however, it did entail an understanding of the ways in which racist language and imagery within the culture helps to create a context where such violence is imaginable, and contributes to its legitimisation or justification. It is instructive that the same understanding has had little traction with regard to pornography, where extreme and blatant racist imagery, language and narratives are commonplace (Forna, 1992; Dines, 2010).

The prevalence of pornography within the culture means that 'pornographic fictions continue to shape our culture's sexual and social imagination more thoroughly and powerfully than competing discourses can' (Cameron and Frazer, 1992: 379). For anti-porn feminists, the struggle against pornography is nothing less than the struggle to change the 'normal and normative sexual practice of our culture' (*ibid*.: 381). Far from being a distraction from issues of 'real' violence against women, it is inextricably bound up with the struggle to end the reality of male violence in women's lives, not least the lives of those abused in the production of pornography itself.

Objectification

> She becomes symbol of this, symbol of that: mother of the earth, slut of the universe; but she never becomes herself because it is forbidden for her to do so. No act of hers can overturn the way in which she is consistently perceived: as some sort of thing. (Dworkin, 1981: 128)

> Women are the generic object of culture, culture is the monologue of the male gender. (Kappeler, 1986: 215)

'Objectification' is a critical concept for anti-porn feminists, since it extends the scope of analysis from a consideration of explicitly violent pornography to include a broader consideration of the problem of the pornographic representation of women as sexual objects. The construction of women as objects of the male gaze and male pleasure is a commonplace within a wide range of cultural and media products, from the canon of English Literature to fashion advertising. However, nowhere is the reduction of woman to object status more direct and unequivocal than within pornography.

The construction of the woman as object in pornography is crucial to what Dworkin identifies as the main theme of pornography: male power. '[S]he is the thing in contradistinction to which the male is human' (1981: 128). Woman's identity is reduced to a fetish whose sole purpose is to provoke a sexual response in the male viewer. Without the woman as object, the male 'would be unable to experience his own selfhood, his own power, his own penile presence and sexual superiority' (*ibid.*). Objectification is the woman's purpose, what she exists for; within and outside of pornography, women are rewarded proportionately to the

77

degree with which they comply with their own objectification, such as through subscribing to beauty practices: 'beauty is rewarded and lack of beauty is punished' (*ibid.*: 118). Women are therefore constantly at risk of internalising their object status, negotiating a devastating paradox in which social approval is won at the expense of full human status. Within pornography, financial incentives are offered to the female porn performer corresponding precisely to the degree and extent to which her body is subjected to sexual use by men.

The objectification of women in pornography is vital to the broader discursive construction as woman as object: 'Man fucks woman. Subject verb object' (MacKinnon, 1989: 124). The prevalent sexual acts of pornography signify female absence in relation to the male presence: she is a series of holes to be penetrated. Symbolically, she needs the penis to give her meaning, and so ultimately is grateful to it, no matter how violent the act or how much she might resist initially.

The objectification of women has its corollary in 'the subjectification of man' (Kappeler, 1986: 50). In Kappeler's analysis of the process of objectification, she identifies the pornographer as the speaking 'I' of the pornographic representation. Although the woman is foregrounded as the displayed object, the subject of the representation is male (whether he is within the picture or not: if the representation is an image of a naked woman, he is an implied presence only). This subject is, according to Kappeler, in direct communication with another male subject, the spectator or reader (1986: 52). This 'man to man' communication is strikingly conveyed in many examples from pornography: from 'readers' wives', through to contemporary revenge porn, and ex-girlfriend porn. In 2005, a British lads' mag ran a competition for readers to 'win a boob job for your girlfriend', thus inviting men to take up subject positions as consumers and owners not just of the magazine but of the bodies of women with whom they were in a personal relationship. The magazine therefore very explicitly constructed male subjectivity through the ownership and instrumentalisation of women.

Martha Nussbaum (1995: 257) identifies a number of characteristics that might be involved in the treatment of a human being as an object. These include:

Instrumentality: The objectifier treats the object as a tool of his or her purposes.

Denial of autonomy: The objectifier treats the object as lacking in autonomy and self-determination.

Inertness: The objectifier treats the object as lacking in agency, and perhaps also in activity.

Fungibility: The objectifier treats the object as interchangeable with other objects.

Violability: The objectifier treats the object as lacking in boundary-integrity, as something that it is permissible to break up, smash, break into.

Ownership: The objectifier treats the object as something that is owned by another, can be bought or sold, etc.

Denial of subjectivity: The objectifier treats the object as something whose experiences and feelings (if any) need not be taken into account.

Rae Langton adds three features to Nussbaum's list: *reduction to body*, which involves the treatment of a person as identified with their body, or body parts; *reduction to appearance*, which involves the treatment of a person primarily in terms of how they look, or how they appear to the senses; and *silencing*, involving the treatment of a person as if they are silent, lacking the capacity to speak (Langton, 2009: 228–9).

For Nussbaum, instrumentality is 'especially problematic', since it 'involves denying what is fundamental to them as human beings, namely the status of being ends in themselves. From this one denial, other forms of objectification ... seem to follow' (Nussbaum 1995: 265). This focus on instrumentality as a key element of objectification is particularly relevant to pornography, where the instrumentalisation of women for men's sexual use is the defining and endlessly repeated narrative of pornography. A superficial perusal of the kinds of mainstream porn sites described by Gail Dines in *Pornland* (2010) reveals that, within this dominant narrative, women are routinely presented as lacking in autonomy and agency (she does not determine the sexual script); as inert (she is acted upon, 'done to'); as fungible (she is anonymous and interchangeable with other 'sluts', 'bitches', 'MILFs' and so on); as violable (she is penetrated in multiple ways, and the breaking of her physical boundaries is celebrated); as owned (access to her body can be bought); and as lacking subjectivity (she has no history, experience, personality or identity beyond her sexual use). In the same vein, as part of the instrumentalising process, women in pornography are reduced to body parts (she is 'pussy', 'ass') and appearance (whole sub-genres of pornography centred around a woman's physical attributes, including racialised characteristics such as 'ebony', 'Asian' and 'blonde'). Finally, she is silenced: she has no autonomous voice, her only articulation is to respond to being acted upon either through articulating pleasure – an insatiable desire for more – or pain.

A key argument for anti-porn feminists is that objectification is harmful without additional violence, since the cultural violence of instrumentalising a whole class of people in this way is in itself harmful, involving a denial of subjectivity and personhood. The objectification of women in pornography also has to be seen in the context of a general asymmetry in the culture, where men are consistently constructed and represented as active human subjects across all media and cultural forms, from children's literature, where the lack of female characters effects the 'symbolic annihilation' of women (McCabe *et al.*, 2011) to news media and public life (Cochrane, 2011).

Choice, coercion and consent

For pro-porn and anti-censorship feminists, the notion of 'free choice' is crucial as an explanation and justification for individual women's participation in pornography and desire to consume pornography. In fact, a vocabulary of 'choice' is often used rhetorically as part of a discourse of justification by those wishing to defend the porn industry, deployed in order to silence debate around pornography, as if establishing that a woman freely chooses to perform in porn is the last word on the subject. What is striking about this position is how closely it chimes with neoliberal understandings of 'choice' as a dominant explanation of all human behaviour and social phenomena. Anti-porn feminists, by contrast, point out that choice only meaningfully exists when one is choosing from a set of options: the options must be available, visible and intelligible (and even then, the choice is still only a possibility in relation to the finite set of possible options):

> even a perfectly rational, freely choosing individual is con-strained by the fact that she must choose from the options that are available to her, and that are cast as appropriate for her. These options themselves may be limited; or they may violate an individual's well-being or her equality, since in order to access some benefit, the individual may be required to harm herself, and she may be required to harm herself when no such requirement is placed on other types of individuals seeking to access the benefit. (Chambers, 2008: 263)

The idea that women simply 'choose' to perform in pornography takes no account of women's social and economic position in relation to men in a male-dominated society. Anti-porn feminists therefore question the adequacy of a decontextualised concept of individual choice in explaining gendered social phenomena. Assuming for the time being that a woman has not directly been forced or coerced into performing in pornography or posing for a pornographic magazine, let us consider the implications of the assertion that she has simply and unproblematically exercised free choice in so doing. Such an assertion immediately raises a number of problems. First, as Gail Dines points out, 'choices' are never made outside of a specific context:

> All choices are made within a set of social, economic and political conditions that are often not of our own making. The more real power a person has, then the more they get to re-articulate the conditions of their lives, and the less powerful (such as young women) end up being constrained and limited by forces that are beyond their control. Radical feminism is not about individual choices so much as about changing the very conditions under which these choices are made. (Dines, 2009)

The question raised by anti-porn feminists, then, does not focus on the individual woman's choice, but rather on the meaning, nature and function of the practice in which she is engaging. Does the practice harm the individual woman, or women as a group? Does it help maintain male domination of women? How are relations of power configured in this practice? Such questions reveal that not only does an emphasis on choice tend to overplay women's agency in this scenario, but it similarly obscures the male demand that underlies why such a choice should be offered in the first place. For in a male-dominated society, where the sexual objectification and commodification of women are routine and normalised, and where male demand for pornography dictates that a pool of women must be available to participate in its production, it is both inevitable and predictable that some women – often in the absence of other viable choices – will choose to participate in the porn industry. However, establishing that an individual woman has made a particular choice is not necessarily the last word on the debate, for the key question of harm remains: 'That something is chosen or consensual is perfectly consistent with its being seriously oppressive, abusive and harmful – to oneself and/ or to a broader group of which one is a member (e.g. women)' (Whisnant, 2004: 23).

Problems with the 'free choice' argument also include a notable failure to focus on men's choice and agency and the respective positions of men and women in relation to porn production and consumption. Whilst 'she chooses to do it' is a common refrain in relation to women's participation in porn, it is seldom heard in relation to men's choice to produce or consume porn.

Similarly, a focus on individual choice fails to take account of specifically gendered social patterns and trends. For example, while participating in many Student Union debates on pornography I have noticed what appears to be a fixation with women's choice to perform specific acts that are commonplace within pornography, such as facials (see Chapter 3), anal sex, double penetration, double anal, throat-gagging and so forth. Interestingly enough, the consensus that invariably emerges in the debating chamber on such occasions is that some hypothetical woman somewhere can be assumed to choose or like such acts. This hypothetical woman is then referenced triumphantly, as if to suggest that questioning her choice to be repeatedly penetrated in multiple ways and ejaculated upon in multiple ways is to reveal yourself as an enemy of both freedom and womankind, as opposed to the benevolent and woman-loving porn industry, which generously provides her with numerous opportunities to exercise her hypothetical choices and desires. Of course, there is much that is problematic about this line of argument. First, as noted, the preoccupation with the woman's choice or preference erases male demand from the picture. Second, the focus on individual choice fails to take account of the way that social forces and norms work, for if the porn industry did not exist and did not demand the participation of thousands of women in such acts, how likely is it that each one of those thousands of women would 'freely' and autonomously choose to participate in painful, risky and body-punishing acts anyway? And in the rather unlikely event that they did, would that 'free choice' render those acts any less painful, risky and body-punishing? Finally, a focus on choice woefully fails to take into account the cultural and symbolic meaning of those acts, within the porn narrative. Images of facials and double anal, for example, can hardly be read as polysemic, open to infinite interpretations; they are not *constructed* to be read as powerful expressions of individual women's sexual choice and agency. Rather, they form part of a consistent pornographic narrative of degradation and humiliation of the woman, constructing her as a slut who can't help herself, who needs to be taught a lesson, whose sole purpose is to serve as a receptacle and exhibit for male power and potency. Such meanings then circulate within the culture, shaping ways of understanding what it means to be a woman or a man, which in turn form part of the conditions of more 'free' choices.

Of course, regarding many women's involvement in the porn industry, the use of the word 'choice' is entirely inappropriate. Force, exploitation and coercion are common routes into the porn industry (Everywoman, 1988), or routes to submitting to more 'extreme' acts once inside the industry (Jensen, 2007; Jeffreys, 2009). Force might include the use of drugs, physical violence or threats of violence, grooming, trafficking and abduction. Exploitation might include the manipulation of vulnerabilities such as age, economic vulnerability, a personal history of abuse, lack of family, friends and social supports, and periods spent in the care system. This absolute lack of even the most basic notion of choice needs to be recognised and understood before any questions of choice and consent are addressed. Coercion might include economic, psychological or emotional pressure: an open secret within the industry, as the following British porn industry advice to potential performers illustrates:

> Far too many girls get put off because they regret doing something they should not have done at the time because of pressure from producers. Not only will you have to live with that decision but also it could sway the rest of the industry to demand more of the same from you. ... A common tactic I've seen to manipulate girls to consider going harder is to deprive them of work so they consider upping their levels ... a girl who does everything is more likely to get bookings over one that does not offer as much. (UK Adult Producers website)[8]

The construction of adult women as 'girls' in this statement is telling.

The payment structure of the UK porn industry illustrates how women are financially incentivised to participate in more extreme acts, with fees on the UK Adults Producers website ranging from 'Solo girl' (£200–£250) and 'Girl/ Girl' (£200–£300), through 'Boy/ Girl' (£250–£300) and 'Boy/Girl w anal' (£300–£400) up to 'Boy/Girl w dp [double penetration]' (£350–£450).

In order to emphasise that women have *not* been coerced into performing, the porn industry and pro-porn feminists rely heavily on the notion of consent. There are of course blatant examples of non-consensually produced pornography: for example, within some amateur and 'revenge' porn where women are unwittingly filmed whilst participating in sex acts; or where a woman is filmed or her image distributed without her consent, as in the case of 'sexting' and 'upskirting', or as part of sexual abuse or rape. However, even leaving aside such clear instances, the notion of consent – like that of choice – is hugely problematic. First, under patriarchal power relations, women's consent to heterosexual penetration is constructed as the norm.

The word 'consent' – from the Latin meaning 'with feeling' – suggests the lack of determination of a situation: various dictionary definitions include 'to give assent, as to the proposal of another', 'to acquiesce', 'acceptance or approval of what is done by another', 'acquiescence', 'compliance', 'to permit, approve, or agree'; 'comply or yield, to give assent or permission (to do something)'; 'acquiescence to or acceptance of something done or planned by another'. One consents to something that someone else has proposed or decided will happen; the consenting party does not initiate the situation, but agrees to it. We seldom hear talk of male consent because it is rarely an issue (unless between men): the individual in the subject position is going to be the one deciding or proposing. This norm of the male dictating or driving the sexual scenario, and the woman reduced to granting or withholding consent, is amply illustrated by an important study on teenagers and sexual relationships that came to the conclusion that both young women and young men experience 'the male in the head': 'the elusive but entrenched ways masculinity is privileged within conventional heterosexuality' (Holland *et al.*, 1998: 30). Janet Holland and her colleagues found that there was no equivalent 'female in the head': 'Neither those women who resist conventional femininity nor the men who resist masculinity appear to have a 'female-in-the-head' as the basis of their identity ... male needs, male bodies, and male desires are dominant' (*ibid.*: 189). The findings of Holland *et al.* regarding teenage sexual relationships and experiences have important implications regarding the question of consent:

> The social construction of femininity encourages young women not only to cede agency and submit to this male power, but also to contribute to it through their own disembodiment ... the successful construction of femininity in relation to masculinity requires women to enable the exercise of men's power. (*Ibid.*: 127)

If, as Holland and her colleagues found, 'the dynamics of heterosexual relationships effectively silence an embodied and desiring female subjectivity' (*ibid*.: 29), then the lessons learnt in socialisation into normative heterosexuality raise serious questions regarding the consent of women in the porn industry, who have been subject to this socialisation – a socialisation to which, of course, the porn industry itself contributes significantly. Given the aggressive performance of male heterosexuality that is the mainstay of hegemonic porn, how can women's consent to such a performance be meaningful, if the very performance presupposes and is predicated upon her silence and lack of subjectivity? Other research has reached similar conclusions regarding difficulties experienced by young women in asserting themselves and their desires in heterosexual relationships. In her study of adolescent girls and their experiences of sexual desire, Tollman identifies the impossible situation that her research subjects inhabit. One young woman, Barbara, has learnt to repress her desires through 'fear of being humiliated, feeling embarrassed, being laughed at' whilst simultaneously being 'filled with regret and frustration at having silenced herself' (1998: 109–10). While these studies concern adolescent girls and young women negotiating specific sexual situations, and therefore do not map straightforwardly onto the commercial porn production scenario, what is pertinent to the question of consent regarding the latter is that male aggression and assertiveness along with female passivity and silencing are the norms of heterosexuality that both male porn producers and female porn performers have learnt in adolescence, and which porn itself helps to construct and perpetuate. Given that both have been 'shaped by social norms rendering problematic a girl's agency in general and her sexual agency in particular' (*ibid*.: 114), and given the fact that within the pornographic scenario the woman is involved not in negotiating a scenario of desire but rather a commercial transaction within a profit-driven industry, how meaningful is her consent when she is financially incentivised and quite possibly pressurised to perform certain acts, and when expectations are freighted not only with the kinds of norms into which both she and the male pornographers have been socialised, but with the demands of the industry? When the entire genre of hegemonic pornography is based on the permanent and unconditional sexual access to all parts of women's bodies, how useful is the notion of consent?

Of course, there are many examples where pornography is created and disseminated without the woman's consent: her sexualised image – or a record of her abuse – may have been recorded without her knowledge, or in a situation of force where she had no choice. Even if initial consent is given, as one radical feminist blogger points out, once a woman has participated in a porn scene, it is impossible for her to revoke this consent: instead, her image and videos 'remain masturbatory aids for any man who finds them'.[9] The trauma from having a record of one's abuse permanently available for the pleasure and gratification of future consumers needs to be integrated into any consideration of 'consent'.

What is peculiarly absent from the pro-porn appeal to notions of consent is any understanding of the praxis of cultural hegemony. In relation to news media and advertising, theories of how the consent of the powerless is *manufactured* by the powerful (Chomsky and Herman, 1988) enjoy longstanding respect and credence within academia. It is strange, then, that in relation to pornographic media, the term 'consent' is deployed so unreflexively, and that such burden of meaning is placed on such a fragile concept. Notions of choice and consent are of course completely consonant with neoliberal discourse and their prevalence is therefore unsurprising in the current political climate; however, the unproblematised deployment of such terms within academic debates on pornography betrays a curious and anomalous lack of sophistication in theorising the political and social functions of media and culture.

Free speech and censorship

> The answer to bad porn isn't no porn ... it's to try and make better porn!
> (Annie Sprinkle)[10]

> The growing power of the pornographers significantly diminishes the likelihood that women will ever experience freedom of anything – certainly not sexual self-determination, certainly not freedom of speech.
> (Dworkin, 1988: 225)

As we saw in Chapter 1, pro-porn feminists, including those who are critical of some aspects of the porn industry, are opposed to legal interventions that would increase the censorship of pornography. In making this argument, they appeal to the liberal notion of free speech as a supreme social value to be upheld (Strossen, 1995), apparently accepting the highly problematic conceptualisation of pornography as 'speech'. This unproblematised notion of free speech is one that is deployed emphatically and relentlessly by the porn industry itself, as indicated by the name of the industry lobby group in the USA – the Free Speech Coalition. As well as uncritically championing the notion of free speech, pro-porn feminists warn that any state intervention that increases censorship would be likely to have an adverse effect on the freedom of women and minority groups, and would obstruct feminist advances in the area of sexuality (Duggan, Hunter and Vance, 1988; Duggan, 1988; Parmar, 1988; Rubin, 1993; Gorna, 1993; Segal, 1993a, 1993b; Duggan and Hunter, 1995; Strossen, 1995).

Anti-censorship feminists argue that we watch violence in other contexts – war films, action movies – and also other media where women are seen in subordinate roles such as advertising, so the fact that sexually explicit images are being singled out indicates morality around sex rather than a concern about sexism and violence (George, 1988; Rubin, 1993). In the view of anti-censorship feminists, the problem is a lack of honest discussion around sex, which a more censorious climate would inhibit still further (George, 1988).

A wariness around state intervention is understandable, given the patriarchal nature of the state, and the potential for greater powers to be used against women. Pro-porn feminists argue that censorship would endanger the rights of women and oppressed minority groups, and there is therefore a danger in the state determining what is permissible or prohibited. As we saw in Chapter 1, this was a particular concern in the 1980s, when deeply conservative governments were in office in the USA and the UK.

A central pro-porn argument is that, rather than advocate for censorship – which is understood as a denial of speech – the feminist response should be to meet the sexism of mainstream pornography with what Nadine Strossen terms 'counterspeech'. For Strossen, '[m]ore speech about sex – education, information, and the development of critical viewing skills – not less, is the answer' (1995: 273).

Judith Butler frames attempts at censorship as 'representational violence' which she claims should be countered with the promotion of 'a proliferation of representations, sites of discursive production which might then contest the authoritative production produced by the prohibitive law' (2000: 502). Pro-porn feminists argue that women need to produce their 'own sexually explicit narratives and images of female desire and sensuous engagement' (Segal, 1993a: 19). Part of this project involves the production of a 'feminist' pornography. Such a move would entail developing a 'transgressive cultural politics'

(McIntosh, 1993: 168), which could 'play a part in the formation of a feminist-centred sexuality' (George, 1988).

The challenge of developing 'counterspeech' has been taken up enthusiastically by a number of third wave and queer feminists in the project of developing 'feminist' pornography. The claims and contradictions of 'feminist porn' will be addressed briefly later in the chapter.

The pluralist idea that the production of such images could seriously challenge the porn industry – the view that all ideas and images can compete in the cultural marketplace – does not take account of women's lack of economic and cultural resources in respect of a multi-billion dollar, globalised porn industry, so that even if the production of such images did constitute a feminist project, it is unlikely to have a serious effect or influence on the mainstream industry under present economic and social arrangements. Certainly, to date, the project of creating counter-images has not succeeded in posing any significant challenge to the commercially dominant, hegemonic porn industry, which continues to expand, diversify and extend its reach into the mainstream, as we will see in Chapter 3.

It should be noted that while pro-porn feminists such as Strossen and Rubin habitually refer to anti-porn feminists as 'pro-censorship', this appellation is distinctly misleading. As discussed in Chapter 1, the pioneering legal challenge to pornography developed by anti-porn feminists, the Dworkin-MacKinnon ordinance, did not propose censorship through the 'prior restraint' of pornography, but as a civil rather than criminal law it instead sought to provide a means via which women could seek restitution for harm that they had experienced due to pornography. As we have seen, the definitions of what would constitute pornography and specific categories of harm were set out very precisely and in great detail in the ordinance. However, pro-porn feminist literature of the time consistently misrepresents the ordinance: interpreting the law as involving prior restraint, claiming that educational and feminist self-help books like *Our Bodies, Ourselves* would be 'censored' (Strossen, 1995: 204); questioning whether any image of a woman would be 'safe' from the censors (Segal and McIntosh, 1993: 25); and stating that anyone could bring a civil suit against 'anything deemed to be offensive' (Parmar, 1988: 126). As noted in Chapter 1, the misrepresentation seems to indicate an unwillingness to engage with the anti-porn arguments behind the ordinance.

The argument that the state is male-dominated and serves specific interests is of course valid, but by this logic no feminist or oppressed group would campaign for legal interventions; there would have been no campaigns for changes in legislation regarding domestic violence or rape in marriage, for example. And if the state is male-dominated, so too is the market, so rejecting an engagement of the state does not leave a level playing field where women can express themselves in a pluralist society; it simply means other male-dominated institutions, such as the porn industry, will prevail, as has patently been the case since 1980s.

There is an obvious problem with seeing porn as speech: porn is produced through a set of practices, involving real people and real acts happened upon and within real women's bodies. It is hard to see how what constitutes the mainstream of contemporary pornography could be understood straightforwardly as 'speech'. So, the appeal to the concept of free speech is in fact an appeal for certain practices to be treated as speech, and to take place without restraint. Such a stance is clearly libertarian rather than liberal, since most versions of liberalism acknowledge that freedom is not absolute, but needs to be balanced alongside other social values such as justice or equality. The freedom of the porn industry to act without restraint must be balanced with considerations of justice for women and women's equality.

Libertarianism, on the other hand, positions individual liberty as the foundational moral principle of society: interpreted and promulgated in this instance by the porn industry and, apparently, pro-porn feminists, as the right of the industry to conduct its business uncurtailed and regardless of its consequences on the rights or freedoms of others. Significantly, the freedom of women to live without restraint from the porn industry appears to be unintelligible within libertarian approaches.

The notion of free speech, like the notions of choice and consent discussed in the previous section, is ironically enough consistently deployed rhetorically by the porn industry to silence dissent. Following Monbiot's critique of rightwing libertarianism (2011), it can be understood that the 'free speech' get-out-of-jail-free card is the means by which the porn industry frames its desire to exploit and abuse without restraint as a fundamental right to be protected, and characterises any attempt to curb that right as tyranny. Pro-porn, anti-censorship approaches perpetuate the illusion that the state is the only threat to liberty. It renders invisible the myriad ways in which the practices of the multi-billion dollar porn industry impinge on women's freedoms. These framings also ignore the fact that, as a society, we agree to all kinds of restraints on our individual liberty all the time, for the sake of what is held to be a greater social good – from the existence of criminal laws against violence and murder, to prohibitions on smoking and the enforcement of wearing of seatbelts, for example. These restraints also include restraints on speech, in the form of laws on incitement to racial hatred, for example, and laws around public order. Not all 'free speech', therefore, is seen as 'good' and unconditionally worthy of protection under the law. The idea of 'free speech' as an absolute and non-negotiable good is also challenged by problematising the term 'free' and introducing the term 'fair' (McLellan, 2010, 2011). For example, the concept of 'free trade' can be understood as being unfair in serving the interest of wealthier nations to the detriment of the interest of poorer nations; the term and practice of 'fair trade' is thus introduced as a means of challenging and exposing that self-serving version of freedom. In a parallel move, one might highlight the interested and oppressive nature of 'free speech' through introducing the concept of 'fair speech': a move which brings the lack of fairness of pornographic speech into sharp relief (*ibid.*).

Setting aside the question of whether pornography can be counted simply as speech, for anti-porn feminists pornography is not simply an expression: pornography does certain things. For MacKinnon, pornography both subordinates and silences women (1994). Although pornography might not explicitly state that women are inferior or that sexual violence is legitimate, the narratives of pornography presuppose such propositions, because they are 'required for the hearer to make best sense of what is said' (Langton and West, 1999: 9). Through these narratives – for example, that women say no when they mean yes, or that women enjoy rape – pornography makes certain kinds of illocutionary utterances impossible or unintelligible for women: it therefore 'makes moves which subordinate and silence women, moves which women, as subordinate and silent, cannot then adequately challenge' (*ibid.*: 16). To characterise the anti-porn feminist as a tyrant who threatens the freedom of the porn industry to 'speak' is to presuppose that both feminists and pornographers are equally able to speak, whereas in fact women are silenced and rendered powerless in innumerable ways in society, including by pornography (Dworkin, 1998).

One of the key ways in which pornography 'speaks' is through the naming of women: 'The history of representation is the history of the male gender representing itself to itself – the power of naming is men's' (Kappeler, 1986: 53; see also Dworkin, 1981: 17–18). The one-way process of men naming women through pornography is evident in the lexicon of misogynist terms by which women are referred to in pornography (Dines, 2010), that have no male equivalent. This naming then enters the culture, becoming part of the spectrum of ways in which it is possible to think about women. An analysis of hate speech suggests that pornography can also be classed as such. Hate speech can be identified through four features: it aims to inflame emotions; it aims to denigrate the designated out-class; it aims to inflict permanent and irreparable harm to the opposition; it aims to conquer (Whillock, 2005). The misogynistic and aggressive nature of mainstream pornography, along with its aim to be sexually stimulating, can be understood as aiming to inflame the emotions of the reader (this might include sexual arousal, feelings of power, hatred towards women, the shoring up of masculine identity and male bonding). Denigration of women is achieved through the stereotyping of women as sluts and bitches, and through the acts to which they are subjected, which are intended to be understood as degrading. The aim to inflict irreparable harm on the opposition can be understood as the effect of positioning women as objects. Finally, the aim of conquering can be read in the endlessly repeated narratives of women being violated, instrumentalised and denied subjectivity – she is conquered by the man, or any number of men, and also by her own inescapably 'sluttish' nature.

It is worth noting that whilst the reach of hegemonic pornography continues to expand, there is plenty of evidence that feminists who criticise porn are silenced in myriad ways (Dworkin, 1988; Jeffreys, 1988; Sere, 2004). As we will see in Chapter 3, many of the women I interviewed experienced attempts by friends and family to silence them when they tried to articulate a porn-critical, feminist perspective.

Finally, a recognition of the material realities of pornography as a practice and an industry needs to inform and challenge any framing of pornography of speech. The real, lived experiences of women abused in the making of pornography give the lie to the idea that pornography constitutes individual expression. In assertions by pornographers of their right to free speech, the voices of these women remain unheard.

Fantasy and reality

A central argument of pro-porn feminists is to assert the importance of sexual fantasy, and to locate pornography within that realm (Vance, 1984; Rubin, 1984; Segal, 1993b). Since women's sexual subjectivity has been repressed, the argument goes, a feminist goal should be the liberation of women's sexuality, and sexual fantasy should be recognised as an important part of such a project. Whilst the goal of women's sexual liberation is one which anti-porn feminists would share – as part of a broader project of women's liberation – anti-porn feminists nonetheless challenge the uncritical celebration and demand for recognition of any version of sexuality that does not also incorporate a critical reflection on where desires and fantasies originate. Where pro-porn feminists tend to embrace the left-liberal idea of sex, and therefore sexual fantasy, as being an inherently good impulse that must be liberated, anti-porn feminists see sex, sexual practices and sexual fantasies as constructed under patriarchy and subject to political scrutiny.

Anti-porn feminists point out that pornography is not simply a 'fantasy'; it is a product produced through specific, material practices, and therefore embedded in the *realities* of the globalised marketplace. Real women are used in the making of pornography, the acts recorded in pornography are real, not 'fantasy'. Women harmed in the production of pornographic images live with the consequences, effects and trauma of those experiences in the real world (Farley, 2011). The industry generates profits; porn production and distribution involves complex networks of subsidiary and related industries, such as billing companies, internet service providers, mobile phone companies and hotel chains. The porn industry holds trade fairs, conventions and summits; porn consumers engage with the industry through attending such events, and through posting reviews of videos onto user sites. Far from being located in the realm of the 'fantasy', pornography is part of social reality: produced within specific situations and economic relationships; distributed, sold, circulated and consumed. The narratives and language of pornography become part of the stream of culture, its terms entering the vocabulary, its images referenced in advertising, fashion and music videos, its practices contributing to norms and expectations about sex that are replicated in personal relationships and sexual encounters. The idea of porn existing only in a 'fantasy realm' flies in the face of all that is known about the interrelationships between desire, language, images and the construction of 'reality': the existence of the advertising and fashion industries, for example, testify to the fact that images help to shape attitudes, desires and behaviour. In Afghanistan, frontline British troops were reportedly shown footage of Apache attack helicopters killing people in order 'to boost morale' (Dutta, 2011): such a project obviously rests on the assumption that viewing certain images will have some kind of consequences in 'reality'. 'Fantasy' arguments rely heavily on the liberal distinction between the public and the private: the idea that absolute freedom is appropriate regarding fantasy, because it takes place within the sacrosanct realm of the private. However, such arguments are troubled by the mainstreaming of pornography and processes of pornification: as we shall see in the next chapter, it is evident that pornography is increasingly contributing to the shaping of social reality; becoming part of what is experienced as 'real'. This is evident through its role in creating normative ideas around the nature of masculinity, femininity, sex and desirable sexual practices, as well as through its very real effects regarding women's freedom and equal participation in society.

Empowerment and agency

In current British and US society, few situations elicit the word 'empowerment' from commentators as predictably as that of a woman taking her clothes off in public. 'Sherlock's nude "dominatrix" says she found the role "empowering"' (Plunkett, 2012); 'Women feel empowered', says daytime television host Richard Madeley, of his daughter Chloe's photoshoot for lads' mag FHM (Clements, 2009). The term is also commonly used in association with women's participation in other activities predicated on their objectification, such as beauty contests[11] and pole-dancing classes.[12] Entire reality TV series are dedicated to helping women to achieve the unique empowerment that can only come from baring all in front of millions of strangers.[13]

The current usage of the term 'empowerment' in relation to women's participation in the sex industry is instructive. A legalistic term dating from the mid-seventeenth century, the word originally meant 'to authorise or license' (Allen, 1991). It gained a more collective meaning at the time of the civil rights and women's liberation movements, and its origin as a social theory is traceable to Paolo Freire's plan for education as a means of liberation from oppression (Hur, 2006). Since then, it has continued to be used in this collective sense in relation to community programmes and strategies addressing disadvantage and oppression. However, in the minority world any potential sense of collectivity in the term has been eclipsed by its increasing usage from the early 1990s to denote a highly individualised rather than collective experience. In this sense, the term 'empowerment' is extremely problematic, as it incorporates and de-politicises the crucial word 'power', manoeuvring it into a kind of linguistic headlock where it is no longer useful for or amenable to feminist analysis. An important project for anti-porn feminists is the reinstating of serious discussions and analyses of power in relation to women, men and the sex industry; a discussion which a preoccupation with individual 'empowerment' impedes.

As discussed in an earlier section, radical feminist analyses of patriarchal power are central to anti-porn feminism (Millett, 1970; Dworkin, 1981). From an anti-porn perspective, it is clear that pornography acts as an instrument of patriarchal power, in terms of the ownership and control of the industry, how it functions to subordinate women, how it constructs and reinforces an oppressive male sexuality and how it presumes and requires the availability of a class of women for its production. An understanding of this structure of domination highlights the inadequacy of the concept of 'empowerment' as an analytical tool to theorise women's relationship to pornography.

Given that hegemonic pornography is a product produced and consumed by men, it is hard to see how it can be empowering to women, who are positioned as the commodity in the scenario. At best, it appears there are two consequences that a woman may experience as beneficial: financial reward and an approving male gaze (a satisfied customer). The first of these *is* likely to constitute a significant benefit for the individual woman, particularly if she is economically disadvantaged and unable to secure a decent income by other means. The second relies on the woman being heavily invested in the approving male gaze for her sense of identity and self-worth; an internalisation of her objectified status under patriarchy. In neither case does the benefit effect any kind of shift in the structure of domination; no *actual* empowerment is evident. While there is a material benefit in the first case, this is minimal compared to the profits enjoyed by the male owners and producers. The need for the material benefit also makes the woman particularly vulnerable to both the producer and consumer in the scenario, since as they both have economic power in relation to her they can influence the level and nature of her participation through financial pressure and rewards. In the second case, the woman simply experiences a feeling of approval or validation (of being 'sexy' or 'hot', for example) as her body or performance is reflected back to her through the male gaze. In this case, she also has gained no real power; any *feeling* of power is totally dependent on the male gaze, which can be withdrawn or become hostile at any point, and is in fact premised on her own debasement and object status. In both cases, the structure of domination remains untroubled – rather, it is reinforced – and any sense of empowerment attributable to the female performer pales in the face of the actual financial empowerment enjoyed by the producer (who can of course profit repeatedly from product sales), and the sense of power enjoyed by the consumer, whose masculinity has been buttressed through viewing the sexual use and debasement of a woman.

Claims that pornography affords opportunities for women's empowerment are further belied by an understanding of the way in which the industry functions. Jennifer Johnson's important analysis of the online porn industry reveals the highly complex and sophisticated ways in which the industry works to extract money from male consumers and potential consumers (2010). Johnson's work reminds us that the industry was hardly intended to serve as an empowerment programme for women, but functions rather as a fundamentally and supremely *commercial* enterprise, operating at the nexus of patriarchy and capitalism. Johnson's social network analysis of the online industry leads her to draw the conclusion that 'at its core, commercial pornography is a system where men manipulate other men for money' (2011). An understanding of this scenario – where women are the product at the heart of a homosocial, commercial transaction – is a crucial starting point from which to evaluate claims regarding women's empowerment in the industry.

A particular danger of a focus on empowerment is that it erases the experiences of women abused within the industry (Dines, 2010: xxvii–xxviii). A dominant discourse of empowerment creates myths that serve to silence survivors of the porn and sex industries, or to render their accounts unintelligible. The same is true in relation to the currently much-favoured focus on 'agency': the idea that individual women are exercising 'agency' through participation in porn not only obscures the wider power structures within which they are located, but also obscures the coercion and force to which many women are subjected within the industry. The problem of how to theorise agency in relation to societal norms, cultural forces and regimes of power is the subject of considerable academic debate regarding women and pornification (Duits and van Zoonen, 2006, 2007; Gill, 2007a; Whitehead and Kurz, 2009; Evans *et al.*, 2010). These debates address questions such as how to represent and respect the choices and voices of women who participate in what might be seen as 'pornified' practices such as cosmetic surgery or recreational pole dancing, whilst at the same time subjecting such accounts to feminist intellectual scrutiny. Gill advocates a stance of 'critical respect' towards women's individual voices, emphasising that this does not involve abdicating 'the right to question or interrogate' their accounts:

> Respectful listening is the beginning, not the end, of the process and our job is surely to contextualise these stories, to situate them, to look at their patterns and variability, to examine their silences and exclusions, and, above all, to locate them in a wider context. (Gill, 2007a: 76)

The key phrase here is 'a wider context'. Any attention to women's 'agency' with regard to porn or 'pornified' practices needs to be informed by the recognition of women's lack of power as a class, and the fact that it is men, not women, who dictate the conditions within which any such agency is exercised. The limitations of such agency are clear: as Miriam notes in relation to prostitution, 'one aspect of the sexual order remains *non*-negotiable ... namely, men's right to be sexually serviced' (Miriam, 2005: 14). On an individual basis, women's agency can only ever be exercised *within* these conditions; since structures of domination can only be addressed through a collective response, individual agency poses no threat. As Miriam pertinently observes: 'The question is, what is the *meaning* of agency – and indeed "empowerment" – when these terms are defined as a capacity to negotiate within a situation that is itself taken for granted as inevitable?' (*ibid.*: 11).

For anti-porn feminists, drawing on the insights developed by second wave consciousness raising, the structural nature of women's oppression can only be addressed through collective struggles to challenge the material basis of that oppression. In relation to pornography,

> radical feminism must be expanded to theorise freedom in terms of women's collective political agency ...: this task requires an understanding that freedom is not negotiating within a system taken as inevitable, but rather, a capacity to radically transform and/or determine the situation itself. (*Ibid.*: 14)

Porn as a feminist project?

Since the focus of this book is the resurgence of feminist anti-porn activism, and in turn the focus of such activism is pornification and hegemonic pornography, there is not the space here to enter into a full analysis of so-called 'feminist porn'. However, since it is a phenomenon increasingly invoked as evidence of the diversity and heterogeneity of the porn industry, I will briefly consider such claims.

Recent years have seen a growth of queer and 'feminist' porn production, though it still remains marginal to the industry. The Good For Her Feminist Porn Awards, set up by a Toronto women's sex shop, Good For Her, in 2006, offer an insight into the ethos and values of the enterprise. The awards are said to be 'feminist' and 'sex positive', constituting 'the longest running celebration of erotica focused on women and marginalised people', celebrating 'feminist smut', and showcasing 'those who are creating erotic media with a feminist sensibility'. The organisers' rationale for the awards is:

> We believe the world is inundated with cheesy, cliche, degrading, and patronising porn. But we also believe that erotic fantasy is powerful, and that women and marginalised communities deserve to put their dreams and desires on film, too.[14]

The choice of vocabulary and priorities expressed are somewhat surprising. Given what is known about mainstream content, one might have imagined that any 'feminist' project in relation to pornography would primarily be concerned with countering the violence against women that is its mainstay. However, the awards are framed primarily as a response to the perceived *aesthetic* qualities of the porn industry – 'cheesy', 'cliche' – which are not generally notable concerns of a feminist struggle. Similarly, a concern for the positive regard of men, expressed further down the same webpage – 'We love it when men get what we are doing' – is likewise rarely a prominent feature of feminist projects.

In order to be considered for a Feminist Porn Award, a pornographic product must meet at least one of a number of criteria: that a woman had a hand in the production, writing, direction, et cetera of the work; that it depicts genuine female pleasure; and that it expands the boundaries of sexual representation on film and challenges stereotypes that are often found in mainstream porn. 'And of course, it has to be hot!' The awards include 'hottest gonzo sex scene' and 'boundary breaker of the year' – again, perhaps not the most obviously feminist categories to include: one might not expect feminists with an awareness of rape, abuse, violence and sexual assault to endorse 'boundary breaking' through an awards ceremony.

Advocates of 'feminist' porn make appeals to notions of authenticity ('genuine') and 'healthy' sex:

Getting people together who are brave enough to reveal their authentic sexuality in a really hot way...

Let's keep fucking and keep documenting it and keep doing it in a super healthy, sex-positive way.

As we will see in the next chapter, such statements are subject to critique for their normative and unexamined assumptions.

Apart from a declared focus on women's 'pleasure' and an element of female participation in the production of the film, the Feminist Porn Awards offer little evidence of anything that could be construed as feminist in a political sense. Dana Bialer (2011) scrutinises claims made positioning the female porn producer as a feminist revolutionary, and interrogates what she sees as the four foundational claims of queer pornography: subverting capitalism; presenting diverse or queer bodies; porn as a political move; and embracing sexuality as part of a holistic lifestyle. Bialer finds that, whilst there is evidence of a greater diversity of body types than is to be found in mainstream pornography, there are various contradictions around the other claims, due to the normalisation of violence, and failure to connect with the realities of trafficking and inequalities of gender, race and class. Bialer also finds commercial crossovers between queer 'feminist' producers and the mainstream industry, which undermine the image of the producer as a feminist revolutionary. According to Bialer, queer 'feminist' porn producers utilise a post-modern/queer theory vocabulary of transgression, the terms of which do not in fact move beyond established porn norms and inequalities. Whilst research in this area is in its early stages, there is supporting evidence that porn made by 'feminist' producers is not markedly different in content or approach from that made by other female porn producers (Liberman, 2009).

The example of Queerporn.tv provides a further insight into the feminist and queer porn enterprise. Set up in 2010 by producers Courtney Trouble and Tina Horn as a project of their porn company, Trouble Films, the website won an 'Honoured website' award at the 2011 Good For Her Feminist Porn Awards ceremony, thus endorsing its credentials in the 'feminist' porn stakes. Queerporn.tv offers '[p]ublic access to queer kink, gritty sex-positivite hardcore porn, and real queer sex ed', performed by a cast of characters advertised as: 'proud modern sluts, feminist porn stars, sexy amateurs, trans men, trans women, genderqueers, cisgendered folks, fags, dykes, tops, bottoms, switches, real couples, sex educators, non-normative heterosexuality, sado-masochists, perverts, activists, punks, and artists at their kinkiest, raunchiest, filthiest, rawest, most passionate, radical, and real'.[15] Within the Queerporn.tv world, then, there is no contradiction between the term 'feminist' and the eroticised inequality and domination inherent in terms such as 'sado-masochists'.

Queerporn.tv is keen to respond to with potential criticisms regarding the consent of their performers and the 'authenticity' of their pleasure, to the extent that they include a video of performer testimonies enthusing about how much they 'loved' participating in the productions:

> I just fucked the hottest queer chick for queerporn.tv and I LOVED it.

I banged my boss for queerporn.tv and I loved it.

Today I got fucked by Sophia St James wearing the Sophia St James harness, and I fucking loved it.

I cried my face off for queerporn.tv, and I loved it.

I bled for queerporn.tv and I fucking loved it.

I had an orgasm in bondage for queerporn.tv and I loved it.

I fucked a girl with a handmade wooden double dildo and I loved it.

I got fucked on camera for the first time for queerporn.tv and I fucking loved it.

The video demonstrates the paradox at the heart of any claim or assertion of authenticity: the repeated *performance* of the assertion of the pleasure experienced only serves to highlight the fact that the assertion *is* inescapably a performance; the 'authentic' is asserted and performed, according to a certain formula – and with a slightly jarring element of product-placement – thus undermining its own claims to authenticity.

Queerporn.tv also offers an 'x-rated trialer [sic]' montage of video clips interspersed with text, again invoking authenticity, this time mixed with commercial messages: 'real queer bodies'; 'real queer sex'; 'real queer voices'; 'VOD – Digital Downloads – VIP membership' 'free member uploads on QuTube: the world's first queer adult tube site'; 'www.Queerporn.tv: a new hardcore website from Courtney Trouble & Tina Horn'. The trailer includes a number of short scenes featuring a range of sex acts, including the suggestion of dog performing oral sex on a woman ('that's a good dog'); a woman being instructed to 'suck me you little slut'; acts involving ropes and bondage; cunnilingus; vaginal penetration with fingers and hands; rimming; toe licking; fellating a banana; whipping with a flogger; slapping; penis-slapping on a woman's vulva; snapping an elastic band on a woman's stomach; a man slapping a woman's buttocks;

suggestion of urination on woman's belly; nipple pinching of a woman; a woman in a bondage scene told 'pussy looks like it's ready for some cock'; fisting; a woman gagged with a gag ball apparently crying out (incomprehensible); a woman apparently scooping white liquid out of her anus onto a bowl of cereal. Inclusion in a trailer obviously suggests that the above scenes are indicative of the content that Queerporn.tv has to offer. While a variety of body types are in evidence, and more attention is given to cunnilingus than is generally in evidence in mainstream pornography, there is little that could be construed as 'feminist' in any meaningful sense of the word. Relationships of power inequality and domination are eroticised, with misogynist language, s-m scenarios and scenes of violence and aggression towards women forming part of the repertoire. Any version of feminism that is invoked, therefore, is one that eschews a political analysis of the eroticisation of inequality and acts of violence against women.

In addition to the problematic of the sexual instrumentalisation and commodification of the performers for the paying consumer, it would seem that the imperative to 'hot'-ness – key adjectives featured on the site include 'hot', 'filthy', 'kinky', 'pervert', 'raunchiest' – inevitably involves the representation of an unequal power dynamic. As Reeves and Wingfield noted regarding a lesbian magazine in the 1990s, 'pornography without inequality [is] impossible to make', and simply would not 'work' (1996: 67); a conclusion also reached by Andrea Dworkin who considers that pornography by definition is 'based on sexualised inequality of women, whether expressed as dominance or expressed as violence against women. You couldn't sell diddly-squat of anything that had to do with equality' (1990: 211). Queerporn.tv's very reliance on the representation and performance of inequality, then, appears to sit uncomfortably with the attempt to frame the content as 'feminist'.

Any consideration of claims made regarding 'feminist' porn should also bear in mind its marginality in terms of the mainstream market. For Dworkin, the question of feminist 'erotica' is a 'diversionary question':

> I don't have any objections to people devoting their lives to creating it, if that's what they want to do. But I think that the Women's Movement should stop pretending that it's some kind of essential bread and butter or even bread and roses kind of question. (*Ibid.*: 211)

This sentiment was also prevalent among my research participants, who generally felt that the project of developing 'feminist' porn was not a priority in the face of the more urgent political struggles.

Conclusion

This chapter has outlined some of the main issues of contention that featured in feminist debates on pornography in the 1980s – issues to which a new generation of feminists are returning with renewed urgency over twenty-five years later. The chapter has made the case for a feminist analysis of the porn industry informed by radical feminist theory and insights, explaining why liberal theories that focus on the individual are inadequate when trying to understand and challenge the structural inequalities within which pornography is rooted and which it helps to maintain. As we will see in Chapter 4, it is striking how resonant the language of second wave anti-porn feminists is with a new generation of activists: activists within groups like OBJECT and Anti-Porn London utilise concepts such as objectification, and take issue with notions of choice and agency. Why then, after a period of relative silence, is pornography back so emphatically on the feminist agenda? The answer appears to lie in the fact that, since the decline of anti-porn feminism in the early 1990s, the global expansion of the porn industry and its reach into mainstream culture has accelerated on an unprecedented scale, creating a tipping point where the distress and anger it has provoked in young women has demanded a voice. It is to the story of this mainstreaming of pornography that we shall turn in the next chapter.

Notes

1 Although the term has Greek origins, it was actually coined in the mid-nineteenth century, in order to categorise rediscovered sexually explicit artefacts from classical antiquity (Kendrick, 1997).

2 'Gonzo' porn, discussed in Chapter 3, is a genre of pornography which places the camera directly into the action, and which largely dispenses with conventions such as plot, characterisation and extended dialogue.

3 *Xbiz EU 2011* was an international adult entertainment digital media conference, held in London, 23–25 September 2011.

4 Say No: Unite to End Violence Against Women, <http://saynotoviolence. org/issue/facts-and-figures> (accessed 20 January 2012).

5 End Violence Against Women Coalition, <http://www.endviolence againstwomen.org.uk/pages/the_facts.html> (accessed 20 January 2012).

6 'It is never her fault', <http://sianandcrookedrib.blogspot.com/2012/01/it-isnever-her-fault.html> (accessed 23 January 2012).

7 For example, at a UK conference on sexual exploitation, presentations on sexual exploitation and internal trafficking consistently referred to victims as 'children and young people' in spite of the fact that 100 per cent of cases referred to involved female victims (*Sexual Exploitation in the North East: Prevalence and Practice*, Northern Rock Foundation, Newcastle, 20 January 2010).

8 From <http://www.ukadultproducers.com/ukap/pornschool/?page_id= 62> (accessed 16 January 2012).

9 From 'Womononajourney', <http://womononajourney.wordpress.com/ 2011/08/15/critiquing-the-consent-positive-movement/> (accessed 16 January 2012).

10 Sprinkle and Harlot, 1999.

11 'Plea to call off Miss World feminist protest in London', <http://www.bbc. co.uk/news/uk-england-london-15605862> (accessed 26 January 2012).

12 Pole Dancing School, London, <http://www.poledancingschool.com/ index.php?option= com_content&task=view&id=1&Itemid=80> (accessed 26 January 2012).

13 'How to look good naked', <http://www.channel4.com/programmes/how-to-look-good-naked> and 'Miss Naked Beauty', <http://www.channel4.com/programmes/miss-naked-beauty> (accessed 26 January 2012).

14 Feminist Porn Awards, <http://goodforher.com/feminist_porn_awards>, (accessed 10 January 2012). All quotes relating to the awards are taken from this website.

15 <www.queerporn.tv> (accessed 24 January 2012). All material quoted is drawn from this site.

CHAPTER 3
Pornification and
Its Discontents

The mainstreaming of pornography has been a galvanising factor in the re-emergence of anti-porn feminism: as we will see, activists cite the phenomenon of the 'pornification' of society as a key motivation for their activism. The concepts of 'pornification' and the 'mainstreaming' of pornography have gained attention in both media and academic debates. What is the evidence for the 'mainstreaming' of pornography? And what does such mainstreaming look like?

The term 'pornification' refers to the phenomenon of certain versions of sex – those constructed and distributed by pornography and the sex industry – being mainstreamed into culture. The phrase 'pornographication of the mainstream' (subsequently expressed more succinctly as 'pornification') originated in the field of media studies, introduced by Brian McNair (1996, 2002) in the context of his concept of 'striptease culture', and taken up in journal articles and collections (Paasonen *et al.*, 2007; Attwood, 2002, 2006, 2009b; Boyle, 2010; Tankard Reist and Bray, 2011) as well as academic seminars and conferences. It has also received considerable attention in popular, journalistic accounts (Paul, 2005; Levy, 2005; Sarracino and Scott, 2008), the mainstream press and internet blogs. McNair's 'pornographication of the mainstream' denotes the transformation of mainstream culture through what he terms 'porno-chic' – the influence of pornography on aspects of culture

– a process which has developed in tandem with the expansion of the 'pornosphere': the realm wherein pornographic texts are produced, disseminated and consumed. McNair locates both these developments in the broader context of what he terms a 'striptease culture', a term he coins to refer to the disruption of boundaries between private and public within Western culture, 'the media of sexual confession and self-revelation' (2002: 88).

What is being mainstreamed?

When we speak of the 'mainstreaming of pornography', what is the nature of the material that is currently being mainstreamed? What, in fact, constitutes the 'mainstream' of pornography at this point in the twenty-first century, and in what ways does this 'mainstream' manifest itself within the broader culture? The vast amount of ever-changing sexually explicit material – that may or may not be considered under the rubric of 'pornography' – currently available across a range of media makes any attempt to define 'mainstream' pornography challenging. Nonetheless, there is a striking consistency in much contemporary pornography in terms of its production, intended or assumed audience, and content. Ana Bridges argues that 'the pornographic film genre requires that characters demonstrate *indifference to or erotic pleasure from aggression*' (original emphasis) (2010: 36). She also argues that, in the face of the vast expansion of the industry in recent years, there is increasing competition between producers to attract consumers, and that such competition is likely to result in the production of 'novel material'. Not only will competition result in a tendency towards more explicit material, but the process of *habituation* as a result of repeated consumption (*ibid.*: 37) will similarly fuel the drive for novelty. Whilst such novelty may take a number of forms – 'unusual sex acts, increasingly violent or aggressive behaviour, a focus on particular fetishes or characters, seemingly taboo subjects' – Bridges claims that her own research findings evidence the 'increasing appetites for more violent and degrading pornographic media in more habitual users' (*ibid.*: 38). Other research into the industry similarly finds a prevalence of aggression and misogyny (Jeffreys, 2009; Dines, 2010; Tyler, 2011a, 2011b), and industry representatives acknowledge that content has become more 'extreme': according to Sharon Mitchell, former porn performer and founder of the Adult Industry Medical Healthcare foundation, 'Short of driving a train up her ass, there's nothing left to do to a woman's body' (in Samuels, 2009). Taking as her starting point Susanne Kappeler's observation that 'The pornographer himself is more honest and astute about pornography than are the cultural experts engaged in defending it' (Kappeler, 1986: 61), Meagan Tyler's analysis of porn industry reviews reveals that the industry is hardly reticent regarding the woman-hating nature of its products; rather, misogyny and the subjugation of women are selling points for mainstream porn videos (2010). One Adult Video News (AVN) review cited by Tyler (2011a: 127, 2011b) hails the video *Fuck Slaves 3* as 'a misogynistic gem': 'an exercise in dignity extraction' in which 'female performers surrender mind, body and spirit to participate in disturbing acts of debasement'. Refreshingly devoid of convoluted attempts to frame the product as an exemplum of the rich opportunities afforded by the porn industry for women's empowerment, AVN anticipates that it will 'appeal to men who have survived the social castrating of their gender.' Undoubtedly so.

Whilst looking at 'best-selling, best-renting videos' (Bridges, 2010: 45) is illuminating, it is also the case that much current pornographic content is freely available online. Claims are increasingly made asserting the distinct nature of 'amateur' porn, aiming to dismiss decades of research on industry porn content as redundant, since the content in question is supposedly now marginal and unrepresentative. The division between rental and for-sale material and freely available material should not be over-emphasised, however: many websites offering free content also aggressively push site-membership and paid content at the viewer (Johnson, 2011). It should also be noted that the amount of internet porn content that is genuinely 'amateur' is questionable. Given the commercial imperative behind much pornography – and the fact that there are commercial implications and opportunities even where 'amateur' porn is involved – it is not surprising that one commentator claims: 'The bulk of pornographic imagery online is professionally produced – including, at this point, the bulk of so-called amateur porn, at least on the corporatised Web sites' (Patterson, 2004: 110).

As Gail Dines points out, so-called 'amateur' porn is in fact an *industry genre*. Within the industry, the term 'amateur' signifies particular styles and features of the product: the film looks homemade and features an unknown female performer, but nonetheless is industry-produced (Dines, 2011b). A number of the main tube sites delivering free content are owned by Manwin, 'owner of the largest network of adult websites in the world', which includes high-profile paid porn sites (Dines, 2011b). Of course, much free internet porn is not amateur but in fact pirated industry content, and this is of far greater concern to the industry than anything DIY-produced. Panel sessions and discussions at the *Xbiz EU* adult entertainment convention revealed a far higher degree of industry anxiety regarding loss of profits due to piracy rather than anything produced by amateurs (Richter *et al.*, 2011; Duke and Phinney, 2011). Reference to amateur content was conspicuous by its absence in the discussions: when I inquired about this, the consistent message I was given by delegates was that amateur producers were considered to be small-scale and marginal, posing no serious threat to the industry.

It seems, then, that claims regarding the prevalence of genuinely 'amateur' porn should not be taken at face value and a case could be made for the need for more research in this area, though again perhaps the words of Florynce Kennedy regarding research quoted at the beginning of this book are pertinent here. None of this is to deny the existence of amateur content altogether. However, claims regarding its distinctive nature in relation to industry porn are also open to question. First, the conditions of its production are not known to the consumer. There is disturbing evidence from women's sector organisations that victims of rape and abuse are presenting with experiences of having their abuse filmed, or of discovering that sexual images of themselves have been circulated on the internet without their consent (Thompson, 2011). Certainly, the prevalence of sub-genres such as 'ex-girlfriend', 'ex-wife' and 'revenge' porn on amateur websites would not appear to indicate content that was mutually produced by two willing partners (by contrast, any parallel 'ex-husband' genre appears distinctly undeveloped). Whether such content is 'genuine' or not, what such sub-genres suggest is that there is often little difference between the misogynist nature of industry content and amateur content. Again, while further research is necessary, it seems that claims dismissing a focus on industry content as marginal or unrepresentative of the majority of online porn have some way to go in establishing credibility. Furthermore, an examination of the ways in which mainstream culture is being influenced by pornography yields ample evidence that the specific images and language shaping the culture are consistent with those of hegemonic pornography.

Technologisation and accessibility
Over the past three decades, the porn industry has expanded to unprecedented levels and now has a global reach, partly as a result

of technological developments (Clarke, 2004; Jeffreys, 2009: 65–85; Dines, 2010: 47; Bray, 2011). Technological advances since the 1980s have resulted in vastly accelerated flows of production, transmission and access to pornographic images and texts. In fact, the porn market has actually driven the development and use of new technologies, such as camcorders and video recorders; the favouring of VHS over Betamax; DVDs; interactive TV; pay-per-view; the internet and 3G mobile phones (Arlidge, 2002).

The result of this technologisation of the porn market means that hardcore, violent or 'extreme' images that previously would have been difficult to seek out are now easily accessed (Gossett and Byrne, 2002; Banyard, 2010: 154–8; Dines, 2010: xvii–xxiii). Aggressive marketing by pornography companies means that unsolicited images and advertisements present themselves in the form of pop-ups and spam email, and a range of techniques are used to 'catch a curious clicker' (Johnson, 2010: 147). Technological developments have also resulted in the production of new forms of pornography, including 'home-produced' pornography or 'realcore' (Hardy, 2009), interactive pornography and sexually violent computer games, such as *RapeLay*[1] (Nakasatomi, 2011); and the circulation of pornographic images via mobile phones and on social networking sites like MySpace (Whisnant, 2009). These new forms of porn production and distribution have occasioned new, related forms of sexual harassment and violence, such as 'upskirting'[2] (Saner, 2009) and media-related forms of sexual bullying, such as so-called 'sexting'[3] (Funnell, 2011), and 'Second Life' (online virtual world) sexual violence and harassment.[4]

Influence of porn on mainstream culture

The second form of mainstreaming manifests in the influence of pornography on mainstream culture: the ways in which mainstream culture is responding to, incorporating and reflecting pornographic images and norms, what McNair has termed 'porno-chic' (McNair, 2002: 61–9). This is evidenced in fashion advertising, magazines and clothing styles (Sorensen, 2003; Merskin, 2004; Gill, 2009a, 2009b; Whisnant, 2009; Tankard Reist, 2009; Papadopoulos, 2010; Hatton and Trautner, 2011), music videos and dance styles (McLune, 2006; Whisnant, 2009); the production of corporate calendars and charity campaigns featuring semi-naked women;[5] pole-dancing classes offered as a health and fitness activity; and intertextual references to pornography in mainstream films and television genres – including makeover shows, sitcoms such as *Friends* (Whisnant, 2004), comedy panel quizzes and chat shows – that assume viewers' familiarity and ease with pornography. Pornography and the sex industry have been glamorised within celebrity culture, through 'porn star' celebrities such as Jenna Jameson and 'glamour model' Katie Price, sex blogs, and TV shows such as the British series *Secret Diary of a Call Girl.* In the UK, stand-up comedy has been particularly influenced by the norms and values of pornography, with jokes about porn use and rape being standard fare amongst male comedians at the 2009 Edinburgh Fringe (Logan, 2009; Lister, 2009), and 'rape jokes' and 'rape talk' becoming generally more prevalent (Cochrane, 2010c). There is evidence that the normalisation of pornography is causing distress within relationships (Paul, 2005; Banyard, 2010; Walter, 2010; Caroline, 2011). The mainstreaming of pornography is also evident in the increase in 'beauty' practices associated with the porn industry, such as the removal of pubic hair, breast augmentation and labiaplasty (Jeffreys, 2005, 2009; Banyard, 2010; Dines, 2010; Davis, 2011; Rogers and Vanco, 2011; Rogers, 2012).

Presence of porn in public space
A third way in which pornification occurs is via the increasing literal presence of pornography and the sex industry within

public space. Examples of this include the proliferation of lap-dancing clubs – and billboards advertising the clubs – in local high streets; the presence of 'lads' mags' prominently displayed in supermarkets, petrol stations and newsagents; the opening of the Playboy 'concept store' on Oxford Street; the presence of Playboy-branded products in high street stores; and the advertising of sex industry jobs such as lapdancer, webcam performer and escort in JobCentre Plus agencies (Department of Work and Pensions, 2008; 2010). Research is beginning to document the use of porn to sexually harass girls in schools (Gillies and Roberts, 2010). The culture of lads' mags has become a part of some aspects of mainstream leisure and entertainment, with magazine promoters targeting club nights (Walter, 2010) and student union events to recruit young women to pose for their magazines. The Fawcett Society has documented the influence and encroachment of the sex industry within workplace cultures (Banyard and Lewis, 2009). These forms of mainstreaming obviously coincide with technologisation: if the internet is considered a form of public space, then the sex industry has a very large and significant presence within that space, as discussed above – as it does on cable TV channels and as a pay-per-view option in hotels. Mobile devices mean that consumers can view porn any time and anywhere, meaning that others may be subjected to viewing it in public spaces; there have even been suggestions of offering porn as inflight entertainment for airline passengers (Lai, 2011).

Global reach and legitimisation of the industry
Finally, the mainstreaming of pornography is illustrated by the global expansion and economic worth of the pornography industry (Samuels, 2009; Banyard, 2010: 152–4; Stark and Whisnant, 2004: 15; Johnson, 2010). Because of its nature, it is very difficult to assess the economic worth of the pornography

industry, although in 2007 industry sources estimated it to be worth $97.06 billion worldwide (Jeffreys, 2009: 66). According to 'Stop Porn Culture', the annual revenues from the pornography industry in the USA are $13.3 billion: 'more than the National Football League, the National Basketball Association and Major League Baseball all combined; more than NBC, CBS and ABC combined; larger than the revenues of the top technology companies combined: Microsoft, Google, Amazon, eBay, Yahoo!, Apple, Netflix and Earthlink'.[6] The industry is now recognised as an important and legitimate player in global capitalism, with porn companies such as Beate Uhse from Germany listed on the Stock Exchange (Jeffreys, 2009: 65). The legitimisation of the porn industry is exemplified in the figure of porn tycoon Richard Desmond, who amassed a fortune as a porn publisher, before going on to become owner of the British Express Newspapers group, along with a number of celebrity magazines and the UK TV Channel Five. The online porn industry functions as an extremely complex network of commercially driven companies and affiliates with sophisticated strategies aimed at extending their markets. Current strategies to generate profit in the industry include the buying and manipulation of online traffic in order to monetise (make profit from) free content; the aggressive targeting of emerging areas such as the BRIC (Brazil, Russia, India, China) economies, and the pursuit of anti-piracy approaches such as the expansion of live webcam pornography.[7] Commercial issues preoccupying industry minds include questions of how to cater to 'local tastes' in a globalised market; the implications of moves to mobile devices, particularly in emerging markets with dense populations (mobiles will help ensure that men can access pornography even in overcrowded living conditions where laptop or desktop access would be visible to others); and the profit potential of combining adult dating sites with online webcam interactive sites.[8] The implications for women and girls as the porn industry aggressively seeks to both create and meet a demand for men's 24/7 access to pornography across the globe are obviously extremely serious.

Pornification: the 'facial'

The phenomenon of the 'facial' is an example of the ways in which practices from pornography enter the mainstream of culture. It is likely that not all readers will be familiar with this term since as both a term and practice it is not common in many social groups, although it is more prevalent amongst younger generations.

The term 'facial' refers to the practice of a man ejaculating on a woman's face. While numerous references to the practice can be found in the pornographic writings of the Marquis de Sade (1785, trans. Seaver and Wainhouse, 2002), in terms of trends it is a relative newcomer to the heterosexual repertoire, delivered courtesy of the porn industry over the past three decades. Facials now feature as a regular part of mainstream pornography (Jensen, 2007; Dines, 2010). There may be particular reasons why the practice emerged: regulation of pornography in Japan, for instance, meant that genitals could only be shown in pixellated form, leading to a focus on other parts of body; the need for male ejaculation to be visible within the genre, in order to represent the male power that is its main theme and to mark the end of a scene (the 'money shot' or 'cum shot'). The AIDS pandemic also contributed to concern for ejaculation to take place outside of the body as a safer sex practice, although this can hardly be a factor in the development of the practice of the facial, since the potential for infected semen to come into contact with broken skin or sensitive mucous membranes in the eyes, nose and mouth obviously renders it a high-risk practice for the recipient in terms of the transmission of a number of sexually transmitted infections.

In order to understand how the image of the facial works, it has to be seen within the context of the visual grammar and dominant themes of pornography. Whilst obviously images can be open to a number of different readings, the meaning of an image is shaped and constructed by its context and relation to other images. The misogynist and often racist titles of scenes featuring facials give a clear indication as to how the scene should be interpreted: 'Amateur Asian girl gets a huge facial', 'Black babes love facials', 'White babes love facials' (Pornhub. com); 'Cocksucker extraordinaire Jayne Oso takes 2 facials!' (xhamster.com); 'Hot Japanese chick gets massive facial' (tnaflix. com); 'Nasty blonde gets her face filled with cum' (Redtube.com). Whole sites such as PeterNorth.com – described as the 'Cumshot Legend' – specialise in the 'cumshot', offering endlessly repeated images of women with their faces covered in semen.

As Dines notes, the ejaculate 'marks the woman as used goods, as owned by the man or men who have just penetrated her' (Dines, 2010: xxvi). She quotes a male porn producer who states that 'The most violent we can get is the cum shot in the face' and a consumer who talks of his enjoyment of scenes that 'end with the girl a total mess, having a huge amount of cum on her face and tits' (Dines, 2010: xxvi). It is clear that the intended and received meaning of the image is the debasement of the woman and the aggrandisement of the man: the facial functions as an act and symbol of conquest and domination.

The journey of the facial into mainstream culture is illustrative of the process of pornification. Far from an image that exists only in the realms of fantasy, the practice of men ejaculating on a woman's face begins as a material practice; an act of abuse upon the female porn performer. From there, as the image is shared homosocially among male consumers, it is given a name, it is brought into existence as part of a range of possible and desirable acts within a sexual repertoire; part of a potential sexual script. Through further instances of cultural references, it becomes discursively established as both a concept and reality in relation to and influencing current sexual norms.

This journey into the mainstream is evidenced by textual references to the facial across culture and media, along with the way in which the practice starts to become the subject of discussion and debate. For example, in 2001 fashion company Sisley carried an advertisement featuring an image of the model Josie Maran spraying milk from a cow's udder onto her tongue, with the milk dribbling down her chin. An advertisement for Clinique moisturiser features a portrait shot of a woman's face with her eyes closed, a splattering of moisturiser sprayed from her left eye across her cheek to her mouth. An advertisement for Lee Jeans by photographer Troyt Coburn features a woman's mouth with glossy red lips parted, with a milky blue liquid being splashed up into it, again, running out messily down her chin. British company The Ice-creamists (makers of 'boutique ice-cream') runs advertisements featuring a black woman smeared with vanilla ice-cream running down her face and body, and a white woman with chocolate ice-cream smeared and dripping in the same way. An advertisement for Bailey's liqueur features numerous disembodied female mouths, with large drops of the liqueur repeatedly splashing on them.

In addition to the normalising effects of such advertisements, textual references, discussion and debate contribute to the discursive construction of the facial as part of the sexual norm. For example, it has been the object of some attention in the blogosphere and in online feminist discussion groups. Articles, blogs and comments generate discussions regarding the nature of facials: primarily addressing the question as to whether they are degrading or not. Often it is agreed that they are, but this is seen by some as what makes them 'hot',[9] part of their appeal: 'I'm occasionally into degradation scenes, and facials feel really degrading to me, so there are circumstances in which a guy can come on my face and it'll be hot.'[10] Comments appear on threads, with women discussing their experiences of facials, including instances where male sexual partners have ejaculated on their face without their consent. In a particularly troubling article, a male lecturer relates how he has discussed facials with students in class – with no commentary on the appropriateness, power dynamics or ethics of such a discussion in that context – concluding the piece with the comments of a male student who claims that what makes facials 'hot' is that they make the male perpetrator of the act 'feel clean', since a 'woman's willingness to accept a facial is an intensely powerful source of affirmation'.[11] What is significant about these articles is the way in which a practice from pornography gains recognition and validation as a practice in the wider culture. In spite of the clear message of woman-hating conveyed in the pornographic construction of the facial scene, each of the above articles validates the facial to a greater or lesser degree, the final one reframing it as an act of generosity and affirmation that a woman might perform in order to reassure her male sexual partner that his body is not 'dirty'. This is a singularly bizarre interpretation of the act; firstly because the male body is generally not depicted as 'dirty' or shameful in any way: both the penis and semen are valorised in pornography. Rather, it is the woman who is consistently depicted as both dirty and shameful: she is shown as voracious in her lust for any amount of degradation involving any variety of body fluid. Her own body is presumed to be filthy and unacceptable; it must be strictly policed and sanitised for male consumption – for example, through the removal of all body hair, including pubic hair. Similarly, historically and outside of the pornographic genre, a woman's body is seen as dirty and shameful in a way that has no parallel in the case of men's bodies. There are numerous cultural and religious taboos around menstruation, for instance; in the fifteenth-century treatise on witches, *The Hammer of Witches* by Kramer and Sprenger, the vagina was named the 'devil's gateway'; and the beauty, fashion and diet industries are based around the notion of women's bodies as inherently unattractive and defective. Given this construction of *women's* bodies as inherently dirty and defective, according to the logic of the male student cited in the blog above, if the facial were to function as an affirmative and lovingly accepting act in the face of bodily insecurities, it would make more sense for a whole reverse sub-genre of *menstruation* facials to exist, with men experiencing ecstasy as menstrual blood drips from their mouths and dribbles down their chin. Such a sub-genre is not particularly apparent – any use of menstrual blood in porn will generally once again show it smeared upon the woman's face and body.

This example of the ways in which the image and act of the facial migrate from the pornosphere into mainstream culture is illustrative of the broader phenomenon of pornification. Beginning as a specific act constructed and enacted within a specific commercially based context, the act and image becomes habilitated, gaining validity and new meanings, and potentially becoming a sexual norm: entering the repertoire of possible and potentially desirable sexual acts and helping to shape ideas of the inherent natures of men and women, their respective desires and the nature of sexuality itself.

Theorising pornification

Sexualisation
Scholarship theorising pornification has only emerged since around 2002. Within media studies, cultural studies, psychology

and the policy arena, pornification has tended to be considered as part of a more general 'sexualisation of culture' (Attwood, 2006, 2009b; Gill, 2009a, 2009b; Papadopoulos, 2010), a tendency which is also reflected in news features (Bell, 2007a, 2007b, 2007d) and popular general literature on the subject. The term 'sexualisation' can be used to refer to different social phenomena: either a general effect on culture, or on individuals, particularly women or children. The different usage can lead to a lack of clarity, and indeed the term 'sexualisation' itself is probably too vague and general to be a useful conceptual tool. Inadequate consideration given to the *nature* of the 'sexualisation' means that there is little detailed examination of what notions or versions of 'sex' are being mainstreamed.

Where the term is used to refer to processes of cultural transformation, it might describe 'the ways that sex is becoming more visible in contemporary Western cultures' (Attwood, 2009: xiii) or refer to 'the extraordinary proliferation of discourses about sex and sexuality across all media forms' (Gill, 2007b: 256). For Attwood, the phrase 'sexualised culture' is used to indicate social and cultural phenomena such as:

> a contemporary preoccupation with sexual values, practices and identities; the public shift to more permissive sexual attitudes; the proliferation of sexual texts; the emergence of new forms of sexual experience; the apparent breakdown of rules, categories and regulations designed to keep the obscene at bay; our fondness for scandals, controversies and panics around sex. (Attwood, 2006: 78–9)

Alongside theories of 'sexualisation of culture' there is a burgeoning literature focusing on the sexualisation of children, particularly girls (Palmer, 2006; Durham, 2008; Tankard Reist, 2009; Levin and Kilbourne, 2008). Within the policy arena, debates around sexualisation tend to reflect the concerns of this body of literature, often rooted in psychology rather than cultural or media studies, and relying on heavily loaded and frequently unexamined concepts such as what is 'healthy' or what constitutes 'adult sexuality'. Government reviews into sexualisation carried out in the United States and Australia typify this approach (Zurbriggen *et al.*, 2007; Australian Senate, 2008). The US report – the *American Psychological Association Task Force on the Sexualization of Girls* – has been particularly influential in the UK, with its definition of sexualisation and many of its key concerns being taken up in the *Sexualisation of Young People Review* (Papadopoulos, 2010), commissioned by the Labour government in 2010, though subsequently jettisoned by the Conservative-Liberal Democrat coalition government and replaced with the *Bailey Review* (2011). Since policy reports on sexualisation tend to come from a psychology perspective, it is perhaps unsurprising that they draw on discourses of 'health' and focus on issues such as child development. Concerns about inappropriate 'adult' sexuality being 'imposed' on children have also been taken up by the media (Bell, 2007b; Toynbee, 2008; Marshall, 2009) and in campaigns carried out by a number of UK organisations and charities, such as the National Union of Teachers, the NSPCC and Girlguiding UK (National Union of Teachers, 2007; NSPCC, 2008; Girlguiding UK/Mental Health Foundation 2008). In April 2010, the 'Let Girls Be Girls' campaign launched by internet-based parents' group Mumsnet was successful in persuading clothing retailer Primark to stop selling padded bikini tops for seven-year-old girls. The then Prime Minister Gordon Brown and leader of the Conservative Party David Cameron both voiced concerns over the sexualisation of children, and at a 2010 general election event featuring women's representatives from each of the main political parties,[12] each representative had a stance on the issue, illustrating how the term has gained currency since the publication of the American Psychological Association report.

The review carried out for the Scottish Parliament (Buckingham *et al.*, 2009) takes a different approach, and is critical of much of the literature concerned with the sexualisation of children. Whilst Buckingham *et al.* agree that there is 'fairly good' evidence that sexual imagery has become widely available within the culture as a whole, they argue that, in terms of drawing conclusions about the effects of such imagery, there are limitations in the scope of the research, as well as in theory and methodology. Particular theoretical limitations that they highlight include: 'a lack of consistency and clarity about the meaning of *sexualisation*, and the crucial distinction between *sexual* and *sexualised*'; and the unexamined 'moral assumptions' evident in the literature, for example about 'healthy' sexuality, 'decency' or about what is 'inappropriate' for children (Buckingham *et al.*, 2009).

I agree that unexamined normative assumptions are problematic, though my concerns are somewhat different from those of Buckingham *et al.* Particularly problematic is the framing of 'sexualisation' – within the US and UK reviews – in terms of the premature imposition onto children of an 'adult sexuality', the implication being that it is problematic only in the sense that it is just happening too early. This approach fails to interrogate the nature of these 'adult sexual themes' (Papadopoulos, 2010: 2). To construct the issue in oppositional terms between notions of 'adult' and 'child' is to ignore feminist scholarship which critiques many aspects of normative 'adult' sexuality. Feminist approaches, attending to questions of sexual politics, identify that, through processes of sexualisation, girls are interpellated as sexual *objects*, which feminists argue is undesirable for adult women, not just girl children.

Bragg and Buckingham criticise implied constructions of children as passive, innocent victims of an all-powerful media, arguing that the young people participating in their research projects presented as both 'media savvy' and 'sex savvy' (2009: 132). Bragg argues that researchers and policy makers need to recognise children as 'competent, self-aware media consumers' who demonstrate reflexivity and self-consciousness about being a child, and an awareness of the 'ethics of relationships' (Bragg, 2009). However, the findings on which these arguments are predicated result from the analysis of personal diaries and scrapbooks kept for the purposes of the study, in which children discuss their experience of the media. The data therefore are produced by children as participants in social research, outside of social situations such as the classroom or playground. Within social contexts, children may not prove to be such sophisticated and competent media consumers: as mentioned earlier, other research shows that porn-related sexual bullying can be a serious problem in schools. Such arguments also beg the question as to how many of us – children or adults – are unfailingly 'competent, self-aware media consumers' under patriarchal capitalism: social norms, trends and behaviour in the context of a market-driven economy would plainly suggest otherwise. A strength of the UK Home Office Review is that it emphasises the *cumulative effect* that exposure to sexualised messages and images has over time. Giving the example of cosmetic surgery, Papadopoulos argues that 'the drip-drip effect is an insidious but powerful mechanism by which the previously unthinkable becomes widely acceptable, often within a relatively short space of time' (Papadopoulos, 2010: 25). Gill also questions the emphasis on individual agency within the context of neoliberalism, arguing that notions such as individual choice, autonomy and agency fail to account for striking similarities in what is 'freely chosen', for example, with regard to fashion and beauty practices. Gill highlights the 'striking ... degree of fit between the autonomous post-feminist subject and the psychological subject demanded by neoliberalism': why, for example, do so many women make choices consistent with hegemonic notions of femininity? (Gill, 2007b: 260). Whilst Gill's argument refers specifically to women, it is equally valid – perhaps even more so – in relation to questions of children's autonomy and agency in their interactions with the media.

The Bailey Review, commissioned by the UK coalition government in 2011, marked a departure from the broadly feminist-informed review carried out by psychologist Linda Papadopoulos, to a more overtly right-wing, moralistic agenda. Carried out by Reg Bailey, the male CEO of Christian group The Mothers' Union, the review called for voluntary regulation by business and the media, with recourse to stronger action if such an approach does not prove effective. The choice of Bailey to carry out the review drew much criticism, since he had few apparent credentials to undertake such a review, offering no expertise in the area of children's or women's rights. Similarly, the review was criticised for failing to provide a gender analysis, and to join up with policy approaches developed as part of the Home Office's strategy on violence against women. Indeed, the titles of both the Papadopoulos Review – *Sexualisation of Young People* – and the subsequent Bailey Review – *Letting Children Be Children: the Report of an Independent Review of the Commercialisation and Sexualisation of Childhood* – indicate another problem with the term 'sexualisation', in that its lack of specificity means that there can be a tendency to elide, or inadequately address, questions of gender. Whilst much of the literature recognises that girls and boys are positioned differentially with regard to processes of sexualisation (Durham, 2008; Coy, 2009; Tankard Reist, 2009; Walter, 2010), as do the campaigns led by Mumsnet and Girlguiding UK mentioned above, policy discussions tend to centre on 'children', 'childhood' and 'young people', quite remarkably failing to engage with issues of gender. Where gender *is* addressed, the lack of a clear recognition of the differential ways in which girls and boys are targeted means that analyses tend to lack specificity, as when Papadopoulos argues that there is an 'idealised notion of beauty for both men and women' (2010: 10): a claim that fails to take into account the huge differences in the ways that the fashion and beauty industries target women and men, and the particular pressures and expectations on women (Wolf, 1991; Brownmiller, 1986; Jeffreys, 2005; Orbach, 2009). Similarly, Papadopoulos's claim that 'the messages we are sending out to boys are just as limiting and restrictive' (2010: 54), fails to take into account the different subject positions boys are encouraged to take up: whilst the construction of masculinity is undoubtedly 'limiting and restrictive', boys are generally being positioned as sexual *subjects* and *consumers*, rather than as sexual *objects* (Whisnant, 2009). This failure to see and name sexualisation as a gendered issue leads to obfuscation and weak policy recommendations. Similarly, the failure of sexualisation debates to look at the social and economic contexts within which 'sexualisation' is happening – the context of women's continuing inequality with men, and the nature of 'mainstream' pornography, as discussed earlier – means that the nature and implications of the process are inadequately theorised.

Commentators coming from an explicitly feminist perspective do distinguish between the different forms that sexualisation takes, pointing out that it is not just 'culture' or 'young people' that are being generally 'sexualised', but that girls and women are being encouraged to see themselves as sexual objects (Gill, 2007b, 2009a, 2009b; Jeffreys, 2009; Coy, 2009; Tankard Reist, 2009; Whisnant, 2009). Gill, for example, highlights the gendered nature of this sexualisation, arguing that what is taking place in contemporary culture involves 'the re-sexualisation of women's bodies' (Gill, 2003, 2009b). Gill's term is specific in pointing out that it is in fact women's bodies that are being displayed and presented in a (re)sexualised manner; furthermore, she argues that current versions of this display are new, in that women are no longer straightforwardly 'objectified', but are represented as actively embracing and participating in their own objectification, through a process she calls 'sexual subjectification': *they must now understand their own objectification as pleasurable and self-chosen* (2009b: 107, Gill's italics). Bell also brings a gender analysis to the debates, seeing sexualisation as a form of normalised sexual harassment, even violence: 'This is not just about sexualisation. Sexual harassment is being eroticised' (2007d).

As debates on sexualisation evolve, some theorists argue that more nuanced approaches are necessary, calling for analyses that incorporate the recognition that sexualisation is neither a singular nor a homogeneous practice. Attwood argues for the need 'to be much more precise about the terms of the debates inspired by sexualisation', stating that '[a] concern with the politics and economics of sex, not only in the West but around the world, is needed to provide a clearer grounding and context for studying particular aspects or manifestations of sexualisation' (2006: 91–2). In similar vein, Gill argues for an intersectional approach that moves beyond a 'general, homogenising notion of "sexualisation".' (Gill, 2009a: 142). As Gill points out, 'sexualisation does not operate outside of processes of gendering, racialisation and classing, and works within a visual economy that remains profoundly ageist and heteronormative' (*ibid*.: 138–9). Gill concludes that 'the term "sexualisation" needs to be used with greater care, specificity and attention to *difference*' (*ibid*.: 155).

'Democratisation of desire'?

McNair argues that 'striptease culture' promotes a 'democratisation of desire' through increasing the accessibility of sexual imagery and the number of forms through which sexual desire and sexual subjectivity can be expressed: 'the process of the sexualisation of culture, from the pornosphere to the public sphere, has included within it a democratisation and diversification of sexual discourse' (McNair, 2002: 205). Similar arguments have been made by other theorists, arguing for example that internet pornography 'offers a site where the full investigations of human ambition, desire and degradation are represented and played out, offering the voiceless and the powerless a vehicle for creating and extending the public sphere' (Breen, 2007: 91). Given the extent of violence against women and the potential harms done to women in the 'degradation' that Breen celebrates so unreservedly, one might wonder what understanding he has of the words 'voiceless' and 'powerless'. Unencumbered in his enthusiasm by any kind of grasp on sexual politics, Breen goes on to celebrate the absence of constraints around internet pornography as marking a process of 'proletarianisation' and even 'the emergence of a new social movement' (Breen, 2007: 91). One wonders whether a woman who has had sexual images of herself uploaded to the internet without her consent would share in Breen's delight at the 'absence of constraints' that makes such abuse possible. In similar vein, Hardy argues that 'media technologies are making it possible for a far greater range of human sexual experience to be reflected' – though he considers this neither 'inherently liberating nor oppressive' (Hardy, 2009: 14–15). In these analyses, the predominance of the term 'human' rather than 'women' and 'men' indicates the striking absence of a gender analysis. Claims for 'proletarianisation' (Breen, 2009) and 'democratisation' rely on the concept of an undifferentiated 'demand', one in which all adults ('humans', 'people') participate: 'None of this technology-driven expansion would have been possible, of course, unless people wanted mediated sex, and if there was not quite widespread *demand* (McNair, 2002: 39). Given the nature of the porn industry and issues with claims around 'amateur porn', the heralding of pornification as the 'democratisation of desire' is hardly justified. The failure of such arguments to engage adequately with gender issues means that questions regarding the subject, object and nature of that 'desire' are not addressed. Since mainstream pornographic content – both professional and amateur – represents women and men very differently, and there are very significant gender differences with regard to the production and consumption of pornography, the unproblematic, undifferentiated use of terms like 'human' and 'people' suggests either extreme naivety or an unwillingness to acknowledge the different subject positions of women and men with respect to the 'pornosphere'. Gill also critiques the notion of 'democratisation' on the grounds that many remain excluded from this process (Gill, 2009a: 154).

Claims around 'democratisation' are unconvincing as they disregard material, patriarchal power structures; there is an inadequate focus on the economic power and influence of the sex industry, a lack of attention to agents, context and questions of who is 'choosing'. McNair underestimates the ongoing patriarchal nature of the media in general – 'our media system can no longer be characterised as an oppressive ideological apparatus relentlessly supportive of patriarchal and heterosexist values' (McNair, 2002: 205) – and the porn industry in particular: 'the pressures imposed by the cultural marketplace have worked for rather than against … progressive trends' (*ibid*.: 206). In the light of content analyses of pornography websites and the increased access to violent pornography afforded by the internet, such claims do not appear to be borne out by the evidence. McNair also argues that the 'institutional sexism' of the culture industries is in 'measurable decline': 'as that decline continues … the media's contribution to the process of sexual democratisation is likely to be consolidated and enhanced' (*ibid*.: 207). Again, there appears to be little evidence to support his claim.

Pornification and sexual politics

It is striking that the unequal nature of pornographic production, representation and consumption in terms of sexual politics tends not to be foregrounded in many media and cultural studies accounts of pornification. Scholars such as McNair (2002) and Waters (2007) place considerable faith in the potential of pornography as a site of female agency and empowerment, with Attwood, for example, choosing to focus on the 'rise of the "sassy, sexy and strong" girl' – a figure that she believes 'presents us with a real opportunity to examine how sexualisation and gender are entwined' (Attwood, 2009b: xxii). This emphasis elides important questions of economic power, how women are represented in mainstream pornography and who produces and consumes pornography. The failure to engage adequately with the sexist nature of mainstream pornography, as discussed in Chapter 2, tends to lead to overemphasis on the potential of 'feminist porn' (Waters, 2007) and overclaiming with regard to the agency of women in transforming porn. Claims emphasising the potential of activities such as pole dancing (Holland and Attwood, 2009), burlesque (Ferreday, 2008) and marginal spaces such as 'altporn' (Attwood, 2007) as sites for the production of new, 'empowered' forms of femininity, risk paying insufficient attention to the economic power and influence of the industry from which these new forms are emerging. As Boyle suggests, it is necessary to analyse processes of pornification through understanding pornography 'as *both* a genre of representation *and* a distinct form of industrial practice' (2010: 2).

The rise in pornified images of women must be seen in the context of the lack of other representations of women: as noted by Papadopoulos, depictions of violence against women and girls have increased dramatically in mainstream culture, alongside the under-representation of women and girls in non-sexualised roles (Papadopoulos, 2010: 8, 40). What is culturally visible – pornified images of women – needs to be seen in the context of what is distinctly *in*visible, such as non-sexualised images of women in politics and other areas of public life: '[t]he visible involves isolating one element from all of the other possibilities; it is often difficult to see what gives rise to that which is present'. In these terms Woodward and Woodward utilise Irigaray's ideas around visibility and invisibility in order to form a persuasive argument regarding how 'the sexualised can serve to erase all other possibilities, as if they are invisible and not present' (2009: 116). This argument is highly pertinent with regard to the pornification of culture: increasingly, narratives and images of female objectification originating in pornography crowd out other narratives, and 'serve to erase all other possibilities'. Studies of women in the media make this point very vividly. A study taking a snapshot of mainstream British media over a single day found that all story narrators on children's television were male and only 30 per cent of main characters were female; in newspapers, there were almost three times as many images of men alone as that of women alone, and women were frequently shown not fully clothed (Redfern and Aune, 2010: 182). Research into British news media in 2011 found that, in a typical month, 78 per cent of newspaper articles were written by men, 72 per cent of the foremost television political discussion show contributors were men and 84 per cent of reporters and guests on the foremost national morning radio news show were men (Cochrane, 2011).

Pornification and its discontents
While the mainstreaming of pornography has generated

academic, media and policy debates, it has also generated huge distress and a growing anger amongst young women living with the day-to-day realities of a pornified culture. The activists that I interviewed for my PhD thesis, and latterly for this book, testified to extremely high levels of distress resulting from the everyday sexism that they experienced, which they saw as intrinsically bound up with the mainstreaming of pornography within all aspects of their lives, from the workplace to personal relationships. Many interviewees cited their experience of the increasing normalisation of pornography within mainstream culture as a key influence and motivating factor in their development as feminists. While they spoke in quite general ways about accessing feminist ideas and becoming a feminist, it was clear that pornography, pornification and the objectification of women had been politicising issues:

> Being a 22-year-old feminist in the UK, it's so much worse, you know, than older feminists have any idea of.... . Friends in Hyde Park, a student area, they said they get leafleted through the post, like, leaflets advertising lap-dancing clubs.... . We are grooming girls into this. (Marilyn, 24)

> What it really was for me was music videos. Music videos which show the women completely naked almost, and dancing for men, being sexual for men, being there for men, not even singing or having any place in the music video in their own right, apart from being sexual objects. (Jenny, 17)

> One of my biggest concerns is the normalisation of the objectification of women, women as sex objects, all of that – the culture is so saturated, there's this huge massive tide of things to tackle. (Laura, 31)

Penny gives an account of her 'pre-feminist' self growing up in what she describes as the 'pornified' environment of a town with a number of lap-dancing clubs and a reputation as a venue for stag weekends. She talks about the sexual harassment that was commonplace in that environment, and how it felt impossible to challenge or dissent from the culture:

> I was pornified ... completely, just going along with it, like on my eighteenth birthday I was in a wet t-shirt competition, that's how pornified I was. I just went along with it.... .

Activist Finn Mackay's longstanding involvement with the London Feminist Network (LFN) leads her to believe that pornified culture is a key politicising influence amongst many young feminists:

> LFN still gets about 3–5 new members every week and a lot of those women will write on their reasons for joining 'I am sick of seeing degrading and porny images of myself all over the place, it's not funny, it's gone too far and I want to do something about it.'

As well as being a mobilising issue, pornification was seen by interviewees as a priority in terms of setting an agenda for feminist activism. Roberta is a 28-year-old activist involved with a number of groups and campaigns, but she is emphatic about her priorities:

> To me, the pornification of society and the objectification of women is key – that is the most important battle that I want to be involved in. I mean, that is the key to everything.

The objectification of women – seen as an intrinsic part of pornography and pornification – was particularly mentioned as a 'crucial' issue:

> [As long as] the judge and the jury are men, and women are the objects to be rated, as long we still have that, women will not be equal; we will not, because even if 50 per cent of Parliament is female – you know, a female President, whatever – if you've still got this attitude that women are rated – as in cattle or merchandise or apples, which is the shiniest one or whatever – just by having that system of evaluation means that women

are not seen as human beings. So that's why I think that the pornification stuff, the objectification stuff, is really crucial to that, um, equality debate. (Sheryl, 30)

Many of the interviewees spoke of their experience of pornography as provoking emotional responses such as anger and distress. The account given by Marie-France encapsulates some key themes that came up in the research. She is frustrated and angry with the ubiquity of porn, the sense of powerlessness she has experienced in the face of it, and a sense of regret in terms of its effects on her:

In the 90s, with the boom of porn, it was just everywhere. There was no escaping it. On TV, at home, at work, in the newsagent, school, university, everywhere. And there was no counter argument about it, no one saying anything against it apart from religious groups. I feel this 'culture' has been imposed on us violently, we have been bombarded for two or three decades with these images. Speaking for myself, the consequences have been very negative, damaging even. I do not know what my sexuality would have been like had I not been exposed to these images. I feel a part of my identity has been stolen from me and I don't think I can ever get it back.

Sheryl, a 30-year-old activist, similarly describes the distressing and subordinating effects of living in a pornified culture. Sheryl talks about how she experienced feelings of inferiority without being able to name and identify the causes of what was making her feel this way. She now attributes those feelings not to her own personality but to cultural messages about women perpetuated in sexist advertising and what she now unhesitatingly identifies as a 'pornified' society:

In my past I just remember feeling something's making me feel 'less than', or a bit inferior, something's putting me down or a bit restricting me in some way, and now I think [pornification] was what it was. You don't realise that that's what it is, because people are like 'oh, it's just a bit of fun' you know, 'it's just a picture, it doesn't represent anything', but if it's everywhere it does! And it does represent stuff, everything means something!

The distress experienced by Marie-France and Sheryl is echoed in Belinda's account:

> It was actually an experience of an ex-boyfriend ... putting porn on, like with me there, for obviously what was planned to be an erotic experience for us both, and it was like one of the most grotesque experiences of my life.... And if I was in a newsagent's, I'd start flicking through these men's magazines and I went through a stage – I've hardened a bit now, but every now and then something will catch me – where I was crying when I saw that stuff, 'cos it was just so heartbreaking to me, 'cos it just makes me feel disgusting, it makes me feel like nothing.... It is just page after page of hatred.

Belinda's account draws attention to how misogyny and violence against women is normalised within commonplace experiences. She experiences the effect of pornography as diminishing her sense of self – 'it makes me feel like nothing'. For Belinda, there are conclusions to be drawn regarding the role of pornography in maintaining women's unequal status in society generally:

> You just think, wow, teenage boys and men read this! And how can a man read that joke and find that funny, and take me seriously? It's just impossible, to think a man who reads that joke and finds it funny can take me seriously as a person with my gender as it is.

Sheryl also refers to distressing emotions in explaining how she became involved in OBJECT. Like Belinda, she describes her response to lads' mags and newspapers such as *The Sun* in terms of feeling diminished:

> I always felt like the kind of things like *The Sun* and Page 3 and lads' mags and things like that, I feel that – I'm just saying a personal thing, of how I got into it – like I used to feel I can do

everything, I can compete with men on all levels and be friends with men blah blah, and all it takes is a copy of *The Sun* and then suddenly – I've lost, I'm not equal anymore, I can't – I'm excluded, I've been insulted, my sex has been kind of, um, made less you know.

Sheryl's repeated use of 'I' statements, and her searching for ways to express how the lads' mags make her feel – 'I've lost', 'not equal anymore', 'excluded', 'insulted' – contrasts with the immediately preceding part of the interview, where she expresses how she 'used to feel' quite directly and straightforwardly. This hesitancy seems to indicate a searching for the right language with which to express the specific effects of the magazines. Importantly, the effects she mentions refer specifically to how the magazines alter her social position in relation to men, as well as the associated emotional effects. She then moves from the 'I' statements to generalising the effects of the magazines on all women – 'my sex has been ... made less'. This appears significant because it identifies the effects on her directly in relation to her membership of the social group 'women', which she goes on to elaborate in terms of the feminist slogan 'the personal is political':

Yeah, that's why I think the slogan in feminism 'the personal is political' is really important ... everything related to that, and it took me quite a while to realise that a lot of the things were because of gender inequality, and including, um, you know the pornification of our media and the sex industry and things like that.

Whilst Belinda and Sheryl express their initial reactive responses to pornography in terms of unhappiness, grief, or a feeling of an erosion of the self, other interviewees cited anger as a primary motivation for them to get involved in activism. Nadia explains her motivation in terms of her anger both at witnessing images of naked women in local shops, and the treatment of MP Clare Short:

I just used to get so angry going into a newsagent's or to buy petrol, and being surrounded by these images of naked air-brushed women at eye level and lower than eye level. Newspapers – that was the first thing that made me angry.... . The first thing that got me going was when *The Sun* had their campaign against Clare Short when she tried to ban Page 3, and that was when I think I really started to take things more seriously, 'cos I was outraged the way she was treated.

Nadia immediately goes on to link these experiences of the mainstream news media with her experiences both of personal relationships and the working environment of her first job after graduation. She explains how an ex-boyfriend was a *Sun* reader ('I soon put a stop to that!') and how his friends would also read *The Sun*, as did work colleagues. She links this to what she describes as sexist and racist attitudes in her workplace, which was in the financial sector:

I've never been more disillusioned than when I started. They were so sexist and so racist – and I couldn't believe how much so, really.

She describes serious levels of sexual harassment in the workplace, linking this to the cultural context of the mainstreamed sex industry:

The guys used to go out at lunch time to strip clubs and then they'd come back from their lunch break and I'd be photocopying and they'd walk past me and slap my bottom and stuff. And one of the old associates who was really respected ... every time I'd take his post to him in his office he'd talk to me about how he used to when he was younger go to lesbian orgies and come out with a sore jaw, and ask me would I like to go to sex cinemas with him at lunch time.

Marie-France also recounts experiencing workplace sexual harassment by her 'porn-obsessed boss', who harassed her with a porn video when she was 23. Nadia describes how in the workplace sexist behaviour was treated as a source of humour, and certainly not as anything to be challenged, perhaps because of the associate's senior status:

> All the other guys knew it was happening, and they said it was quite funny that when I went in his office I'd always have one hand on the door to get out of there, or try and deliver his post when he wasn't there and stuff.

As the above section shows, Nadia identifies a range of reactive emotions – encompassing feeling 'mortified', 'alienated' and 'angry' – in explaining her motivations for seeking out anti-porn activism. However, she also describes her motivation in terms of affective emotions in relation to certain family members, as I will go on to examine in the next section. Rita, a 53-year-old activist whose daughter is also an anti-porn activist, describes a similar range of emotions when talking about her motivations for joining OBJECT. She is emphatic in articulating her angry response to the unequal treatment she has received as a woman employee in male-dominated industries, but also explains that she was motivated to get involved as the mother of a teenage daughter:

> I just became aware of it on pop videos, on adverts, you start to see it all around you, and you start to think 'This is influencing my daughter and her peers all the time!' And I was just getting angrier and angrier at the overly sexual way in which women are shown.

Other activists were also motivated by similar protective or concerned feelings in relation to family members in the context of pornification. Nadia discusses her relationships with her sisters in terms of a sense of protectiveness from what she sees as a damaging culture:

> Because I'm the oldest, I'm very protective of my younger sisters. I'd just hate them to go through what I did, like, just

how I felt about myself.... I'm so protective of my sisters, and I hate the eye-level lads' mags, I just think it's wrong.

For Kathleen, raising awareness of the harms of the porn industry was part of her job as an information officer with a women's sector organisation, but she also expresses a personal commitment to the work in the context of being the mother of a thirteen-year-old son. Kathleen explains that she has found attempting to discuss the issue with her son 'very difficult', but explains her persistence in terms not only of a concern for her son, but also of a sense of responsibility to the women that his son may form relationships with:

> You think, well boys these days, how different are they going to be? Are they going to be decent human beings, with good, real relationships with women?

For Carol, working with teenage girls provided a motivation to try to change the culture:

> What I see is so much pressure, it is so damaging. It's acceptable for girls to be considering things like skin lightening, boob jobs, implants. How they look is the ultimate, it's the most important thing. This is my biggest concern, the effect on self esteem, confidence.... It's coming from the culture, music videos – it's totally normal. It's the likes of Hugh Hefner who've created this culture which is so damaging for young women. I call it the 'dolly' look – it's totally fake. You remember, there was the young woman who died, she went to America for buttock implants. It is so damaging, and it's totally normal. There is this idea of beauty – it's nothing to do with personality or personal qualities. Beauty is in the eye of the beholder, but the beholder has been conditioned to accept distorted images of what is truly beautiful.

For a number of activists, relationships with abusive men and boyfriends' porn use acted as catalysts to their getting involved in activism. These activists consistently located their experience of these relationships in the context of factors such as pornification and misogynist attitudes within the broader culture:

> I was in a relationship with someone I discovered had a porn addiction, and it just completely made me feel like terrible, and drove a divide through the relationship. And that as well as other things – I felt that at the time I was surrounded by a lot of misogynist men, and other people in my life had similar attitudes, and I just felt so unhappy and I felt I can't handle this being everywhere, I don't want to be in a world that's like this.[13]

> Pornography reflects and encourages the attitudes that men have towards women in their personal and public life. It perpetuates and encourages the idea that women exist as sexual slaves to men and are merely masturbatory tools for men's sexual gratification. I was in a relationship with a man who was conditioned to be very sexist and he and his friends openly sexually objectified women in my presence. Comments like 'I'd fuck it' and 'Look at the jugs on that' were commonplace. My ex-boyfriend once told me my breasts were saggy and suggested my labia needed altering. I went on to spend time online researching labiaplasty surgeons – such was the powerful effect his comments had on my self-esteem.[14]

The testimonies of these activists tell a story of the levels of distress and experiences of subordination that are galvanising a new generation of feminists to get involved in anti-porn activism. The process of pornification acts as a constraint on women's freedom, and it is this very constraint which, in provoking increasing unease, distress and anger amongst women, has also generated a new wave of activism, through what might be termed 'reactive mobilisation' (Koopmans, 2007: 27). Of course, for this to happen, pornography must be understood in political terms *as* a constraint: it must be understood as a political issue. Such feelings of unease and distress are otherwise experienced only on an individual level: it is through access to feminist ideas and analyses that this personal experience can be transformed into political motivation. In the next chapter, we will look at what broke the feminist 'silence' with regard to pornography and pornification, and examine how individual discontent was mobilised into collective dissent during the first decade of the twenty-first century.

Notes

1 *RapeLay* is a computer game in which the main aim is to sexually harass and rape women.

2 Upskirting is the term used to describe taking photographs, often on a mobile-phone camera, up an unsuspecting woman's skirt.

3 According to anti-bullying charity Beatbullying, 'sexting' is defined as follows: 'A portmanteau of sex and texting, sexting is the act of sending sexually explicit messages or photos electronically, primarily between mobile phones and/or the internet. Sexting is an extension of cyberbullying when someone (or a group of people) deliberately attempts to hurt, upset, threaten or humiliate someone else. This includes when a recipient is made to feel uncomfortable as a direct result of the content, or asked to do something which makes the recipient feel distressed.' Beatbullying, <http://www.beatbullying.org/dox/media-centre/press-releases/press-release-040809.html>.

4 Rape Crisis Scotland and Women's Support Project (2011) 'Second life', Newsletter 8 (Spring).

5 See, for example, corporate calendars produced by low-cost airline Ryanair, and charity advertising campaigns run by PETA, the Autism Trust and Cancer Research UK.

6 *Stop Porn Culture*, 'Pornography statistics and studies', <http://stoppornculture.org/stats-and-studies/> (accessed 24 May 2009).

7 These strategies were among the main themes addressed in panel sessions at the *Xbiz EU* adult entertainment convention, held in London, 23-24 September 2011.

8 Topics covered in panel sessions at the *Xbiz EU* convention.

9 Dan Savage, 9 April 2009, <http://www.thestranger.com/seattle/Savage Love?oid =1220590>.

10 Clarisse Thorn, 24 May 2011, <http://jezebel.com/sex_crazy-nympho-dream-girl/>.

11 Hugo Schwyzer, 11 January 2012, <http://jezebel.com/5875217/he-wants-to-jizz-on-your-face-but-not-why-youd-think>.

12 'Women's Question Time', organised by Eaves Housing, Westminster Central Hall, London, 16 March 2010.

13 In order to maintain confidentiality, I have not attributed this quotation.

14 In order to maintain confidentiality, I have not attributed this quotation.

CHAPTER 4
Reactivating Dissent:
Feminist Anti-Porn Activism in the UK

Introduction: the resurgence of anti-porn feminism

The first decade of the twenty-first century saw a remarkable resurgence of grassroots feminist activism in the UK. Online feminist blogs and discussion groups appeared, and feminist networks proliferated across the country, the largest of which, the London Feminist Network, grew from just a handful of members in 2004 to a membership of around 1,700 by the end of the decade. The decade saw the revival of 'Reclaim the Night' and the establishing of 'Million Women Rise' marches against male violence; several large-scale feminist activist conferences; numerous actions and campaigns; and the emergence of a national information and resource organisation – UK Feminista – which aims to coordinate and support UK grassroots feminist activism.

A striking feature of this flourishing activism is the centrality of pornography and the sex industry as mobilising issues. Whilst the re-emergent movement is far from homogeneous, anti-porn feminism is nonetheless a significant and high-profile element within the new activism. In particular, the *mainstreaming* of pornography and the sex industry has galvanised many new activists to engage in various forms of resistance – from informal, *ad hoc* actions such as 'stickering' advertisements and disrupting displays of lads' mags, to more formal, and in some cases highly

147

strategic, campaigns. In this chapter, I will map out some of the key developments, approaches and successes of this movement, and consider how groups build solidarity and collective identity amongst their members. There are obvious limitations to any attempt to map grassroots activism: it is the nature of activist groups to be fluid and sometimes quite transient, characterised by process, flux and movement rather than stasis. Groups emerge, grow, flourish or disappear, according to internal factors such as the resources and commitment of the individuals involved, as well as external factors such as opportunities, pressures and constraints. This makes mapping their presence and activities quite difficult; a difficulty exacerbated by the fact that in some cases documentation on group activities is limited. Given the informal and sometimes transient nature of many grassroots groups, my discussion of UK feminist anti-porn activism attempts to be neither exhaustive nor comprehensive, and will focus particularly on two groups: OBJECT and Anti-Porn London.

Activating dissent

Routes into activism
In order for processes of mobilisation to take place, groups, structures and spaces that can serve as sites of political resistance need to be formed and accessed. Anti-porn activism in the first decade of the twenty-first century has taken place within the context of the emergence of a plethora of new grassroots feminist groups, networks, conferences, blogs and websites that have sprung up in the UK since the turn of the new millennium (Banyard, 2010: 207; Redfern and Aune, 2010). Most of these groups and networks were set up in the second half of the decade, indicative of a building momentum.

Continuity and abeyance structures

The backlash following the second wave created the circumstances in which important feminist insight, knowledge and structures were lost (French, 1992; Faludi, 1991; Jeffreys, 1994; Henry, 2004; Woodward and Woodward, 2009). The porn industry flourished in the same decade that such knowledge and insight was submerged, whilst new, neoliberal versions of feminism – which substituted a language of individual agency and empowerment for radical political critique – were contributing to a context in which collective challenges to pornography were less likely to be possible. What, then, are the structures and processes that have supported or engendered this renewed period of collective action?

To an extent, periods of apparent inactivity can serve as 'incubatory stages of mobilisation' (Della Porta and Diani, 1999: 192). Apparently latent periods can be productive; during these times social movements can create new social codes and realities, whilst moments of more visible, overt contention demonstrate these new realities as forms of opposition to dominant political systems (Melucci, 1989). Latent periods can afford opportunities for the creation of social movement networks and structures that 'constitute the submerged reality of the movements before, during and after [visible] events' (*ibid.*: 338). Periods of apparent inactivity might offer a chance to develop 'abeyance structures' that include associated emotions, beliefs and culture, and that serve as ways of maintaining meaning, motivation and purpose through periods of limited political opportunity (Taylor, 1989). Such structures serve to incubate the goals and purpose of the group until a point at which more direct activism can re-emerge. During the 1990s, abeyance structures were evident in the ongoing work of UK women's sector organisations (albeit often seriously underfunded), and increasing numbers of women in government, and in some policy-making and policy-influencing arenas. Thanks largely to the pressure of the women's sector and sympathetic women MPs in the Labour government from 1997 to 2010, some form of an ongoing, public feminist agenda was in evidence, in some policy areas at least. This presence of feminists in key positions in central and local government, voluntary sector organisations, academia, the media, and informal structures helped to maintain the semblance of a 'social movement community' (Buechler, 2000: 205), albeit frequently isolated, fragmented and beleaguered.

Abeyance structures have contributed to the re-emergence of feminist activism in a number of ways. The wealth of feminist literature produced in the 1970s and 1980s formed a rich resource for a new generation of activists, and the ongoing production of anti-porn feminist texts (Dines *et al.*, 1998; Stark and Whisnant, 2004; Levy, 2005; Jensen, 2007; Jeffreys, 2009; Boyle, 2010; Dines, 2010; Tankard Reist and Bray, 2011; Tyler, 2011a) has been of particular value for women living with the realities of a pornified culture. Abeyance structures also supported the new movement in particularly practical and personal ways. For some younger activists, mothers, family friends and teachers provided access to second wave feminist communities and ideas; some older activists bring their own experience of earlier anti-porn activism with groups such as WAVAW and CAP to the new movement. Finn Mackay, founder of the London Feminist Network, attributes her commitment to feminism to the experience of living at a women's peace camp in her teenage years, and from there becoming part of a radical lesbian feminist community:

> Even though I wasn't around in the Seventies and Eighties, I heard all the stories and it gave me a real insight into strategising, what worked, what didn't work, that kind of thing. And some of these women really became family to me, and that's been really important.

This kind of intergenerational knowledge transfer and ongoing support – 'bec[oming] family' – illustrates the role of informal structures in the development of a feminist social movement community.

Alongside a legacy of personal resources and informal structures, the institutionalisation of the women's movement at the global level also produced achievements that were to be utilised in the new millennium by a new generation of feminists. For example, the UN Convention for the Elimination of All Forms of Discrimination Against Women (CEDAW) and the Platform for Action agreed at the UN World Conference on Women in Beijing in 1995 provided levers that have been utilised by groups such as OBJECT in holding the UK government to account in respect of its obligations regarding women's equality. Abeyance structures were also in evidence in the form of established feminist organisations and individuals playing a part in the re-emergent anti-porn activism, with women's sector organisations and feminist politicians, academics and journalists participating in and supporting OBJECT campaigns.

Campaigns

While not all of the new feminist groups and networks are involved in anti-porn activism, or even necessarily take an anti-porn stance, pornography has been a mobilising factor for many groups. In particular, the mainstreaming of pornography and the sex industry in the form of lads' mags, lap-dancing clubs and the expansion of the Playboy empire has galvanised many new activists. While I will discuss campaigns run by OBJECT and Anti-Porn London (APL) in detail, it is important to acknowledge that these campaigns were not conducted in isolation. For example, East Midland Feminists (EM Fems), formed in October 2006, carried out a campaign to encourage the high street store Marks and

Spencer not to sell lads' mags and the tabloid newspaper the *Daily Star*, and were involved in APL's early meetings and their main campaign, as were North West Feminists. Many groups do take an explicit anti-porn stance: Sheffield Fems ran campaigns to get Playboy merchandise removed from John Lewis, and against the opening of a Sheffield branch of the American 'Hooters' franchise.[1] Bristol Fawcett Society have also energetically campaigned against 'Hooters', alongside campaigns regarding the licensing of lap-dancing clubs. The 'Turn Your Back on Page 3' campaign was started by activist Francine Hoenderkamp in response to reading about Clare Short's campaign to get rid of images of semi-naked women in the tabloid press, and the response of women to Short's 1980s campaign (Short, 1991). An Anti-Porn Men Project was set up in 2010. In Scotland, groups with a specifically anti-porn focus include Scottish Women Against Pornography (SWAP), the Women's Support Project and the Scottish Coalition Against Sexual Exploitation, a coalition launched in October 2003 by Rape Crisis Scotland and the Women's Support Project. SWAP are unusual in that they preceded other groups by several years, being formed in 1999, and ran campaigns during 2000–5, including an 'Off the Shelf' postcard campaign, campaigns against the licensing of sex shops, and lobbying the Scottish Parliament to adopt a harm-based definition of pornography. In particular, SWAP ran a campaign against the Bank of Scotland, protesting the bank's decision to loan £4.5 million to Remnant Productions to buy part of Richard Desmond's pornographic empire.

Alongside more formally organised campaigns, much anti-porn activism takes the form of very informal, sometimes spontaneous activism, carried out by individuals as well as groups. Activism carried out on an individual basis includes web-based activism such as blogging; writing to MPs; challenging sexist attitudes expressed by friends, family and colleagues; requesting local newsagents and cornershops not to stock lads' mags, or to place them on the top shelf, stickering lads' mags or sexist posters and advertisements, or disrupting displays of lads' mags in shops. Occasionally, sex shops have been covered in graffiti, as in the case of a sex shop in Bristol in 2011, which was spray painted with the message 'Women's bodies are not 4 sale', but apart from this example and the stickering, illegal activities were not a common feature of the activism.

Connecting and networking: a movement in movement
According to Imelda Whelehan, 'the biggest changes to impact upon the possibilities open to third wavers have been technological ones' (Whelehan, 2007: xvi; see also Baumgardner and Richards, 2000: 77; Kinser, 2004: 137), and certainly feminists of this generation have embraced technological possibilities, using online discussion boards, web-based groups, social networking sites, electronic zines and newsletters, blogs, YouTube and Twitter to create vibrant online feminist communities and to form connections across geographical boundaries (Redfern and Aune, 2010: 216–17). Online discussions, social networking sites, blogs and Twitter are a key element of anti-porn activism, used to raise awareness and discuss issues, circulate petitions and publicise actions and events. Increasingly, in the latter part of the decade, groups began posting videos of successful actions onto YouTube, thus sharing experiences of activism and helping to create momentum around certain issues.

New technologies help to create movement narratives, broaden the base of activists, and enable support, exchange and the sharing of resources between different groups and individuals. However, this kind of connection and networking was not limited to cyberspace: anti-porn actions in London, for example, have been attended by activists from many other UK cities and regions, and events such as Million Women Rise, the national 'Reclaim the Night' and large-scale conferences in different cities attract delegates from across the UK and beyond. Locally based meetings and actions are also much in evidence, including the revival of Reclaim the Night marches in many UK cities. Whilst online communication plays a key role, physical presence and face-to-face meetings are also evidently highly valued.

Telling the story: encultured informants
A number of activists acted as 'encultured informants' (Spradley, 1979), in that they augmented their participation in activist culture with often highly creative and diverse enterprises in telling a feminist, anti-porn 'story' to the wider community: utilising their skills, opportunities and resources in order to create and disseminate narratives that reached out beyond activist circles.[2] Such narratives help to claim a space for oppositional feminist identities and perspectives within an unconducive or hostile mainstream cultural context. Encultured informants raising awareness of anti-porn feminism amongst a variety of audiences include bloggers, journalists and activists involved in the media or creative professions. Rebecca Mordan, for example, combines her participation in feminist activism with her career as a performer and director of an arts production company. Rebecca organises and performs in feminist fundraiser events, and also devised her own show which combines a cabaret aesthetic with an anti-porn message. Blogger Rebecca Mott, a survivor of rape, sexual assault and prostitution, writes powerfully on the devastating harms done to women in prostitution and pornography, the 'relentless attacks'[3] to which vocal women who have exited the sex trade are subjected by those who champion the sex industry, and the

need for exited women to be supported to play a leading role in anti-porn and anti-prostitution campaigns.

Setting the agenda: conferences and key events
Conferences have traditionally been a key mode of organising within the women's movement (Coote and Campbell, 1982; Rowbotham, 1989; Antrobus, 2004; Rees, 2007), forming 'a spur to mass mobilization' (Marx Ferree and McClurg Mueller, 2007: 594). As we saw in Chapter 1, feminist conferences played a key part in mobilising the wave of anti-porn feminism in the 1970s. Rees highlights the participation of revolutionary feminist Sandra McNeill in an international conference as instrumental in the development of anti-porn feminism in the UK in the 1970s (Rees, 2007: 208). Consistent with this beginning, current anti-porn feminists utilise the conference structure as a key way of disseminating their analysis of pornography and mobilising other women to join their campaigns. A number of large-scale conferences have punctuated and accelerated the growth of feminist activism throughout the decade, and have been important in creating a platform for anti-porn feminism. These include the national 'Fem'[4] conferences held in Sheffield (2004–8) and in London (2011),[5] and the 'Feminism in London' (FiL) annual conferences organised by members of the London Feminist Network,[6] which by 2010 were attracting an attendance of around twelve hundred. Both FiL and the Fem conferences have played an instrumental role in helping to put anti-porn perspectives on the developing agenda of the resurgent grassroots movement, featuring panel sessions and workshops on the themes of pornography, prostitution and objectification, and importantly giving a platform to women who have exited the sex industry.

The Women's Support Project[7] in Glasgow held a number of conferences and seminars titled 'Challenging Demand' in the second half of the decade, as part of the Project's work to actively address commercial sexual exploitation as part of the spectrum of men's violence against women. The 'Challenging Demand' conferences tended to attract a practitioner-based audience as well as some grassroots activists, with a variety of service providers and local government representatives participating.

The 'Challenging Demand' conferences played a significant role in forging international links, and in supporting the efforts of grassroots activists. For example, the Women's Support Project was instrumental in introducing the work of 'Stop Porn Culture!'[8] (SPC), a group of US activists and academics, into the UK. At a 'Challenging Demand' conference in 2008, Rebecca Whisnant of 'Stop Porn Culture!' gave a presentation of a new anti-porn slideshow, which was subsequently circulated and utilised by other groups and at other conferences.

The circulation and various presentations of the slideshow at different fora is illustrative of the networking and mobilising potential of feminist conferences with regard to raising awareness around the issue of pornography. In this regard, 'Stop Porn Culture!' has played a leading role in helping to forge an international anti-porn network. In Boston in 2007, a group of long-standing activists held the first feminist anti-porn conference in fifteen years, which attracted around 550 participants and marked 'the beginning of a new era in anti-porn activism' (Dines, 2011a). 'Stop Porn Culture!' was founded that weekend, and from that point onwards has been active in not only leading and supporting feminist anti-porn activism within the USA, but in helping to build an international movement. SPC has produced two anti-porn slideshows, which they have made available free of charge from their website, so that they can be used and adapted within local contexts by other activist groups: a powerful gesture of solidarity and an indication of their commitment to movement building that is strikingly at odds with the current culture of intellectual property rights and the inaccessibility of most academic resources beyond a privileged academic audience. SPC has helped build links between anti-porn activists in Australia, Norway and the UK as well as across the USA, and activists and academics from each of these locations participated at their 2011 conference in Boston. Such links help to strengthen local activism, as Ane Stø from the Norwegian Feminist Group Ottar[9] explains:

> We are going to translate the Stop Porn Culture slideshow and are about to build a Stop Porn Culture network in Norway. We hope to reach out to a much bigger audience for the slideshows when we get the funding to have some paid employees. We also want to start the same training conference as Gail held in Boston, to have more people able to give the slideshow.

The Boston 2011 conference was followed up with a 'Challenging Porn Culture' conference in London in December of the same year. Again there was a distinctly international flavour, with Gail Dines giving the keynote address and speakers from the USA, Australia and Norway, as well as from across the UK. Importantly, the conference included a 'young women speak out' panel, including presentations from Jennifer Hayashi Danns, a woman who has written a book about her experiences of lap dancing (Danns and Lévêque, 2011), a young lesbian and two young women from the women's sector organisation, Imkaan. The contributions of these speakers were valuable in ensuring that experiences of the realities of living in a pornified culture in the context of different communities were shared.

An important aspect of large-scale events such as the conferences discussed above is that they offer an opportunity for socialising, networking and creating a sense of belonging. Participants testify to finding them extremely inspiring and a valuable opportunity to connect with other feminists, as well as to find out more about specific issues.[10] The opportunity for socialising, connecting and celebrating afforded by such events is important in helping build momentum for anti-porn perspectives, and also in helping to create a sense of solidarity and collective identity amongst group members. In addition to this, the opportunity for strategising at the international level is also vital, given the global nature of the porn industry.

In addition to helping to set the feminist agenda at key conferences, UK anti-porn feminism also gained ground in relation to other feminist priorities and campaigns as the decade progressed. A notable example of this is the shifting agenda of the Fawcett Society, a women's rights campaign group which historically has pursued a liberal feminist agenda; it aims to improve women's rights in a number of strategic areas, including women and poverty, women and the criminal justice system, and the representation of women in public life. In 2008, the Fawcett Society launched its 'Sexism in the City' campaign, which addressed issues of objectification and aspects of the sex industry such as lap-dancing clubs, alongside more traditional issues such as employment equality and the gender pay gap. In the same year, Fawcett joined OBJECT in demanding the regulatory re-licensing of lap-dancing clubs through the 'Stripping the Illusion' campaign, and in September 2009 produced a report on 'the sex industry's infiltration of the modern workplace', covering topics such as 'pornography in the workplace' and 'corporate use of lap-dancing clubs' (Banyard and Lewis, 2009). This shift seems to indicate the growing influence of grassroots feminism in shaping and even possibly transforming a more traditional, liberal feminist agenda.

Collective action and use of protest

I get extremely angry about this stuff so I have to do something about it, and because it's doing something, it's not just reading or writing about it, I find that so kind of necessary and therapeutic, and empowering as well. (Sheryl, 30)

Since 2003, UK feminist anti-porn activism has included campaigns against the Playboy empire, lads' mags and tabloid newspapers, the Hooters restaurant franchise and the *Xbiz EU* adult entertainment convention, held in London in September 2011. A related campaign has lobbied for changes in the way that lap-dancing clubs are licensed, to give more power to local authorities and local communities to refuse licences to clubs. These campaigns have utilised tactical repertoires including participating in marches; collecting signatures for petitions; lobbying MPs and local councils; writing to newspapers; 'stunts' and street protests; organising events and fundraisers; producing materials and props for actions; singing and chanting; speaking at events; meeting with key actors in the media and policy arenas; and strategic networking.

'Bin the Bunny': framing the problem

'Bin the Bunny' was a series of protests held by Anti-Porn London against the opening and presence of the Playboy 'concept store' in London's Oxford Street. Anti-Porn London (APL) is a small feminist activist group, with a membership varying from approximately 12 to 30 women during the period of my ethnography. APL evolved organically from the activism and consciousness-raising opportunities afforded by the London Feminist Network (LFN). The key event which catalysed the formation of the group was the screening of a classic feminist anti-porn film – *Not a Love Story* (Sherr Klein, 1981) – as part of a feminist film festival held by LFN.

Through its 'Bin the Bunny' campaign, APL was engaged in framing (Goffman, 1974) the issue of pornography as a political, feminist issue. 'Framing' refers to the process via which we read and interpret events and experience; the ways in which we understand and give meaning to 'reality'. It is an important concept in the study of social movements, since, as Crossley notes:

The notion of framing connects directly with the notion of 'cognitive liberation'... . If we perceive our own misfortune as evidence of personal failing we are much less likely to challenge it politically than if we frame it in terms of broader system failings. (Crossley, 2002: 135)

It is in the interest of social movements, therefore, to frame experiences and 'reality' in ways that will help to promote certain understandings of movement issues and grievances and garner support for the movement. This has long been recognised by feminists, and is neatly illustrated by the feminist slogan 'the personal is political': through this slogan, feminists helped to frame what might have been experienced as issues of personal unhappiness, misfortune or failing as issues of sexual politics.

Within social movement theory, the concept of framing has been extended in several ways (Benford and Snow, 2000; Snow, 2007). 'Frame bridging' refers to ways in which groups reach out to potential constituents, informing them of the issue, using persuasive language and drawing out connections. 'Frame amplification' involves drawing on 'latent' values of potential constituents, showing that if an individual already holds certain values, then adopting this frame is a logical extension. 'Frame extension' refers to the process via which a group extends its own basic frame to include other agendas, or aligns itself with other issues or cultures, in order to attract diverse constituents. Through developing the tactical repertoire of its campaigns, the group built shared frames of meaning in relation to Playboy and pornification, and also pursued goals of 'frame bridging', 'frame amplification' and 'frame extension'.

The film screening that galvanised the formation of APL is significant as the first element of a tactical repertoire that helped to frame pornography as a feminist issue. The event also created a space for discussion, through which this framing could be developed as part of a process of consciousness raising. Following the tradition of the original London Anti-Porn Group of the late 1970s, consciousness raising played a critical role in the development of APL as an activist group. In early APL meetings, space was dedicated to sharing thoughts and feelings around pornography, with these discussions generating ideas for activism. The group worked towards a shared analysis, and broad agreement was reached in relation to the group position and aims – an important first step in framing the issue of pornography as a feminist issue. Similarly, agreement regarding strategic aims and approaches emerged through group discussion. A consensus quickly emerged in identifying the mainstreaming of pornography, and particularly the targeting of young girls by companies such as Playboy, as issues of major concern.

Consumers unfamiliar with the core business of the Playboy Corporation would not necessarily associate its branded merchandise with a global pornography empire, as was obviously the case with the marketing of Playboy-branded stationery, which was already an established aspect of the Playboy enterprise prior to the opening of the store. A key aim of the campaign, then, was frame bridging: raising awareness about the nature of the company among the general public and framing the issue in a way that would highlight Playboy's targeting of girls as potential consumers as a feminist concern. The targeting of Playboy also offered the potential for frame amplification, since Playboy's marketing strategy meant that the campaign was likely to be received sympathetically by those who had a concern around the commercialisation of childhood, without necessarily relating this to a feminist analysis.

Members of APL developed a colourful and imaginative tactical repertoire in conveying the group's messages, framing pornification as a problem, and raising awareness about the activities of the Playboy Corporation. These included the production of a film trilogy – *Bin the Bunny*; a series of demonstrations outside the Playboy Store involving costumes and placards; and the production of resources including leaflets and fliers, badges and t-shirts. Since the group was unfunded, the campaign was developed using the time, energy and financial resources of members of the group, and drawing on social resources in the form of friends and social networks able to offer specific skills, particularly in relation to film making.

The *Bin the Bunny* film trilogy was screened at a London cinema in October 2007, shortly after the first demonstration; copies of the DVD were sold, and the film was then made available on YouTube. The film trilogy attempts to expose the 'real' face of Playboy as a porn empire behind the logo and merchandise aimed at young women, utilising humour and subversion in conveying this message, through the central character of a white rabbit who discovers the 'truth' behind the image; the slogan outside the Playboy store proclaiming 'The things that dreams are made of' is 'subvertised' to read 'The stuff that nightmares are made of'. The film culminates with 'The Rabbit Strikes Back': a boxing match between the rabbit and Hugh Hefner, which the rabbit wins.

The demonstrations were held in a peaceful, non-confrontational way; the local police were always informed prior to an action and protests were conducted lawfully. The actions contained an element of humour and colour provided in the form of the white rabbit and Hugh Hefner costumes used in making the film trilogy, along with humorous slogans. Campaign messages were conveyed via materials such as badges, stickers, placards and t-shirts.

The main activities at the protests were giving out flyers and engaging in discussion with members of the public. Flyers contained information about the group, the rationale for the campaign, information about Playboy and messages about why pornography is harmful. One flyer used at the 'Bin the Bunny' protests, entitled 'About us', was written to raise awareness of the activities of the Playboy Corporation and the group's position with regard to pornography.[11] The flyer used a question and answer format, with the implied voice of a member of the public posing the questions, and responses given by the group. Each question raises what the group considered to be myths or misapprehensions relating to Playboy, the nature of pornography, issues of choice and agency, men in pornography, and stereotypes of feminists. The answers address these questions through presenting a feminist analysis of pornography as a form of sexism and violence against women. The group seeks to draw on a discourse of 'authenticity', through utilising phrases such as 'dishonest' and 'honest' with regard to sexuality.

The flyer is an example of frame bridging: attempting to put forward the group's analysis of the issue in an accessible form, reaching out to potential constituents in the form of an implied dialogue. Some aspects of the flyer might be seen as rather simplistic, whether or not the reader sympathises with an anti-porn position. A straightforward binary is established between 'pornography' and 'sex', declaring that the group is 'pro-sex' and 'anti-porn', and asserting that 'pornography and sex are not the same thing'. This binary opposition of 'authentic' sexuality and 'dishonest' porn is questionable for a number of reasons: first, the notion of an 'authentic' sexuality is inconsistent with a feminist social constructionist approach; and second, if a key anti-porn argument is predicated on the understanding that pornography *does* have certain cultural effects, then presumably it is likely that for some people at least their experience of pornography is in fact quite consistent with their experience of 'actual' sex, rather than distinct or oppositional. There is also perhaps a rather un-nuanced approach to notions of choice and pleasure in the flyer: signs of women's possible enjoyment of participating in porn are dismissed as 'part of the performance' – there is no engagement with the possibility that some women in some circumstances *may* actually testify to enjoying the experience. These messages perhaps reflect the purpose and intended audience of the flyer: unproblematised assertions are common features of campaign materials, since the aim of such materials is to make an impact in an immediate, effective and memorable way, rather than to participate in a detailed and nuanced debate.

The flyer highlights a challenge inherent in framing feminist anti-porn messages. A feminist anti-porn analysis is derived from a deep feminist consciousness, which is not generally shared by the general public. Communication challenges therefore arise, since the two states of consciousness involve vastly different sets of assumptions and vocabularies. The dialogic format of the leaflet was an attempt to negotiate this challenge, and to bridge the different states of consciousness.

Frame bridging presented other kinds of challenges. Activists spoke of their experiences of participating in the 'Bin the Bunny' protests as challenging:

[S]ometimes people can be a bit confrontational when you're standing on the street, especially young people I think, sometimes, 'cos like they've maybe been brought up in quite a pornified society, and they maybe don't think there's another option or way of thinking about things. (Sheryl, 30)

[I]t's certainly challenging, it can be quite intimidating, but it does feel empowering at the same time, because you kind of think, 'Well, here I am stood on Oxford St, and all these people are going past, and you know, we are making a stand against it.' (Roberta, 28)

The 'challenging' aspect of the protests was sometimes quite serious, and on occasion activists experienced insults, abuse, ridicule and aggression. A typical form of this was young men ostentatiously displaying their choice to enter the store, by shouting 'I love porn'. This was always done by young men in a mixed group, never as an individual activity, highlighting the element of display and the importance of being socially positioned amongst their peers in terms of the attempted performance of hegemonic masculinity. The nature of the insults tended to focus on activists' physical appearance and occasionally (presumed) sexuality, as Roberta recounts: 'You do get told to fuck off quite a lot, and "You're only doing this 'cos you're ugly".' The invocation of the 'ugly manhater' stereotype has been well documented as commonplace within anti-feminist discourses (McRobbie, 2009; Scharff, 2010), and the emphasis on activists' physical appearance as a means of attempting to undermine the anti-Playboy activism is particularly significant, as it is the sexualised display of the female body that is central to the issue of contention, whilst the means of protest involves the activist using her physical presence as part of a display of resistance. As the activists attempt to claim a public, political space, attempts to undermine this involve comments about the women's body and appearance, apparently to attempt to relegate women to the realm of objectification. Other hostile responses included the criticism that the issue was a trivial one and the suggestion that activists were wasting their time: the irony of members of the public making this criticism while engaged in Saturday afternoon shopping on Oxford Street was not lost on the activists.

However, alongside the elements of hostility or antipathy, activists also experienced considerable support and appreciation from passers-by:

> [O]ne thing that keeps me going is when you do the protests outside Playboy and people come up to you and say 'It's really great you're doing this', and 'Someone has to do this'. Just

165

handing out flyers, people are really grateful that someone is standing in front of this tidal wave. (Penny)

Other reactions included humour and incomprehension: non-English-speaking tourists make up a large number of the crowds in Oxford Street on a busy Saturday afternoon, and sometimes it was evident from the bemused response of passers-by that they did not understand what the protest was about. The company itself was obviously unhappy at being the target of such a protest: they positioned members of staff in the shop doorway to try to encourage people to ignore the protesters and come into the store.

Following the initial protests and making of the film trilogy, anti-Playboy demonstrations became less frequent. Early in 2010 it became apparent that the store had in fact closed down. Over the 2008–9 period the group's tactical repertoire extended to taking on more educational activities, with group members holding workshops, presenting the anti-porn slideshow and participating in university debates and radio talkshows. In particular, the group participated in discussions with political and social movement groups outside the feminist arena, such as at anti-capitalist events. This afforded the opportunity for 'frame extension' through aligning itself with other social justice issues and presenting its arguments to diverse constituents. The success of such discussions was rather limited, due to the male-dominated leftist audiences tending to be unreceptive to a feminist analysis of the sex industry. Nonetheless, these more discursive approaches contributed to the group's project of framing pornography as a feminist issue; a project which continues to be pursued in the form of an online blog.[12]

'Eff Off Hef!'

Although Anti-Porn London gradually ceased its protest and educational initiatives to become a largely online activist presence, many of its members remained highly active as part of OBJECT and the London Feminist Network, or in other groups. The legacy of the group was evident in June 2011, when OBJECT and UK Feminista coordinated the 'Eff Off Hef!'[13] demonstration, in protest at the reopening of the Playboy Club in London's Mayfair thirty years since the closure of the original club. The 'Eff Off Hef!' protest owed its title – which makes obvious reference to the owner of the Playboy corporation, Hugh Hefner – to the original Anti-Porn London protests, and the demonstration drew on the resources and knowledge that had been developed in the original 'Bin the Bunny' campaign. What was striking about the 'Eff Off Hef!' demonstration was the visible increase in size, confidence and assertiveness of the anti-porn feminist movement in just four years since the inception of APL in 2007. The noisy and passionate demonstration was attended by around two hundred protesters, lasting for several hours; throughout the evening the energetic and angry chanting and singing did not flag, and so forceful was the protest that Hefner was compelled sheepishly to enter the club via the back entrance rather than the red carpet. In contrast to the 'Bin the Bunny' protests, which had attracted no media attention, the demonstration was covered on national and global television networks, and in the national and international press. What was also striking was the growing capacity of the movement and the cooperation of movement groups: while the action was coordinated by UK Feminista and OBJECT, it was also formally supported by the London Feminist Network and Million Women Rise. The event stood as a testimony of the power of such cooperation and solidarity – as a milestone in the re-emerging activism, the 'Eff Off Hef!' protest showed a movement that was increasingly emboldened, confident and vocal.

'Stripping the Illusion': tactical repertoires

'Stripping the Illusion' is a campaign run by OBJECT, 'a human rights organisation which challenges the sexual objectification of women in the media and popular culture' (OBJECT, 2009). OBJECT is more formally established than APL, comprising a management committee, paid staff, a team of activists, a Yahoo group and a membership base of some hundreds. The campaign, co-organised with the Fawcett Society, provides an example of how a varied tactical repertoire can be strategically deployed in order to engage with a range of political and media opportunity structures. OBJECT had previously campaigned to ban sexist advertising on London transport and for the imposition of restrictions on the sales of lads' mags and tabloid newspapers such as *The Star.* The latter campaign was subsequently revived with the launch of 'Feminist Fridays', discussed below. A further campaign – 'Demand Change!' – which called for the 'demand' side of prostitution to be tackled, was launched in June 2009.

'Stripping the Illusion' was launched to change the legislation regarding the licensing of lap-dancing clubs, in line with similar feminist campaigns in Scandinavia. In Norway, The Feminist Group Ottar energetically campaigns for a city free of strip clubs in the capital Oslo and in Bergen. In Iceland, the government passed a law in March 2010 banning all strip clubs.[14]

At the core of OBJECT's campaign was the argument that lap-dancing clubs 'promote the idea of women as sexual objects who are always sexually available and who exist to fulfil the sexual fantasies of men' (van Heeswijk, 2011). OBJECT produced resources outlining the key problems with lap-dancing clubs: that they are sites of commercial sexual exploitation, where performers pay to work and competitive conditions may mean that women end shifts in debt to the club; that sexual harassment is part of the job; and that the presence of clubs creates no-go zones where women feel unsafe walking at night. An important aspect of the campaign was to ensure that the voices of women exploited in the industry were central in the campaign. As the campaign became more high-profile, OBJECT was contacted by numerous women wishing to speak of their experiences of exploitation and sexual harassment in the clubs. OBJECT ensured that the voices of women who had worked as lap dancers were given a platform, either through speaking on panels at campaign events, or through being included in a DVD of testimonials that was used as a campaign resource. Sandrine Lévêque, Campaigns Manager with OBJECT, worked with ex-lap dancer Jennifer Hayashi Danns to produce a book on lap dancing which incorporated Danns's experiences along with those of other women, including lap dancers and a club waitress (Danns and Lévêque, 2011). In the wake of the 'Stripping the Illusion' campaign, OBJECT initiated a project to support women who have exited the industry.

Under the Licensing Act 2003, lap-dancing clubs in the UK were licensed as part of the leisure industry, needing only a 'Premises Licence' in order to operate. This licensing regime made it very difficult for local authorities to refuse licences even when there was strong local opposition to clubs opening. The campaign sought to have the clubs reclassified as 'Sex Encounter Establishments'[15] in order that they could be licensed as part of the sex industry, giving greater power to local authorities to control the number of clubs in their area, and to refuse licence applications. The campaign position was that re-licensing was crucial: it would allow local councils to apply more stringent regulations on lap-dancing clubs to protect the rights of women in the clubs, and also to give local people the right to object to a lap-dancing club opening in their communities.

The campaign aimed to maximise both media and political opportunities through combining highly visual, media-friendly actions with political lobbying and forming strategic alliances. In order to attract media attention, OBJECT developed a tactical repertoire that employed colour, humour and spectacle, with the use of witty visual props. In addition, campaign stunts and actions were characterised by enthusiastic singing and chanting, with the group devising songs and chants relevant to the campaign. The most visible form of protest that punctuated the 'Stripping the Illusion' campaign was 'a stunt a month' – a series of monthly stunts held in strategically chosen locations: outside Parliament; next to the Mayor of London's offices at City Hall; and in front of two of London's largest lap-dancing clubs, 'For Your Eyes Only' and 'Spearmint Rhino's'. The stunts aimed to create a spectacle and were highly successful in generating media interest for the campaign. Ideas for the stunts were generated in monthly meetings, and members of the group showed high levels of commitment, ingenuity and resourcefulness in bringing these ideas into effect. Often the ideas involved drawing attention to central campaign messages in witty and eye-catching ways, as in the case of designing and creating huge 'coffee cup' placards, to highlight the fact that lap dancing clubs were licensed in the same ways as cafes. These placards were designed as 'awards' and utilised to hold a spoof 'Lap Dancing Association Awards Ceremony' outside the club 'For Your Eyes Only', in order to subvert the actual awards ceremony that was taking place inside. The placards were labelled like awards for the spoof ceremony, bearing slogans such as 'Award for promoting sexist attitudes', 'Award for creating no-go zones' and 'Award for greatest misuse of the word "gentleman"'. Activists then acted out the spoof ceremony in front of the club, accompanied by singing and chanting.

Songs and chants are a central part of OBJECT's tactical repertoire. Songs were written by activists for each campaign, customised to convey protest messages with regard to lap-dancing clubs, Playboy, lads' mags and prostitution. The centrality of songs to OBJECT's tactical repertoire follows earlier women's movement struggles such the Greenham Common anti-cruise missile protests, and even the suffrage campaigns, where music played an important role. Suffragettes sang while marching, and practised songs at branch meetings: music and singing 'mixed revolutionary fervour with emotional intensity, and drew the women together' (Crawford, 2012). The power of music and chanting in promoting *ésprit de corps* and collective identity is also much in evidence amongst OBJECT activists at Reclaim the Night and Million Women Rise marches.

The 'Stripping the Illusion' campaign enjoyed considerable media attention and was covered in substantial articles in the national press. The campaign also featured in a Channel 4 'Dispatches' documentary, and OBJECT, APL and the London Feminist Network featured in a BBC4 documentary, 'Women' (Engle, 2010c), screened in March 2010, which showed activists protesting outside the Playboy store and campaigning outside a lap-dancing club. The media treatment of the campaign was largely sympathetic, even celebratory. The mass media obviously have considerable power to further or hinder movement objectives (Gamson 2007), and, given the largely hostile treatment of feminism within mainstream media (Gill, 2007b; McRobbie, 2009), the success of OBJECT in gaining serious, sympathetic media coverage is highly significant. This success may be due to a number of factors, including the nature of the campaign and media interest in young women's relationship to feminism. However, it also possibly reflects an image-conscious approach: the style of OBJECT's stunts was serious but generally good-humoured; impassioned, but celebratory rather than angry; designed to communicate campaign messages clearly and engage a sympathetic response, rather than to display anger in ways that might be alienating. OBJECT staff were particularly conscious of the potential for misrepresentation of media reporting, and were careful to brief activists before each action, to ensure consistency of campaign message, and to avoid any pitfalls such as journalists or photographers misleadingly trying to present the protesters as against the women working in the clubs. All stunts were peaceful and lawful. Social movement groups face a dilemma regarding access to the media and the question of gaining 'standing' – a voice – in the media (Gamson, 2007), in that gaining sympathetic coverage may involve compromising a political position. It seems that in the case of OBJECT, journalists sympathetic to movement goals played a role in communicating the aims, arguments and values of the activism. One journalist in particular participated in the campaign as an activist as well as writing about it; others, whilst remaining outside the campaign, were often supportive of its objectives.

Political opportunity structures
The colourful and eye-catching stunts comprised only one aspect of the campaign. Other aspects of OBJECT's repertoire included producing flyers and information sheets to inform members of the public about the issue, along with more substantial documents and reports, and a DVD of testimonials from women who had worked in the lap-dancing industry. Particular use was made of political opportunity structures, through a highly strategic and informed lobbying dimension, and engagement with parliamentary processes, in order to achieve success in changing licensing legislation. Strategic alliances were formed with Members of Parliament sympathetic to the aims of the campaign, who were active in pushing to get

a clause relating to the licensing of lap-dancing clubs into the Policing and Crime Bill in 2008, using parliamentary procedures including an Early Day Motion and Ten Minute Rule Bill, and holding public meetings in the House of Commons. Speakers at the launch event and subsequent public meetings included feminist academics, writers and NGO representatives, as well as MPs, local government representatives and ex-lap dancers. The support of feminists in positions of authority highlights the importance of abeyance structures, in the form of the professionalised, established versions of feminism discussed in Chapter 1. The testimonials of ex-lap dancers, either as speakers or via the campaign DVD, importantly included the voice of exited women in the campaign, and helped to expose the realities of lap dancing through first-hand accounts of economic exploitation and sexual harassment experienced in clubs. The key work underpinning the campaign involved writing letters to MPs, lobbying local councils to join the campaign, and collecting 8,500 signatures for a petition which was presented to 10 Downing Street in early 2009, on the same day that the OBJECT lobbyist and an ex-lap dancer spoke at a public hearing called by the Select Committee on Licensing Regulation.

Engaging with the parliamentary process and with local government appears critical to the success of the 'Stripping the Illusion' campaign. OBJECT was energetic in forging alliances with central and local government actors that proved highly effective. OBJECT also formed a strategic alliance with a more mainstream and established women's rights campaign group, the Fawcett Society. This strategic alliance was useful to OBJECT in that Fawcett was experienced at working with government ministries and was highly regarded. At the same time, OBJECT, as a relatively young, grassroots organisation, was able to be flexible and responsive to campaign aims in a way not always easy for more established organisations.

Unlike 'Bin the Bunny', with its key aim of raising awareness amongst the general public, 'Stripping the Illusion' was a highly strategic campaign with a very specific goal. OBJECT utilised a range of political, organisational and media opportunities in pursuit of that goal. OBJECT's ability to engage convincingly in high-level lobbying, its willingness to develop strategic alliances and its savviness in dealing with the media proved a successful combination. Clause 27 of the Policing and Crime Bill, which proposed a number of measures that would help to ensure greater restrictions on the licensing of lap-dancing clubs, was passed in the House of Lords on 3 November 2009, becoming Section 27 of the Policing and Crime Act, and coming into effect the following April.

Legislative and policy approaches

The Jane Longhurst Trust is a campaign group set up by the family of Jane Longhurst, a young schoolteacher and musician who in 2003 was strangled in a sexually motivated murder by a man with a strangulation fetish and an obsession with violent pornography. Records taken from the perpetrator's computer showed that he had visited hundreds of sites showing rape, necrophilia and strangulation pornography; reports spoke of his 'self-confessed seven-year addiction to internet pornography' and how he had surfed for images of dead and strangled women on the day before he murdered Ms Longhurst (Press Association, 2004). Following the murder, Graham Coutts stored his victim's naked body for 35 days before setting it alight.

In the wake of the murder, Jane Longhurst's mother Liz Longhurst and sister Sue Barnett, with the support of their local Member of Parliament Martin Salter (Labour), launched a campaign to outlaw 'extreme' violent internet pornography. The campaign was supported by a petition of 50,000 signatures, and gained a sympathetic hearing from the then Home

Secretary David Blunkett. The Labour government proposed new legislation to criminalise the possession of extreme pornography, thereby extending the Obscene Publications Act 1959, which already outlawed the production and distribution of 'obscene' materials, defined as those which may 'deprave and corrupt' the consumer (McGlynn, 2010: 191).

While not specifically feminist, the campaign to outlaw extreme violent pornography drew support from feminist and women's sector organisations. Several feminist organisations participated in the consultation process regarding the proposed legislation, including Justice for Women, Rights of Women, the Women's National Commission and OBJECT. The campaign was opposed by a pro-sadomasochism group, Backlash, along with a range of liberal commentators, such as Holly Combe from Feminists Against Censorship and playwright Bonnie Greer, who deployed familiar liberal arguments regarding the right to privacy and the unalienable right of 'consenting adults' to 'freedom' in sexual matters, and who rejected the idea of any relationship between the viewing of violent pornography and the perpetration of violent acts (*The Guardian,* 2006).

The extreme pornography provisions (Section 63) of the Criminal Justice and Immigration Act 2008 came into effect in January 2009 (McGlynn, 2010: 191). Under the Act, the possession of an 'extreme pornographic image' is a criminal offence, punishable by up to three years imprisonment. There are three elements to the offence under the Act, which are:

1 That the image is pornographic;
2 That the image is grossly offensive, disgusting, or otherwise of an obscene character; and
3 That the image portrays in an explicit and realistic way, one of the following:
   (a) An act which threatens a person's life; this could include depictions of hanging, suffocation, or sexual assault involving a threat with a weapon.

(b) An act which results in or is likely to result in serious injury to a person's anus, breast or genitals; this could include the insertion of sharp objects or the mutilation of breasts or genitals.

(c) An act involving sexual interference with a human corpse; or

(d) A person performing an act of intercourse or oral sex with an animal, and a reasonable person looking at the image would think that the animals and people portrayed were real.

(UK Ministry of Justice, 2009)

The introduction of the new legislation was generally welcomed by feminist campaigners (*The Guardian*, 2006), albeit with some reservations. Pornographic rape sites were not covered under the new law, and the language of the law – 'disgusting', 'obscene' – draws from a moral conservative framework, rather than a feminist perspective. As Clare McGlynn points out, radical feminist perspectives were sidelined in both parliamentary and media debates on the proposed legislation, which were dominated by the familiar language of moralism and liberalism (McGlynn, 2010: 195). There were also concerns from feminist organisations that 'a category of materials that are deemed "extreme" creates unfortunate distinctions between different types of pornography, rendering non-"extreme" pornography harmless, or less serious' (*ibid.*: 196). Nonetheless, in spite of its shortcomings, a law that outlawed extreme violent pornography was broadly welcomed by feminist grassroots groups. The effectiveness of the new law and the extent to which it is implemented is another story: some reports warned that it would be impossible to enforce (Murray, 2009), others that it could potentially 'criminalise millions' (Ozimek, 2008). By the end of 2010 there had in fact been around a dozen cases of men charged with possession of extreme pornography, though the charge was usually made alongside other charges, such as the possession of child pornography or possession of Class A drugs or stolen goods. In at least two cases, the trial resulted in a conviction, with one offender receiving a three-year community order for the possession of extreme pornography and downloading hundreds of images of child pornography (Cassell, 2010).

'Feminist Fridays': breaking the silence

'Feminist Fridays' are direct action protests, organised by OBJECT as part of their campaign for 'lads' mags' to be recognised as part of the porn industry, and, if sold, to be covered up, placed on the top shelf and age-restricted. Held monthly on Friday evenings, 'Feminist Fridays' involve a group of activists targeting a large newsagent such as W. H. Smiths, or a supermarket such as Tesco, and covering the lads' mags on display with brown paper bags on which they have written feminist slogans, such as 'This promotes rape culture', 'Love women – hate sexism', 'Lads' mags are for losers' and – utilizing the names of particular lads' mags – 'MAXIMum Sexism' and 'FHM: For Horrible Misogynists'. The activists do this until the entire display of lads' mags is replaced with feminist slogans, taking the opportunity to circulate petitions and flyers to members of the public.

The disruption of the display is sometimes followed by 'sit-ins' or exuberant chanting, singing and dancing, as on the memorable occasion when protesters danced a conga through a Tesco's supermarket, as described in the vignette that introduced this book. The format of the protests is therefore highly effective at bringing a feminist message into the public realm, and providing an alternative message to that intended by the publishers of the displayed material.

The symbolism of 'Feminist Fridays' in bringing a feminist critique into the public realm is very important, not only through its message to the store owners and the general public, but also in terms of developing an assertive, collective, feminist voice amongst group members. Before getting involved, many activists had experienced being silenced or ridiculed for their objections to pornography.

> I mean, I've got a lot of hassle for saying that I think that [the normalisation of pornography] is wrong.... Culture and society has told [girls] that they should impress boys ... and going against that would just be like social suicide. (Jenny, 17)

> Everyone's scared to speak up first 'cos they're scared of being labelled a prude. (Nadia, 32)

> Saying you were a feminist was a dirty word and I was almost like a closet feminist. (Fran, 26)

> Yeah, I'm kind of 'out' like a feminist activist now. But it took me a while, I was like, it's so controversial and everyone hates people who talk about that.... I do talk about it but I don't talk about it too much in case I get into an argument.... (Sheryl, 30)

Experience of ridicule by friends and family was common. This was sometimes described as 'just' teasing, but nonetheless served as a powerful silencing mechanism:

> When I'm with [non-feminist] friends, I mean, I love them dearly but if I start going on about [feminist] stuff, then it's a kind of, you know, rolling the eyes and raised eyebrows and [pause] they'll humour me to a certain extent, but they just don't connect with feminism in the same way, and so I feel quite constrained in what I can say. (Roberta, 28)

Roberta and Fran describe their negative experiences of being associated with the term 'feminist' at school and at university. Roberta remembers being 'mocked' for expressing feminist ideas, both by boys in her class at school and also by her male peers at university; Fran recounts an experience at university where she felt extremely uncomfortable at being identified as a feminist:

The lecturer said 'Put your hand up if you'd consider yourself a feminist,' and hardly anyone put their hands up, and I put my hand up – I felt really scared to put my hand up, and that was on a feminist course, 'cos the word had such negative connotations, it felt scary to put my hand up, to say I was a feminist, even though I was studying it.

Nadia is also highly aware of the pressure to be silent, but is emphatic in asserting her right to voice her opinions:

I'm always getting this 'be quiet' and I'm fed up of being told to be quiet! I've got just as much right as everyone else you know, I have to see all these things in the media and hear everyone else's sexist opinions!

In some cases, the hostility to anti-porn feminism can also have serious personal consequences for activists. Sandra discusses the effect of comments posted following an article in a newspaper about the anti-porn work of her project:

I can't say it didn't affect me – I mean, I went out and smoked five cigarettes in a row, and I was like 'Jesus Christ!' It did affect me, that impact – it's hard sat there going 'Oh my god' and knowing that this is part and parcel of what I should expect in the job, I was waiting for it but actually I hadn't prepared myself for how personal they could make it to me. (Sandra, 37)

These accounts demonstrate how hostility to anti-porn feminism acts in concrete ways to silence women and inhibit the development of a feminist identity and feminist politics. The fact that women are undeterred by such pressure to remain silent and seek out feminist groups is a testament to their courage and feminist conviction. However, attempts to deny or suppress one's voice are very difficult to deal with on an individual basis, where one is likely to simply encounter ridicule or accusations of being humourless or hysterical. For these reasons, 'Feminist Fridays' are an extremely important way for feminists to break the silence: through the act of writing slogans on the paper bags, and joining in a collective action, activists assert a collective response to the silencing that they have encountered on an individual basis. It is perhaps for that reason that 'Feminist Fridays' are characterised by such exuberance and sense of solidarity.

The issue of breaking the silence, finding a voice and naming oppression was a crucial second wave project (Olsen, 1978; Rich, 1980; Lorde, 1984b). It appears to be no less crucial to young women in the twenty-first century, who, while invited to take up the supposed freedoms and opportunities of the neoliberal social order, are 'called upon to be silent, to withhold critique' (McRobbie, 2009: 18). The denial of one's voice and the pressure to be silent ironically speaks volumes about the nature of any version of freedom that is bought at such a cost.

Educational and training initiatives: activism in Scotland

What we've picked up is that the work in Scotland, including the government agenda, is much more clearly set in a gendered context, and it's clearly acknowledged by the government that the cause of violence against women is gender inequality. Which is not the case in England... . That's providing opportunities for gradually expanding people's ideas of what falls under the spectrum of violence against women. I think that's relevant as well in terms of the recent increased activism in terms of anti-porn work. (Jean, 50)

Anti-porn activism in Scotland has some distinct features, which particularly highlight the possibilities afforded by a government-funded Violence Against Women strategy. The 'new' activism differs from its English counterpart in a number of ways. As mentioned above, Scottish Women Against Pornography bucks the trend chronologically, as it was formed in 1999, prior to other new grassroots groups, and during the 'latency period' where little discernible anti-porn activism was taking place in the UK. Devolution seems to have provided a more sympathetic context and greater political opportunities for anti-porn feminists in Scotland, compared to their sisters south of the border. In 2000, the Scottish government published its 'National Strategy to Address Domestic Abuse in Scotland' (Scottish Government, 2000), and since then has led the way in the UK in broadening this strategy to include sexual violence and other forms of violence against women. In 2009, the Scottish government became the first national government in the UK to publish a violence against women strategy, 'Safer Lives, Changed Lives: A shared approach to tackling violence against women in Scotland' (Scottish Government, 2009). The strategy adopted a comprehensive definition of violence against women, making specific reference to 'commercial sexual exploitation', including pornography and lap dancing. However, the progressive nature of this strategy, and the accompanying funding, is also attributable to the key role played by the women's voluntary sector – a sector staffed by long-term committed and tireless activists. In the Strategy, the Scottish government acknowledges 'the vital role of the voluntary sector', stating that 'There is no doubt we would not be in the position we are in Scotland without their tireless, and often thankless, work over the past three decades' (Scottish Government, 2009: 1).

The existence of a funded Violence Against Women strategy was significant in the development of feminist anti-porn approaches in Scotland. The Women's Support Project (WSP) received funding to develop a national post to challenge the demand for prostitution and commercial sexual exploitation, including pornography. It was significant that of the activists I interviewed, the majority of those whose anti-porn work constituted part of their paid employment were based in Scotland.

Much anti-porn work in Scotland takes place within professional settings. The work of the WSP includes anti-porn awareness raising in education, working with a range of organisations and sectors. The Project has also worked with Zero Tolerance to develop a new online campaign for young people, which involved engaging with a core group of young people trained as 'peers' who were responsible for developing the online presence of the project.

The WSP also works with local authority groups, such as child protection committees and technical colleges, to look at their policies and to develop new policies around porn and explicit materials being viewed, shared, and produced in college settings. The project is responsible for the Scottish Coalition Against Sexual Exploitation (SCASE), which is used as a platform to disseminate information and encourage people to take action.

The variety of work covered by the WSP means that the organisation reaches diverse audiences – from groups of parents, community events and small groups of young people up to large assemblies and conferences. The work is usually well received, and the strong Violence Against Women sector means that the project has good links with strategic organisations such as Rape Crisis Scotland and their network members, Scottish Women's Aid and Zero Tolerance.

Diversity and representation
As my PhD research involved qualitative ethnography, I did not collect formal or quantitative profile data on feminist groups beyond my interviewees, and given that the membership of groups changes over time, it is not possible to make definitive comments about the profile of activists involved in this area of campaigning. My interviewees included mixed heritage and black women, though the majority were white British; the ages

of participants ranged from 17 to 53, with most being in their 20s and 30s; most were university-educated, but came from a variety of class backgrounds. APL had a more visibly lesbian profile than OBJECT, with lesbians comprising up to half of the active group membership at certain points. Most active members did not have children (see Long, 2011).

The relative youth and high levels of education among group members is quite typical of the demographic of new social movement participants generally, since 'age and education appear as the most widespread structural determinants of political participation' (Gallego, 2007: 13). The demographic profile of the activists that I interviewed and encountered in my ethnographies gives some substance to the claim that protest is 'the domain of the politically active, well-educated middle class' (van Aelst and Walgrave, 2001: 462). However, the fact that the activists were overwhelmingly women is in itself significant, given the under-representation of women in formal politics, and the powerful social forces militating against women's collective organisation. Nonetheless, a lack of diversity within the groups was an issue that activists were committed to addressing. Anna van Heeswijk, OBJECT CEO (Grassroots Coordinator at the time of my ethnography), voiced her ambitions for OBJECT and the broader feminist movement to include different groups of women:

> If we are to be effective long-term as a movement, we have to be accessible to all women, and to be representative of the diversity of women's experiences and women's voices. This is how we will move forward as a group, and this is how we will move forward as women.

Anna's acknowledgement of the ways in which the current movement is not fully representative indicates her awareness of how the underrepresentation of certain groups 'prevents us from speaking about genuine democratisation of street protest' (van Aelst and Walgrave, 2001: 482), but also that the movement itself is weaker as a result of these exclusions. For Anna, the goal of an inclusive movement that unites different groups of women is central to her vision of its success: 'then we'll be a really formidable force'.

Activist groups, however, are not static, and what has been noticeable since the period of my original research has been the increasing involvement of black, Asian and minority ethnic women in anti-porn activism. This has been particularly due to the participation of activists from Million Women Rise in actions including the protests outside the new London Playboy Club and the *XBiz EU* adult entertainment convention. Million Women Rise[16] is an activist group of diverse women including a high proportion of black, Asian and minority ethnic women, who organise an annual national International Women's Day march against male violence. Million Women Rise also participated – along with the London Feminist Network, UK Feminista and OBJECT – in a protest held outside the finals of the Miss World beauty content in London in November 2011. While not an anti-porn demonstration, it was a protest against the sexual objectification of women, and protesters made links between beauty pageants, pornography and male violence. Speaking to *The Telegraph* newspaper, founder of Million Women Rise Sabrina Qureshi stated that, far from harmless fun, beauty pageants were a sign of a society that trivialises women in a way that leads to violence:

> 'We have read that the murderer of Joanna Yeates was using pornography which contained images very similar to how he murdered Joanna,' said Ms Qureshi. 'To stop such heinous crimes against women and girls, we need to stop trivialising what may appear to be harmless practices and start joining up the dots of women's treatment, representation and discrimination.' (Mason, 2011)

The press statement also released by Million Women Rise highlights the vital importance of ensuring that voices of all women are heard in feminist debates and activism around pornography and objectification. Referring to the 'freedom trash can' which was a feature of the protest (recalling the one used outside the 1968 Miss America beauty pageant), the statement reads:

> Million Women Rise actions are symbolic of saying no to the violation of all women and our continued experiences of violation and discrimination, which includes race and class.

> Say no,

> Bin bleaching cream, symbolic of racism Bin fake tans. Women are beautiful as they are. Bin handcuffs, symbolic of women trafficked for sexual exploitation. Bin feather dusters for women domestic workers who are often sexually exploited as well as work under horrendous conditions. Bin weighing scales for the relentless pressure to diet, conform to media, fashion, celebrity and porn images of women. Bin scalpels for the cutting of women's breasts, vaginas and clitoris.

The statement incorporates a consciousness of women experiencing racial and class oppressions, and a range of harmful practices across diverse cultures. Similarly, OBJECT literature incorporates an awareness of difference and the specific oppressions experienced by women in different groups and locations: the OBJECT leaflet on beauty pageants, for example, refers to ideas of beauty that are 'based on sexist, racist, homophobic and able-bodied notions of what constitutes beauty'.[17] The anti-porn literature that informs the activism also integrates considerations of race, class and other oppressions into analyses of sexual objectification and pornography (Dworkin, 1981; Jeffreys, 2009; Dines, 2010). It is also significant that the Miss World protest saw a greater visibility of older women than is generally common at such events, with a number of women from the original 1970 protest taking part, bringing a presence and knowledge that similarly enriched the action immeasurably.

It is fair to say that a commitment to including all women in feminist anti-porn groups in the UK is reflected in the visible efforts groups are making to support this inclusion. The same women active in anti-porn campaigns have also been involved in the Feminism in London (FiL), Fem and Challenging Porn Culture conferences, which have consciously supported and valued the inclusion, as both participants and speakers, of black, Asian, minority ethnic women and asylum seekers, lesbian and bisexual women, disabled women, older women, young women and teenagers, and women from a range of class backgrounds. In particular, efforts have been made to support the inclusion of women who have been exploited in lap dancing and the sex industry, with exited women Jennifer Hayashi Danns and Rebecca Mott speaking powerfully at the FiL and Challenging Porn Culture conferences.

It is relevant to note that all groups involved in feminist anti-porn activism are generally either seriously under-resourced or completely unfunded, and rely almost entirely on the commitment of unpaid activists in organising campaigns. This lack of resources has obvious implications with regard to capacity in terms of the work that groups do and the opportunities for participation that they can offer, for example, with regard to crèche provision, flexibility of meeting times and accessible venues. Without their own fully accessible premises and adequate levels of staffing, efforts towards being fully inclusive are hindered by a lack of material and human resources, as well as extremely highly pressurised time schedules. The essential work to include all women in campaigns, and to support diverse women in different campaigns, is undertaken in extremely inhospitable and unconducive circumstances.

Women-only?

The biggest difference between UK feminist anti-porn groups inheres in their respective approaches to women-only organising. Of my case study groups, APL was a women-only group in terms of meetings and core membership, although men were welcome to attend protests; OBJECT is open to both women and men, and in fact for a number of years had a male chairperson on its management committee. Of the other groups mentioned in this chapter, both the London Feminist Network and Million Women Rise are women-only, while UK Feminista positively welcomes male participation and ensures that men are formally represented at their conferences and events. UK Feminista also has men on its board of directors. Even many of the regional Reclaim the Night marches are mixed: the London Reclaim the Night and Million Women Rise marches are unusual in maintaining their women-only status.

A preoccupation with involving men in feminism is a striking feature of the broader resurgent grassroots movement. Women-only groups are a rare breed in twenty-first-century Britain: many of the new feminist groups and networks are mixed, and the topic of how to 'engage' men is often on the agenda. Media articles, online blogs and discussion threads appear to have a high boredom threshold when it comes to debating men's involvement in feminism: within the space of two days, three separate articles on the topic came up on my Facebook newsfeed page. 'I don't think feminism is about the exclusion of men but their inclusion ... we must face and address those issues, especially to include younger men and boys,' advises Annie Lennox in a *Guardian* article on International Women's Day (Martinson, 2012), having taken the opportunity at the previous year's International Women's Day to suggest replacing the word feminism with the word 'FeMANism', in order to more 'inclusive' (Lennox, 2011). 'Girls and women cannot achieve equality *without* the participation of boys and men' opines Soraya Chemaly in the *Huffington Post* (Chemaly, 2012), only a week or so following a Canadian feminist radio show devoting an entire programme to the issue of the role of men in feminism.[18]

Women-only spaces and modes of organising were the defining feature of second wave feminism. For the women's liberation movement, as the name suggests, the feminist project was one of liberation from patriarchy, the very starting point for which involved a separation from men. This separation might begin simply in a woman's head as the attempt to clear a space in which to think about her oppression; it might mean establishing women-only caucuses within mainstream political organisations; it might mean a wholesale separatism. Marilyn Frye considers 'feminist separation' to mean the 'separation of various sorts or modes from men and from institutions, relationships, roles and activities that are male-defined, male-dominated, and operating for the benefit of males and the maintenance of male privilege – this separation being initiated or maintained, at will, *by women*' (1983d: 96). Frye argues that whilst '[m]ost feminists, probably all, practise some separation from males and male-dominated institutions', a separatist 'practises separation consciously, systematically, and probably more generally that the others' (*ibid.*: 98).

For the original London Anti-Porn Group of the late 1970s, the idea of involving men would have been unthinkable. As revolutionary feminists, the group had a clear politics around the necessity of women-only organising. The consciousness raising on which the group was based – vital in enabling members to develop a political understanding of pornography, and accessing the feminist rage that was to fuel their activism – would obviously have been completely impossible with men present, even those who were sympathetic to feminism. A key principle for the group was the necessity for women to liberate themselves within the context of their own movement.

Coming from the women-only tradition of London Feminist Network (LFN), APL meetings were women-only. It is significant that the women-only status enabled consciousness raising to form a core part of these meetings. Louise considered that involving men in APL would have impeded this process:

> If it was a mixed group I just don't think we would have got to where we are now.... I just don't think it would have worked, 'cos you'd have certain personalities taking over perhaps, or you'd have to append everything – a disclaimer, not all men are like this, blah di blah.

However, APL was open to allowing men to attend protests and actions. Some women involved in women-only organising also felt that women 'should' be involving men:

> I really, I really do believe in the idea of women-only space. Um, however, if there are men who want to get involved ... I think we should celebrate that in a way, because ... I think we should be working together. (Roberta, 28)

Other women shared this ambivalence, or saw a need for both women-only and mixed organising:

> I love that LFN is women only ... but I like that OBJECT is mixed. I think it's good, it needs to be inclusive when we're talking about sexism in the media and objectification of women. (Nadia, 32)

OBJECT historically has involved men across most areas and at different levels of the organisation, although latterly this position appears to be changing.[19] During my fieldwork, no men attended activist meetings, and some informal consciousness raising did take place in the meetings as women shared and discussed experiences and feelings around pornography and the sex industry, sometimes particularly in relation to male partners or ex-partners. However, it was noticeable that when men did start attending meetings later in the year, such consciousness raising was far less in evidence: usually only one man would be present in the room, but shifts in group dynamics were evident.

Women in OBJECT expressed a range of feelings about the involvement of men in the group's activities. Views ranged from a sense of gratitude that men attended protests to high levels of anger and frustration at the presence and sometimes behaviour of male activists. It was generally women who were newer to feminism who expressed the former opinion, with more longstanding feminists frustrated at the presence of men.

Within OBJECT, a discourse of pragmatism tended to dominate considerations of men's role in feminism: it was felt that because society is composed of women and men, it was necessary to involve men in challenging sexism. There was little evidence of awareness of the obvious problems of involving the oppressor group in women's liberation, such as how patterns of male domination may be replicated within the activist arena, or the ways in which consciousness raising would be impossible in a mixed group. There was also little awareness in either OBJECT or UK Feminista of how the media would be likely to give more attention to men on protests, so this situation was not anticipated and managed. The result of this was that a media article in the London *Evening Standard* following the 'Eff Off Hef!' protest featured a photograph of a man – who was not a regular activist – at the centre of the picture, flanked on either side by women activists, in a manner disturbingly replicating the structure of pictures of Hugh Hefner, flanked on either side by women in bunny costumes (Urwin, 2011). Similarly, there was little consideration or acknowledgement given to the advantages of women-only organising; the discourse of pragmatism rested on unquestioned assumptions about movement effectiveness being reliant on the participation of men within feminist groups. I did not witness men being challenged to develop their own groups or join established men's organisations such as the White Ribbon Campaign. In fact, a male member of OBJECT did go on to set up the Anti-Porn Men Project, a website providing resources and a space for men to share anti-porn sentiments and perspectives. This kind of organising on the part of men is clearly a necessary development; while there is plenty of attention given to the role of men in feminism, there is little evidence of men autonomously and actively challenging the porn industry or other men as porn consumers. However, a politics that considers how men can best work as allies of feminist anti-porn activism appears quite undeveloped. Significantly, the need for an autonomous men's space was unquestioned by women activists. By contrast, women's participation in women-only organising drew resentment and sometimes hostility from men who 'feel a bit sidelined': 'I got a bit of jip about the Million Women Rise march, 'cos that was women only' (Nadia).

Challenges and adversaries

There are many challenges involved in anti-porn activism, both in terms of strategic organising, working (often unpaid) in often high-pressured situations, with extremely limited resources, and dealing with the stress and trauma of working closely with misogynist material and attitudes. There is often huge demand on unpaid activists to deliver training, participate in debates, give talks and organise protests. Due to the extensive and relentless nature of the campaign issue, activists can easily succumb to burn-out.

Trainers responsible for delivering anti-porn awareness-raising sessions developed practical strategies for dealing with pornographic content and its potentially distressing effects. These strategies included delivering the training in pairs, providing details of support agencies dealing with sexual violence and offering participants the chance to opt out at any point. While most of the women I interviewed were not generally involved in this kind of work, all groups recognised the need for women to share and discuss feelings and experiences regarding porn in a safe space. Another challenge of presenting the slideshow were the ethical issues involved in showing images of women abused in pornography, and also actually being able to show the extent of misogyny and women hating in porn when there are concerns that groups could be breaking the law, either with regard to copyright or 'indecency'.

The challenges of frontline activism also led groups to developing practical supports. These, often informal, helped with managing emotions and group dynamics. For example, Lydia spoke of 'having to have de-brief sessions' after group actions:

> I always made sure I sent round emails afterwards that were positive and upbeat. Often, even when an action had gone well, there would always be a confrontation, obviously usually with a man, or there would be an incredible adrenalin crash because you really had to build yourself up to these things. (Lydia, 34)

In other groups, there was a desire to create a structure where emotions could be explored and women could support each other. However, time pressures and limited resources meant that these kinds of structures did not always get beyond the ideas stage. In the meantime, activists developed personal friendships and informal support networks within groups. It was evident that great attention was given to recognising and valuing the contribution of individual activists, perhaps in recognition that their activist work was not always valued by friends and family outside the group.

For some anti-porn activists, isolation can be a significant and ongoing problem. For women in small communities or rural settings, feelings of isolation and the stigmatisation of the 'anti-porn' label can be acute. Measures taken to combat this included online communication with other feminists, and reading online blogs and feminist books. Sharing the company of other women at feminist events such as marches and conferences was especially valued, particularly if this was a rare opportunity. Endemic cultural misogyny and hostility to feminist anti-porn perspectives is a challenge to all activists involved in the work. The fear of being exposed to hostile attitudes can lead to a reluctance to get involved, although generally the activists I encountered were grateful of the supportive environment that activism created for dealing with such attitudes. The need for support is clear, given the deep-seated cultural resistance and hostility to feminist anti-porn perspectives. In my own experience, media interviews that I have given on issues of sexual objectification have generated comments that are generally hostile and antipathetic to a feminist viewpoint. The dominant vocabulary of 'choice', 'free speech' and 'consent' means that it is very difficult – particularly in a short interview – to convey more complex analyses that problematise these terms. The experience of constantly being misheard or misrepresented as a 'prude', or having your passionately held convictions trivialised, is one that can be accommodated and overcome – but nonetheless at times will take its toll. Compounding this, a pro-porn stance in some versions of third wave feminism, and particularly within queer politics, means that anti-porn feminism is under siege not just from a vocal and well-resourced pro-sex industry lobby, but from groups and individuals claiming to be feminist. Of course, such groups are entitled to voice their opinions, but what is deeply frustrating is the way that anti-porn feminists are consistently and seriously misrepresented in their arguments. Anti-porn feminists are repeatedly accused of being engaged in a 'moral crusade', and accused of perpetuating stereotypes of 'good' and 'bad' women.[20] OBJECT has been accused of 'plac[ing] the blame on women for their own objectification' (O'Hara and Kent, 2010). This is clearly a gross misrepresentation of OBJECT's stance, and no evidence was provided to support it. In similar vein, a paper delivered at the 'Pornified?' conference,[21] held at the Institute of Education in December 2011, claimed that groups such as OBJECT and the London Feminist Network 'castigate sex workers', 'reinforce a female victim/male oppressor scheme' and thus 'reduce women to objects'. Again, the accusation of these groups as 'castigat[ing] sex workers' is a gross misrepresentation of the stance of both OBJECT and LFN, who make it quite clear that the targets of their campaign are the male pimps and punters who exploit women in the sex industry; both groups do considerable work to support women exploited and abused in prostitution. The erasure of male violence and accusation of anti-porn feminists of 'objectification' of women is a leap of logic that defies all evidence and reason; that it should have endured since the early 1980s is dismaying, to say the least. The misrepresentation and marginalisation of anti-porn feminist voices is not uncommon within academic debates on sexualisation and pornography, where in some cases a pro-porn lobby is distinctly evident. The public funding of academic conferences and seminar series that give a platform to industry players and representatives is extremely concerning, serving as it does to legitimise the industry and de-legitimise a feminist critique of its harms.

Collective identity and solidarity

There are particular pressures on feminist activism, since patriarchal and heteronormative social practices militate against women's collectivism and political solidarity (Buechler, 2000: 138). The role played by commitment and solidarity in creating and sustaining collective identity is a topic that has received attention from a number of scholars researching women's activism (Roseneil, 1995; Taylor and Rupp, 1993; Della Porta and Diani, 1999). The importance of 'female' values, separatist strategies and female bonding has been noted in relation to the development of women's collectivism (Taylor and Rupp, 1993), and Bianchi and Mormino found a number of elements important for women organising collectively, including the relationship between collective action and personal identity; identity as a social process, involving personal change and empowerment, and the transformation of negative feelings into positive; group action; solidarity; affective elements; and developing new forms of interpreting the world (cited in Della Porta and Diani, 1999: 83–4). These elements all have some resonance with themes that emerged in my interviews, although as mentioned above the predominance of mixed organising in some cases prevented women organising collectively. Social activities and celebrations were also seen as important in promoting a sense of collective identity and belonging.

Creating solidarity and a sense of collective belonging are recognised as important elements in achieving movement goals and fostering commitment to group aims (Della Porta and Diani, 1999; Polletta and Jasper, 2001; Hunt and Bedford, 2007). Eschle and Maiguashca assert the 'importance of emotional attachments to the construction of solidarity – and, by extension, to the making of collective subjects of resistance'. They argue that 'shared experiences and feelings of empathy are vital to the politicisation process as well as to the development and maintenance of movement infrastructure' (2007: 293).

These perspectives are borne out by my findings: relationships of friendship and solidarity were highly valued by the activists I interviewed, and play a clear role in fostering group commitment and movement development:

> I feel I can just talk about [feminism] for hours, and a lot of the people I've met at the meetings doing the activism are the same,

like after the meetings ... [we] can't stop talking, like missing tube stops, 'cos it's just like fresh air – like, 'I've finally found someone I can talk to, who understands what I'm talking about, and AGREES even!' (Sheryl)

Penny is enthusiastic about the 'feminist friends' she has made through her activism: 'I do just really value my feminist friends; I've got this space I can go to and talk in, and we're not judging each other, and we're all angry about the same things.' Penny's valuing of these friendships has a direct impact on her commitment to group activities:

there have been times I've thought, ooh maybe I'm putting too much time into this, and I've thought I don't want to continue. But a lot of it's to do with making friendships within the group, and spending time with people and that motivates me to keep going back to meetings.

For Anna van Heeswijk, solidarity is a major strength of OBJECT. She considers that it is 'something really important to hold on to': 'what I love about [the OBJECT activist group] is everyone really has a direct role in it, and we all think about things together and move together as a group'.

Participating in collective action plays a role in fostering a sense of solidarity and collective belonging: 'protest actions are one of the means by which challenging groups develop an oppositional consciousness and collective identity' (Taylor and van Dyke, 2007: 270). Taylor and van Dyke point out that tactical repertoires offer a number of different levels of participation – from 'low risk' activities such as signing a petition to 'high risk' activities such as participating in blockades. The tactical repertoires adopted by OBJECT and APL offered a range of opportunities for participation, and a sense of belonging was fostered through engaging in activities such as chant practice, prop-making sessions and sharing practical tasks, as well as participating in protests and stunts. The sense of solidarity was highly valued by Annette:

> I quite enjoy the sense that there's a real solidarity between people, compared to campaigning I did on other issues ... it doesn't feel like you have that same bond that I feel you do when you're campaigning on women's issues.
>
> I notice with the OBJECT campaign the fact that there's quite a core group of women who are really supportive, who take time out to help with protests, and who really, really help the campaign ... so it really felt like there was a collective effort there which is what I really like about the OBJECT campaigns ... it's nice that people are passionate enough about things to try and do that.

The role of collective action in fostering group solidarity was evident throughout the period of my field work with OBJECT. Group coordinators and members developed a range of practical strategies to ensure that activists felt supported and able to cope with the challenges of a public demonstration. These included planning and preparation prior to the action; meeting up beforehand to make sure new people were welcomed; using resources such as 'comeback sheets' to build confidence in dealing with members of the public; building group spirit through chant practice, banner-making sessions and sharing practical tasks; working as a team and 'looking out' for each other; providing training for dealing with the media; dividing up tasks and agreeing roles (one person to deal with media interest while a demonstration is taking place, for example); de-brief sessions after the actions; building informal support networks, including through phone, email and online discussion; socialising and celebrating.

Whilst even early campaign actions featured chanting, singing and spectacle, activists became visibly bolder and more confident in the stunts as they developed an ease and familiarity with protest repertoires, along with a strong sense of *ésprit de corps* and group identity. As mentioned earlier, this was particularly evident in the increasingly exuberant 'Feminist Friday' protests, and protests outside the Playboy Club, *Xbiz EU* and the Miss World contest.

It is unlikely that such extrovert and assertive protests would have been possible in the early stages of the group's campaigns; rather, practice of collective actions within a supportive environment meant that group solidarity was fostered to enable new forms of protest to be undertaken. The development of OBJECT's repertoire of protest over the period of my research is indicative of the mutually reinforcing relationship between tactical repertoires and *ésprit de corps*: a movement's repertoire constitutes a mutually constructed and performed language that serves to foster collective identity (Tilly, 1995). In this way, repertoires contribute to collective identity within a movement; at the same time, the fostering of group identity and a sense of belonging (Blumer, 1969), through the kinds of support structures and modes of organisation discussed earlier in the chapter, enables and supports the development of more ambitious tactical repertoires.

Anti-porn feminism and the 'third wave'

In this chapter, we have seen that pornography and pornification are significant mobilising issues in the development of twenty-first-century feminist activism in the UK. Feminist networks and a number of formal and informal abeyance structures have provided opportunities for feminist anti-porn agendas to be developed and communicated. The importance of routes of access to feminist anti-porn perspectives and groups raises questions about how young women outside the movement, who are invited to adopt a postfeminist stance and who hold largely negative attitudes to feminism, might respond if accessibility to feminist ideas is increased through the continued expansion of the movement.

I have shown that, throughout the decade, anti-porn perspectives have been communicated in diverse, imaginative and dynamic ways through a variety of media and technologies, within and between networks, and beyond the activist community. Whilst this new period of activism is distinct, following a period of latency, there are important continuities and links which connect twenty-first-century activism with that of the second wave; new forms of activism build on past strategies and analyses in important ways. As the decade progressed, anti-porn activists acting in a number of capacities ensured that pornography and pornification were placed emphatically at the centre of the developing feminist agenda, in relation to broader grassroots activism, more liberal versions of feminism, and indeed mainstream politics. Viewed in terms of historical cycles, this claiming of the agenda may indicate a parallel to Rees's description of how, in the 1980s, 'revolutionary feminists claimed, and were ceded a hegemonic position within feminism regarding anti-pornography politics' (2007: 227). At the time of writing, it is too early to say whether anti-porn feminist perspectives have indeed achieved a 'hegemonic position' within the broader resurgent movement: whilst my mapping exercise suggests that anti-porn perspectives are in the ascendancy, as has been noted, not all groups share this perspective.

Debates around 'third wave feminism' did not emerge as particularly useful in mapping the development of anti-porn feminism, partly because of the lack of consensus around what the term actually signifies, particularly in relation to confusion between 'postfeminism' and third wave feminism. New millennium anti-porn feminists might be described as 'third wave' only in the chronological sense of the word, and in respect of their creative utilisation of new technologies. Regarding ideological positions, the term does not seem to be particularly relevant or useful; in fact, the ideological positioning of 'new' anti-porn feminists is probably more accurately explained in relation to long-standing differences between radical and liberal feminism. Consideration of 'waves' was not a feature of activist accounts, although some activists identified strongly with second wave feminism, and several cited second wave texts as inspirational and influential. Activists engaged in 'cultural activism' such as stickering may be seen as representative of third wave tactics, but it should not be forgotten that this form of cultural intervention was also very much a part of second wave activism. Furthermore, whilst stickering may often be carried out on an individual basis, as an act of resistance it is far from 'individualistic' and indeed involves some personal risk to the individual activist. In fact, there is evidence of striking continuity between certain forms of second wave and post-millennial feminist activism: both 'waves' demonstrate a sense of collectivity, a desire to communicate feminist messages and a commitment to challenging the status quo, with conferences and other collective events playing a key role in developing the movement.

The activism that I mapped often seemed at odds with much academic writing on the third wave, young women and feminism, possibly suggesting a divergence between the resurgence of feminist activism and academic feminism. McRobbie, for example, writes persuasively about how young women are positioned and invited to take up certain identities within the neoliberal social order (2009), but, as Woodward and Woodward point out, she 'fails to acknowledge how young women are themselves critical of the popular culture they consume and inhabit' (2009: 18). In the course of my mapping exercise and during my ethnographies, the gap between much academic feminism and feminist activism was striking, although work produced at the end of the decade is beginning to address this (Holyoak, 2008; Woodward and Woodward, 2009; Redfern and Aune, 2010).

The activist groups that I have discussed provide evidence that anti-porn feminists 'see their efforts as part of a larger feminist project ... rather than adopt[ing] a postfeminist stance of opposition to the second wave' (Kinser, 2004: 140). Not only do my findings support those of Redfern and Aune (2010), in suggesting that 'third wave' feminism has much in common with the second wave, but the activism that I researched also offers a challenge to what Kinser refers to as 'weak' feminism: a version of feminism which uncritically sees plurality and multiplicity as inherently good. Whilst theorists of the third wave have celebrated the ways in which 'complexity, multiplicity, and contradiction can enrich our identities as feminists and the movement as a whole' (Bailey, 1997: 18; see also Baumgardner and Richards, 2000; and Braithwaite, 2002: 342), the stance taken by my research participants suggests that a more critical view of pluralism is necessary in order to face the challenges of a pornified society. As Kinser argues:

> *Everything* cannot be feminism... . If we invite every cause and point of view under the purview of feminism, then it is spread so thin that it disintegrates altogether, coming to mean nothing at all, since it cannot possibly mean everything. (2004: 145)

An uncritical celebration of multiplicity and contradiction as unproblematically 'enriching' of the feminist movement glosses over the ideological tensions existing between various versions of feminism. For example, it is not convincing to assert that seeing pornography as a form of violence against women, and seeing it as a site of empowerment and liberation can *both* be feminist positions. Whisnant's consideration of the kind of feminism necessary to meet the challenges of pornification

(Whisnant, 2007) is useful in reflecting on this point. As I mentioned in the Introduction, Whisnant emphasises that a movement of significant numbers articulating a feminist critique of porn must be generated. Such a critique needs to demonstrate the distinctiveness of a feminist argument in relation to both moral right and liberal, pro-porn positions. The critique of pornography and the porn culture must be connected to a broader critique of the commodification of everyday life and, must promote a non-marketised conception of freedom. Finally, a vision of alternatives must be imagined and supported. In relation to Whisnant's initial point about generating a movement, OBJECT, APL and other UK anti-porn groups have certainly been mobilising activists, promoting a feminist anti-porn analysis and helping to shape the agenda of twenty-first-century activism. Similarly, both OBJECT and APL have carefully negotiated both 'moral right' and 'liberal left' perspectives, and framed their arguments and campaign messages carefully as rooted in issues of women's equality and liberation.

There is less evidence from my research in relation to Whisnant's second and third suggestions. The focus of both OBJECT and APL has been very much on providing a critique of pornography and the sex industry, and lobbying for change or raising awareness around these issues. Little work has so far been done to link an anti-porn agenda to broader critiques of the commodification of everyday life, or to providing visions of alternatives. There are indications that such approaches may be developed: for example, the slogan 'Pro-sex, anti-porn' suggests a desire to distinguish and celebrate non-pornographic versions of sex from pornified versions. Also, a crucial part of the creation of feminist solidarity and the building of group culture involves a deep respect for and valuing of women, in a way that women seldom experience in a misogynist culture. The relationships nurtured within the activist community potentially provide a model of loving, respectful and egalitarian modes of relating. But overall, visions of alternatives were implicit in campaign messages rather than explicit, and were not much discussed in group meetings or informal conversations amongst group members. If UK-based anti-porn feminism is to develop the 'vision of alternatives' that Whisnant considers to be necessary, perhaps spaces for consciousness raising will be where these new visions can be imagined, developed and articulated.

Reflections: activism then and now

The organisational repertoires developed by OBJECT and APL follow traditions of feminist organising that had been established in earlier decades. Similar arguments and differences arose relating to organisational issues, such as the desirability of maintaining women-only space as opposed to mixed-membership groups. However, apparent departures from second wave modes of organising are also evident. The prevalence of women-only consciousness raising in the second wave seemed to lead to more integrated approaches than are evidenced in twenty-first-century activists: accounts of second wave feminism document wide-ranging personal transformations associated with developing a feminist consciousness. These transformations included, for some, a rejection of 'beauty practices' (as symbolised by the 'Freedom Trash Can' action outside the Miss World beauty pageant in the USA in 1970); experiments with unconventional forms of living, such as housing cooperatives, collectives and communes; and a rejection of heterosexuality and embracing of separatism and political lesbianism. These broader, radical transformations were not much in evidence amongst my interviewees. It would be interesting to explore why, for many twenty-first-century activists, a stance against pornification does not necessarily involve a more thoroughgoing critique of heterosexuality. It may be that, since the groups and resurgent movement are at a relatively early stage of development, more radical analyses and transformations will indeed emerge in due course, assuming that the current movement trajectory continues; or it may be that the different social and cultural context within which this new movement has emerged is less conducive to more radical departures. For example, in the current economic climate, factors such as student debt, housing costs and lack of access to education, social housing and public services may create a culture of anxiety that encourages a certain social conservatism; conversely, such straitened economic circumstances may actually contribute to the pursuit of radical alternatives. Future research would be needed to examine such questions. It may also be that the wholesale rejection of beauty practices and heterosexuality are seen as neither necessary nor desirable: again, future research would be needed in order to investigate this.

In terms of the tactical repertoires of groups, there are again parallels and differences to the previous wave of anti-porn feminism. The framing of pornography is broadly similar, and the focus of campaigns and use of spectacle to attract media attention is evident in both waves. However, the tactical repertoires deployed by twenty-first-century activists have obviously been influenced by the new opportunities created by technological developments, so blogging, e-lists, e-zines and online discussion groups have become dominant forms of communication, replacing the earlier media such as hard-copy newsletters and magazines. Twenty-first-century anti-porn activism has also tended not to involve illegal or violent actions: the actions of my case study groups were always conducted lawfully, and stickering was generally the only example of unlawful behaviour mentioned by activists in relation to their individual activism, apart from the spray painting of the sex shop in Bristol. Both UK Feminista and OBJECT pursue a reformist agenda in seeking to influence policy and legislative changes. There is no obvious militant strand akin to WAVAW or Angry Women, supergluing the locks of sex shops, pouring cement down toilets of cinemas showing pornographic films, carrying out widespread graffiti of sexist advertisements and, in the case of Angry Women, arson attacks. It is also notable that, at the point of writing, although demonstrations have been held within and outside stores selling lads' mags, and outside lap-dancing clubs and the Playboy store, twenty-first-century anti-porn activists have not to date picketed the offices of porn publishers, stockists or distributors.

It seems likely that the more formalised structures of activism provided by funded groups such as UK Feminista and OBJECT have shaped the nature of the tactical repertoires employed. It also seems significant that women-only consciousness raising does not play such a key role in the re-emergent movement as it did in the 1970s and 1980s. What was crucial about consciousness raising in the second wave was that it led to both the production of theory and activism. Through consciousness raising, women involved in the original Anti-Porn Group developed a revolutionary feminist analysis of pornography that informed the campaigns of WAVAW and Angry Women. While a wealth of anti-porn literature is available to and accessed by twenty-first-century feminists, activists largely focus on campaign strategies, goals, and the practicalities of organising protests and events; there is little time and space devoted to theoretical discussions and searching analyses of pornography. A factor in this may simply be the frequency of meetings: London WAVAW activists met twice weekly, planning actions on Wednesdays and carrying them out on Fridays. This is in marked contrast to OBJECT's 'Feminist Fridays', which happen monthly, or less frequently. Overall, this seems indicative of a different level of involvement in activism; whilst some key group members are heavily involved in activism, it does not perhaps have quite the central role in the lives of many activists as it did in the second wave. The accommodation of men in some feminist groups and the lack of a visible and supportive women's culture in the form of women's cafes, bars and bookshops militates against activists accessing and embracing a deeper feminist identity and community. Whatever the factors, the deeply politicised rage that fuelled the anti-porn activism of the second wave does not yet seem to have been fully accessed in the re-emergent movement. It should be remembered, of course, that movements are constantly in movement, and modes of organisation and tactical repertoires are likely to change over time.

The above comments notwithstanding, groups with anti-porn aims and objectives, in the context of grassroots feminist networks, are adopting organisational forms and processes that activate those aims through developing a range of effective tactical repertoires. With extremely limited financial resources and in a short space of time, groups are proving adept at mobilising activists and running high-profile campaigns that engage with the general public, and with political and media opportunity structures. These campaigns have produced a range of impacts including remarkable successes in achieving legislative change and expanding the movement. Key activists demonstrate a willingness to invest considerable amounts of personal energy, time and in some cases material resources in group projects and sustaining groups through difficult times. Groups have been successful in generating high levels of solidarity and a sense of collective belonging amongst members.

There are two emerging features of the new activism that seem particularly important. The first is the indication of an increasingly diverse constituency of anti-porn feminists in the UK, which has the potential to enrich the movement through the inclusion of a wealth of perspectives across differences of class, race, sexuality and age. A key element of this diversity is the inclusion and support of women with direct experience of the sex industry, whose voices are vital and need to be at the forefront of the movement. The second feature is the beginnings of an international network of anti-porn feminists, which is facilitating exchange of knowledge and strategies, and enabling activists in different locations to share experiences and learning. If the movement is to pose a serious challenge to the globalised porn industry, which it must, such international networking is vital.

Notes

1 Hooters is an international restaurant franchise that originated in Atlanta, USA. The company states that 'the element of sex appeal is prevalent in the restaurants' and that 'Hooters hires women who best fit the image of a Hooters girl to work in this capacity': <http://www.hooters.com/About.aspx> (accessed 25 April 2010).

2 Spradley uses the term 'encultured informant' in the context of ethnographic research, to refer to a research participant who plays a useful role in imparting knowledge of the research culture to the ethnographer. I have expanded the term here to refer to activists who play a similar role in creating narratives which render the activist culture accessible and intelligible to a wider, non-activist community.

3 Rebecca Mott, 'We see through you', <http://rmott62.wordpress.com/2012/02/27/we-see-through-you/>.

4 <http://femconferences.org.uk/>.

5 <http://ukfeminista.org.uk/2011/11/fem-11-a-storming-success/>.

6 For reports on the 2008, 2009 and 2010 conferences, see the Feminism in London website: <http://www.feminisminlondon.org.uk>.

7 The Women's Support Project works on a broad range of issues, including sexual violence, child sexual abuse and incest; support for women whose

children have been sexually abused; domestic abuse; prostitution and other forms of commercial sexual exploitation.

8 <http://www.stoppornculture.org>.

9 See Rogg Korsvik and Stø (2011) for these plans and the background to 'the Nordic approach'.

10 Comments from participants at the FiL 09 conference are available at: <http://www.feminisminlondon.org.uk/p_Home.ikml> (accessed 25 March 2010). A conference report on Fem05 is available at<http://www.femconferences.org.uk/Downloads/FEM05PostConferenceReport Summary.pdf> (accessed 25 March 2010).

11 The text of the original flyer is available at <http://antipornfeminists. wordpress.com/about-us/>.

12 <http://antipornfeminists.wordpress.com/>.

13 <http://www.object.org.uk/home/3-news/128-eff-off-hef-press-release>.

14 <http://www.guardian.co.uk/lifeandstyle/2010/mar/25/iceland-most-feminist-country>.

15 A 'Sex Encounter Establishent' (SEE) is defined as a venue which provides 'visual entertainment for the purpose of sexual stimulation'. Venues already classified as SEEs at the time of the 'Stripping the Illusion' campaign included sex shops, sex cinemas and peep shows.

16 <http://www.millionwomenrise.com>.

17 <http://www.object.org.uk/campaigns/beauty-pageants>.

18 <http://rabble.ca/podcasts/shows/f-word/2012/02/men-feminism-hugo-schwyzer-controversy>.

19 In late 2011, OBJECT began to define itself as 'woman-led', and a motion to this effect was proposed at its 2012 annual general meeting. At the time of going to print, the proposal had yet to be voted on by the membership.

20 Speech given at the London Slutwalk, 2011.

21 'Pornified? Complicating the debates about the "sexualisation of culture": An international conference'. Institute of Education, 1–2 December 2011, <http://www.ioe.ac.uk/research/50360.html>.

CONCLUSION

Pornography and pornification pose profound challenges for the feminist movement. According to Jensen, pornography is 'what the end of the world looks like':

> [I]f we have the courage to look honestly at contemporary pornography, we get a glimpse – in a very visceral, powerful fashion – of the consequences of the unjust and oppressive systems in which we live. Pornography is what the end will look like if we don't reverse the pathological course that we are on in patriarchal, white-supremacist, predatory corporate-capitalist societies. (Jensen, 2010: 105)

Of course, many women are already living with the direct consequences of the devastating injustices perpetrated by the porn industry. For them, the end of the world is here. Crimes of sexual violence are committed against women involved in the production of porn; others are victims of sexual violence committed by men who have been influenced by porn. Porn is not an issue of fantasy removed from 'real' injustice experienced by women, rather, it is acutely bound up with other forms of oppression experienced by women, including economic and racial oppressions. 'Fantasies' have consequences. Men's actions and men's choices have consequences. Fantasies do not stay fantasies for long; and we are seeing the effects of porn 'fantasies' of eroticised subordination in the real world. They do not look like freedom.

In order to build an effective resistance to pornography, feminists need to develop a movement that can tackle the industry and the demand on a number of fronts. As this book has shown, many groups are already organising against porn in a variety of ways. The movement is growing and continually changing in response to the hydra-like entity that is pornography. The mixture of unpaid activist groups, third sector funded initiatives and the actions of individuals all result in a plethora of ways in which porn is being challenged. Funding is vital for this work to continue, and the innovative work being done in Scotland illustrates the potential of what can be achieved with adequate funding and an integrated Violence Against Women strategy.

For groups taking a reformist path, there are legislative approaches to combating pornography that might be pursued, such as exploring the potential of a law to combat incitement to hatred on the basis of sex, and looking at how legislation might be used for women harmed by pornography to seek restitution. Similarly, educational initiatives such as those developed in Scotland are essential in trying to help young people – and girls, in particular – to negotiate the violent, sexualised images that are widely available on the internet and consumed by many of their peers. Consumer actions and boycotts, akin to the early WAVAW and WAVPM activism in the USA, could target industries currently profiting from the porn industry. Governments need to recognise pornography and commercial sexual exploitation as violence against women, and develop appropriate, funded strategies to combat it, in consultation with women's groups. In attempting to take a responsible stance towards the porn and sex industries, governments need not only to implement measures to combat the industry and male demand, but also to ensure that women exiting the industry are fully supported, with access to training, employment and education.

A promising and important aspect of the new activism is the increasing presence of the voices of black and minority ethnic women, young women, older women and lesbians. Such diversity is essential, and also needs to include other groups of women experiencing multiple oppression. Women with direct experience of abuse and exploitation in the porn industry need to be supported and facilitated to take their rightful place at the forefront of the movement. Funding bodies need to support the work that under-resourced groups are doing, and in particular to help to facilitate the inclusion of voices of marginalised women within these groups and in wider arenas.

Academics researching the porn industry and porn use need to take a responsible view of their topic that recognises the harmful and oppressive nature of mainstream pornography. Academic grant-making bodies and those in positions of academic standing need to consider their privileged position and access to resources in relation to those of the women whose voices are not heard and who are harmed by the industry. Any academic work on pornography needs to be mindful of the context of endemic male violence against women and structural oppression of women within which the industry thrives and which it perpetuates. Marginal aspects of the industry such as 'alt' porn and 'feminist' porn need to be considered in relation to the dominant industry, and a sense of proportionality should be incorporated into such analyses.

There is crucial and urgent work that male allies need to be doing to challenge the porn industry and porn consumption. However, men need to think carefully about how they can best challenge other men and act as responsible and useful allies to anti-porn feminists. Such thinking needs to be informed by a fully politicised understanding of men's position in relation to feminist struggles. In taking action, male allies need to ensure that the work that they do is useful and fully supportive of feminist goals, that it supports rather than undermines women's leadership, collectivity and solidarity; that it does not reproduce patterns of male domination, or drain energy from the feminist movement.

However, anti-porn feminism cannot simply be reformist. As members of the London Anti-Porn Group observed in the late 1970s, the project of dismantling the porn industry is deeply bound up with the ultimate feminist project of dismantling patriarchy. Anti-porn feminism cannot, therefore, be a single-issue feminism, but must be fully integrated into a radical feminist politics that brings a thoroughgoing critique and programme of resistance and transformation to all aspects of male domination. A fundamental part of such a project is the rebuilding of a radical feminist movement, which claims, ensures and supports women-only spaces, within which women can organise for our own liberation. The transformative effects of women-only organising are currently not available within many groups in the UK, to the serious – possibly fatal – detriment of the movement, and to the personal loss of those women who are denied the vital opportunity to experience women's politicised collectivity and solidarity. The joy of women engaged in collective struggle throws into sharp relief the alienated and sterile nature of the consumption of pornography: one-dimensional, endlessly repetitive and deeply solipsistic, as well as deeply woman-hating.

•••

Women must ask not only what we are fighting against but also what we are fighting for. (Janice Raymond)

The meaning of our love for women is what we have constantly to expand.
(Adrienne Rich, 1980)

I would like to finish with a consideration of the language that we use in our struggle, and in our imagining and creation of alternatives that reject a pornographic model of sexuality. In her fascinating account of participant observation in a community of North American nuclear defence intellectuals and security affairs analysts in the early years of the Reagan presidency, Carol Cohn offers a chilling analysis of the ways in which the gendered discourse of such a community renders certain ways of thinking unspeakable and unintelligible. Cohn discusses the ways in which a hyper-masculinised discourse prevailed in the group and functioned in order to silence any perspective that might have called into question the values that informed the group's discussions on nuclear military strategies. Within this hyper-masculinised environment, concerns regarding the implications and potentially devastating consequences of such strategies were silenced and dismissed through being labelled as 'feminine'. To articulate such concerns was to be labelled emotional and irrational: a 'wimp' and a 'pussy' (Cohn, 1993). Unsurprisingly, then, such concerns were rarely articulated, quickly silenced and ultimately rendered unthinkable as well as unspeakable.

Something akin to this takes place in the way that debates on pornography are conducted. The hyper-masculinised world of pornography renders certain values and modes of relationship – respect, equality, empathy – unthinkable, unspeakable and unintelligible. What is noticeable is the ways in which such values become framed as somehow inadmissible to the debates themselves. The pro-porn lobby attempts to frame values such as respect and intimacy as 'conservative' and 'moralising', and to dismiss sexuality based on eroticised equality as 'vanilla'. In debates around pornography, the very notion of *love* has been framed as somehow moralistic and conservative, and has been replaced by the less substantial language of desire and pleasure.

We are greatly impeded if the most important aspects of our values and our politics are rendered unspeakable or unimaginable. What we must unapologetically affirm is that any liberation struggle begins with love. bell hooks asserts the centrality of love in anti-racist struggles through her belief in 'beloved community', which must be nurtured, grown and valued in order to transform a racist society (1995). Before one can feel rage at injustice, one has to love and fully recognise the humanity of the person to whom the injustice is being done, in order to perceive it as an injustice. To find pornography offensive, you would have to believe in women.

It is significant that in struggles where male voices have dominated, ideas of 'brotherly love' and 'brotherhood' are treated seriously, even reverentially. When women unite against the porn industry, however, our love of women is ridiculed. The word sisterhood is used in scare quotes and spoken in a mocking tone. This response is deeply misogynistic, because women's love for other women is deeply feared.

In our anti-porn struggles, we need to speak the unspeakable, and we need to note what the ridicule tells us, for it is highly instructive. It tells us exactly how threatening we are, and where the most intense patriarchal insecurities, vulnerabilities and – let us make no mistake – violent responses lie. A radical feminist critique of pornography is threatening not only to the porn industry but to the very nature of patriarchal capitalism itself. Such a critique shows porn not only to be misogynist, oppressive, harmful and abusive – though it is all of these things. It also shows it to be deeply irrelevant and antithetical to experiences of love and solidarity.

Feminists engaged in the passion, rage and joys of collective struggle are likely to approach sex and sexuality from a very different place and with a very different set of values from those of the patriarchs who first created, desired and consumed pornography. The idea that the purpose of porn is to 'stimulate sexual arousal' is telling, suggestive as it is of the consumer as an inert mass, needing external stimulation to bring him to life. There is no passion in porn, which centres around the fulfilment of desire through an act of consumption, and relies on the ephemeral experience of the 'hot' – the thrill of dominating or being dominated. All are perceived as 'necessary' in order to mask the dead, empty space at the centre of the subject as constructed by the act of pornographic consumption: he who is unconnected, who cannot recognise, listen, empathise, connect, change and grow. For feminists fully alive and engaged in passionate collective struggle, a product offering external 'stimulation' is entirely redundant. A feminist sexuality is not one that is separate from life and human connection, but is part of it. It is not based on a hierarchical relationship that reduces another to an object, in order that the subject can act out their solipsistic sexual fantasies or desires on her. On the contrary, anti-porn feminists are engaged in a struggle to create a world where the pornographic itself is rendered unthinkable and unimaginable.

Audre Lorde describes the different uses of 'the erotic' in feminist struggle. Such experiences of 'the erotic' include 'the power which comes from sharing deeply any pursuit with another person', as 'the open and fearless underlining of my capacity for joy' and as 'self-connection' (Lorde, 1984c: 56, 57). For Lorde, 'Recognizing the power of the erotic within our lives can give us the energy to pursue genuine change within our world' (*ibid*.: 59). For feminists, such a struggle grows from a rage at the injustices of patriarchy, but even more fundamentally than that, from a love of women and love of oneself as a woman. Part of the feminist anti-porn project must be to place love and respect for women at the centre of the struggle, and to think deeply about the implications of this for all aspects of our organising, strategising and envisioning. 'The meaning of our love for women is what we have constantly to expand.'

Such a project is hardly 'conservative': on the contrary, it is revolutionary.

BIBLIOGRAPHY

Aitkenhead, Decca (2003) 'Net porn', *The Observer*, 30 March, <http://www.guardian. co.uk/theobserver/2003/mar/30/features.review7> (accessed 25 February 2008).

Allen, R. E. (ed.) ([1964] 1991) *The Concise Oxford Dictionary of Current English*. Oxford: Oxford University Press.

Altbach, Edith Hoshino (ed.) (2007) *From Feminism to Liberation*. Piscataway NJ: Transaction Publishers.

Amnesty International (2004) *Stop Violence Against Women*. London: Amnesty International Publications.

Antrobus, Peggy (2004) *The Global Women's Movement: Origins, issues and strategies*. London: Zed Books.

Anzaldúa, Gloria and Cherrie Moraga (1984) *This Bridge Called My Back*. New York NY: Kitchen Table: Women of Color Press.

Arlidge, John (2002) 'The dirty secret that drives new technology: it's porn', *The Observer*, 3 March, <http://www.guardian.co.uk/technology/2002/mar/03/internetnews.observer focus> (accessed 18 January 2010).

Arnold, June (2000) 'Consciousness-raising' in B. A. Crow (ed.), *Radical Feminism: A documentary reader*. New York NY: New York University Press, pp. 282–6.

Attwood, Feona (2002) 'Reading porn: the paradigm shift in pornography research', *Sexualities* 5 (1): 91–105.

—— (2005) 'Fashion and passion: marketing sex to women', *Sexualities* 8 (4): 392–406.

—— (2006) 'Sexed up: theorizing the sexualization of culture', *Sexualities* 9 (1): 77–94.

—— (2007) 'No money shot? Commerce, pornography and new sex taste cultures', *Sexualities* 10 (4): 441–56.

—— (2009a) 'Intimate adventures: sex blogs, sex "blooks" and women's sexual narration', *European Journal of Cultural Studies* 12 (1): 5–20.

—— (ed.) (2009b) *Mainstreaming Sex: The sexualisation of culture*. London: I. B. Tauris.

Australian Senate (2008) 'Inquiry into the sexualisation of children in the contemporary media environment', <http://www.aph.gov.au/SENATE/committee/eca_ctte/sexualis ation_of_children/report/report.pdf> (accessed 19 February 2010).

AVN (2005) 'The directors', *Adult Video News*, August.

Bacchi, Carol and Joan Eveline (2010) *Mainstreaming Politics: Gendering practices and feminist theory*. Adelaide: University of Adelaide Press.

Bailey, Cathryn (1997) 'Making waves and drawing lines: the politics of defining the vicissitudes of feminism', *Hypatia* 12 (3) (Summer): 17–28.

Baker, Joanne (2010) 'Claiming volition and evading victimhood: post-feminist obligations for young women', *Feminism and Psychology* 20 (May): 186–204.

Balding, Val, Julie Bindel and Kat Euler (eds) (1996) 'Violence, abuse and women's citizenship', final report on international conference, Brighton, 10–15 November.

Banyard, Kat (2010) *The Equality Illusion*. London: Faber and Faber.

Banyard, Kat and Rowena Lewis (2009) *Corporate Sexism: The sex industry's infiltration of the modern workplace*. London: Fawcett Society.

Barnes, Samuel, Max Kaase, *et al.* (1979) *Political Action: Mass participation in five Western democracies*. Beverley Hills CA: Sage.

Barrett, Michèle (1980) *Women's Oppression Today: The Marxist/feminist encounter.* London: Verso.

Barron, M. and M. Kimmel (2000) 'Sexual violence in three pornographic media: toward a sociological explanation', *Journal of Research* 37 (2): 161–8.

Barry, Kathleen (1995) *The Prostitution of Sexuality.* New York NY: New York University Press.

Barter, Christine, Melanie McCarry, David Berridge and Kathy Evans (2009) *Partner Exploitation and Violence in Teenage Intimate Relationships.* London: National Society for the Prevention of Cruelty to Children (NSPCC).

—— (2011) *'Standing on My Own Two Feet': Disadvantaged teenagers, intimate partner violence and coercive control.* London: NSPCC.

Bartholomew, A. and M. Mayer (1992) 'Nomads of the present: Melucci's contribution to new social movement theory', *Theory, Culture and Society* 9 (4): 141–59.

Bartky, Sandra Lee (1990) *Femininity and Domination.* New York NY: Routledge.

Baumgardner, Jennifer and Amy Richards (2000) *ManifestA: Young women, feminism and the future.* New York NY: Farrar, Straus and Giroux.

BBC News London (2011) 'Plea to call off Miss World feminist protest in London', 5 November, <http://www.bbc.co.uk/news/uk-england-london-15605862> (accessed 29 February 2012).

Beatbullying (2009) 'Truth of sexting amongst UK teens', 4 August, <http://www.beatbullying.org/dox/media-centre/press-releases/press-release-040809.html> (accessed 18 January 2010).

Bell, Rachel (2006a) 'Porn creep in the corner shop', <http://www.thefirstpost.co.uk/2785,news-comment,news-politics,porn-creep-in-the-corner-shop> (accessed 13 November 2008).

—— (2006b) 'Objecting to lads' mags', <http://www.bettybandit.co.uk/readCopy.asp?ID=219> (accessed 13 November 2008).

—— (2007a) 'Students move into pole position', <http://www.thefirstpost.co.uk/2769,news-comment,news-politics,on-campus-pole-dancing> (accessed 13 November 2008).

—— (2007b) 'Love in the time of phone porn', *The Guardian*, 30 January, <http://www.guardian.co.uk/education/2007/jan/30/sexeducation.schools> (accessed 13 November 2008).

—— (2007c) 'University challenge', *The Guardian*, 9 February, <http://www.guardian.co.uk/education/2007/feb/09/highereducation.uk> (accessed 13 November 2008).

—— (2007d) 'Sexualisation damages boys as well as girls', *The Independent*, 22 February, <http://www.independent.co.uk/opinion/commentators/rachel-bell-our-sexual-obsession-damages-boys-as-well-as-girls-437307.html> (accessed 13 November 2008).

—— (2008) 'I was seen as an object, not a person', *The Guardian*, 19 March, <http://www.guardian.co.uk/world/2008/mar/19/gender.uk> (accessed 13 November 2008).

Bell, Diane and Renate Klein (1996) *Radically Speaking: Feminism reclaimed.* Melbourne: Spinifex Press.

Benford, Robert D. and David A. Snow (2000) 'Framing processes and social movements: an overview and assessment', *Annual Review of Sociology*, 26: 611–39.

Benn, Melissa (1988) 'Page 3 – and the campaign against it' in G. Chester and J. Dickey, *Feminism and Censorship: The current debate.* Bridport, Dorset: Prism Press.

Bennett, Catherine (2010) 'One thing the parties agree on – keep women out', *The Guardian*, 8 May, <http://www.guardian.co.uk/commentisfree/2010/may/08/catherine-bennett-women-politics> (accessed 8 May 2010).

Bialer, Dana (2011) 'If you can't beat 'em, join 'em: reflections of lesbian/queer pornography contextualised within an anti-pornography framework', presentation to the conference on 'Challenging Porn Culture', London, 3 December 2011.

Bidisha (2010) 'Women's mass awakening', *The Guardian*, 4 August, <http://www.

guardian.co.uk/commentisfree/2010/aug/04/women-mass-awakening> (accessed 4 August 2010).

Bindel, Julie (2004) *Profitable Exploits: Lap dancing in the UK*. London: Child and Women Abuse Studies Unit, London Metropolitan University.

—— (2007) 'Fighting fear', *The Guardian*, 23 November, <http://www.guardian.co.uk/ commentisfree/2007/nov/23/fightingfear> (accessed 23 November 2007).

—— (2011) 'Joanna Yeates murder: legislation needed on incitement to gender hatred', *The Guardian*, 28 October, <http://www.guardian.co.uk/commentisfree/ commentisfree+uk/joanna-yeates> (accessed 10 June 2012).

Bindel, Julie, Kate Cook and Liz Kelly (1995) 'Trials and tribulations – justice for women: a campaign for the 1990s' in G. Griffin (ed.), *Feminist Activism in the 1990s*. London: Taylor and Francis.

Blumberg, Rhoda Lois (2003) 'The civil rights movement' in J. Goodwin and J. M. Jasper (eds), *The Social Movements Reader: Cases and concepts*. Oxford: Blackwell, pp. 15–21.

Blumer, Herbert (1969) 'Collective behaviour' in A. McClung Lee (ed.), *Principles of Sociology*. New York NY: Barnes and Noble.

Bouchier, David (1983) *The Feminist Challenge: The movement for women's liberation in Britain and the USA*. London: Macmillan.

Botham, Deric (2008) Interview with Rowan Pelling in *The Crisis on the Top Shelf*, directed by Rowan Pelling, BBC Radio 4, 4 November.

Boyle, Karen (2000) 'The pornography debates: beyond cause and effect', *Women's Studies International Forum* 23 (2): 187–95.

—— (ed.) (2010) *Everyday Pornography*. London: Routledge.

—— (2011) 'Producing abuse: selling the harms of pornography', *Women's Studies International Forum* 34: 593–602.

Bragg, Sara (2009) '"Too young to understand"? Children and "sexualised" media', paper presented at conference on 'Porn Cultures: Regulation, Political Economy, Technology', Leeds, 15–16 June.

Bragg, Sara and David Buckingham (2009) 'Too much, too young? Young people, sexual media and learning' in F. Attwood (ed.), *Mainstreaming Sex: The sexualisation of culture*. London: I. B. Tauris, pp. 129–46.

Braithwaite, Ann (2002) 'The personal, the political, third-wave and postfeminisms', *Feminist Theory* 3 (3): 335–44.

Bray, Abigail (2011) 'Capitalism and pornography: The internet as a global prostitution factory' in M. Tankard Reist and A. Bray (eds), *Big Porn Inc: Exposing the harms of the global pornography industry*. Melbourne: Spinifex Press.

Breen, Marcus (2007) 'Internet pornography: another step towards proletarianization.' *The International Journal of Technology, Knowledge and Society* 3 (5): 91–8.

—— (2009) 'Mikhail Bakhtin's "fanciful anatomy": internet pornography and the politics of pleasure within a theory of proletarianization', paper presented at conference on 'Porn Cultures: Regulation, Political Economy, Technology', Leeds, 15–16 June.

Bridges, Ana J. (2010) 'Methodological considerations in mapping pornography content' in K. Boyle (ed.), *Everyday Pornography*. London: Routledge, pp. 34–48.

Bristol Feminist Network (no date) 'Representations of women in the media', <http:// www.bristolfeministnetwork.com/representations-of-women-in-the-media.html> (accessed 3 August 2010).

Bronstein, Carolyn (2011) *Battling Pornography: The American Feminist Anti-Pornography Movement, 1976–1986*. Cambridge and New York NY: Cambridge University Press.

Brown, Wendy (2003) 'Neo-liberalism and the end of liberal democracy', *Theory and Event* 7 (1): 4–25.

Brownmiller, Susan (1975) *Against Our Will: Men, women and rape*. New York NY: Simon and Schuster.

—— ([1984] 1986). *Femininity*. London: Paladin.

—— (1999) *In Our Time: Memoir of a revolution*. New York NY: Dial Press.

Buchwald, Emilie, Pamela Fletcher and Martha Roth (eds) (1993) *Transforming a Rape Culture*. Minneapolis MN: Milkweed.

Buckingham, David and Sara Bragg (2004) *Young People, Sex and the Media: The facts of life?* London: Palgrave.

—— (2005) 'Opting into (and out of) childhood: young people, sex and the media' in J. Qvortrup (ed.), *Studies in Modern Childhood: Society, agency and culture*. London: Sage.

Buckingham, David *et al.* (2007) 'The impact of the media on children and young people', review of the literature prepared for the Byron Review, Department for Children, Schools and Families (DCSF), <http://www.dcsf.gov.uk/byronreview/ (Annex G)>.

—— (2009) 'External research on sexualised goods aimed at children', Report to Scottish Parliament, <http://www.scottish.parliament.uk/s3/committees/equal/reports-10/eor10-02.htm#2> (accessed 14 July 2010).

Budgeon, Shelley (2001) 'Emergent feminist(?) identities: young women and the practice of micropolitics', *European Journal of Women's Studies* 8 (1): 7–28.

Buechler, Steven M. (2000) *Social Movements in Advanced Capitalism*. New York NY: Oxford University Press.

Bulbeck, Chilla (1997) *Living Feminism: The impact of the women's movement on three generations of Australian women*. Cambridge: Cambridge University Press.

Bulbeck, Chilla and Anita Harris (2007) 'Feminism, youth politics, and generational change' in A. Harris (ed.), *Next Wave Cultures: Feminism, subcultures, activism*. London: Routledge, pp. 221–43.

Butler, Judith (1990) *Gender Trouble: Feminism and the subversion of identity*. London: Routledge.

—— (2000) 'The force of fantasy: feminism, mapplethorpe and discursive excess' in D. Cornell (ed.), *Feminism and Pornography*. Oxford: Oxford University Press, pp. 487–508.

Byrne, Paul (1996) 'The politics of the women's movement', *Parliamentary Affairs* 49: 55–70.

Cameron, Deborah and Elizabeth Frazer (1987) *The Lust to Kill*. Cambridge: Polity.

—— (1992) 'On the question of pornography and sexual violence: moving beyond cause and effect' in C. Itzin (ed.), *Pornography: Women, violence and civil liberties*. Oxford: Oxford University Press, pp. 359–83.

—— ([1985] 2010) 'The liberal organ: porn in *The Guardian*' in D. Cameron and J. Scanlon (eds), *The Trouble and Strife Reader*. London: Bloomsbury Academic, pp. 134–41.

Cameron, Deborah and Joan Scanlon (2009) *The Trouble and Strife Reader*. London: Bloomsbury Academic.

Campbell, Beatrix (1987) 'A feminist sexual politics: now you see it, now you don't' in *Feminist Review* (ed.), *Sexuality: A reader*. London: Virago, pp. 19–39.

Caputi, Jane (2003) 'Everyday pornography' in G. Dines and J. Jumez (eds), *Gender, Race, and Class in Media*, second edition. Thousand Oaks CA: Sage Publications, pp. 434–50.

Caroline (pseudonym) (2011) 'The impact of pornography on my life' in M. Tankard Reist and A. Bray (eds), *Big Porn Inc: Exposing the harms of the global pornography industry*. Melbourne: Spinifex Press, pp. xxix–xxxiii.

Cassell, Paul (2010) 'Extreme porn paedophile spared jail', 30 June, <http://www.getreading.co.uk/news/s/2073650_extreme_porn_paedophile_spared_jail> (accessed 29 February 2012).

Castro, Ginette (1990) *American Feminism: A contemporary history*. New York NY: New York University Press.

Chambers, Clare (2008) *Sex, Culture and Justice: The limits of choice*. University Park, PA: Pennsylvania State University Press.

Chancer, Lynn S. (1998) *Reconcilable Differences: Confronting beauty, pornography and the future of feminism*. Berkeley CA: University of California Press.

Channel 4 Television (2009) *The Sex Education Programme v. Pornography*, 3–6 March.

Chemaly, Soraya (2012) 'International Women's Day: 10 reasons why feminism is good for boys and men', <http://www.huffingtonpost.com/soraya-chemaly/international-womens-day_b_1324219.html> (accessed 8 July 2012).

Chester, Gail and Julienne Dickey (eds) (1988) *Feminism and Censorship: The current debate*. Bridport, Dorset: Prism Press.

Chomsky, Noam and Edward S. Herman (1988) *Manufacturing Consent: The political economy of the mass media*. New York NY: Pantheon Books.

Ciclitira, Karen (2004) 'Pornography, women and feminism: between pleasure and politics', *Sexualities* 7 (3): 281–301.

Clarke, D. A. (2004) 'Prostitution is for everyone: feminism, globalisation and the "sex industry"' in C. Stark and R. Whisnant (eds), *Not for Sale: Feminists resisting prostitution and pornography*. Melbourne: Spinifex.

Clavero, Sarah (2005) 'The development of gender mainstreaming as a concept and practice of equal opportunities' in A.-M. McGauran and A. MacNamara (eds), *Administration: Gender Equality Phase 3 – The theory and practice of gender mainstreaming*. Dublin: Institute of Public Administration of Ireland, pp. 7–23.

Clemens, Elisabeth S. (2003) 'Organisational repertoires' in J. Goodwin and J. M. Jasper (eds), *The Social Movements Reader: Cases and concepts*. Oxford: Blackwell, pp. 187–201.

Clements, Jo (2009) '"Don't worry Mum, I'm MEANT to show my bra": Judy Finnigan's daughter turns lingerie model', *The Daily Mail*, 20 January, <http://www.dailymail.co.uk/tvshowbiz/article-1123112/Dont-worry-Mum-Im-MEANT-bra-Judy-Finnigans-daughter-turns-lingerie-model.html> (accessed 29 February 2012).

Cochrane, Kira (2008) 'Now, the backlash', *The Guardian*, 1 July, <http://www.guardian.co.uk/world/2008/jul/01/gender.women> (accessed 1 July 2008).

—— (2010a) 'Feminism isn't finished', *The Guardian*, 24 July, <http://www.guardian.co.uk/lifeandstyle/2010/jul/24/feminism-not-finished-not-uncool> (accessed 24 July 2010).

—— (2010b) 'Why Kat Banyard is the UK's most influential young feminist', *The Guardian*, 10 September.

—— (2010c) 'The Rise of "Rape Talk"', *The Guardian*. 10 September.

—— (2011) 'Why is British public life dominated by men?', *The Guardian*, 4 December, <http://www.guardian.co.uk/lifeandstyle/2011/dec/04/why-british-public-life-dominated-men> (accessed 29 February 2012).

Cohn, Carol (1993) 'Wars, wimps, and women: talking gender and thinking war' in M. Cooke and A. Woollacott (eds), *Gendering War Talk*. Princeton NJ: Princeton University Press.

Collins, Patricia Hill (1990) *Black Feminist Thought: Knowledge, consciousness, and the politics of empowerment*. Boston MA: Unwin Hyman.

Cooper, A., J. Morahan-Martin, R. M. Mathy and M. Maheu (2002) 'Toward an increased understanding of user demographics in online sexual activities', *Journal of Sex and Marital Therapy*, 28: 105–29.

Coote, Anna and Beatrix Campbell (1982). *Sweet Freedom: The struggle for women's liberation*. Oxford: Picador.

Cornell, Drucilla (ed.) (2000) *Feminism and Pornography*. Oxford: Oxford University Press.

Cowan, G., C. Lee, D. Levy and D. Snyder (1988) 'Dominance and inequality in X-rated videocassettes', *Psychology of Women Quarterly* 12: 299–311.

Coward, Rosalind (1987) 'Sexual violence and sexuality' in *Feminist Review* (ed.), *Sexuality: A reader*. London: Virago, pp. 307–25.

Coy, Maddy (2009) 'Milkshakes, lady lumps and growing up to want boobies: how the sexualisation of popular culture limits girls' horizons', *Child Abuse Review* 18 (6): 372–83.

Crawford, Elizabeth (2012) Interview in 'Archive on 4: The lost world of the suffragettes', BBC Radio 4, 11 February 2012, <http://www.bbc.co.uk/programmes/b01bw7hv> (accessed 8 July 2012).

Crossley, Nick (2002) *Making Sense of Social Movements*. Buckingham: Open University Press.

Crow, Barbara A. (ed.) (2000) *Radical Feminism: A documentary reader*. New York NY and London: New York University Press.

Croydon Guardian (2009) 'Jobcentre "Pimpcentre" for carrying sex ads, anti-trafficking campaigners say', *Croydon Guardian*, 16 April, <http://www.croydonguardian. co.uk/search/4291258.Jobcentre__Pimpcentre__for_carrying_sex_ads__vice_ campaigners_say/> (accessed 20 November 2009).

Danns, Jennifer Hayashi and Sandrine Lévêque (2011) *Stripped: The bare reality of lap dancing*. Sussex: Clairview Books.

Davis, Angela (1982) *Women, Race and Class*. New York NY: Random House.

Davis, Flora (1991) *Moving the Mountain: The women's movement in America since 1960*. New York NY: Simon and Schuster.

Davis, Rowenna (2011) 'Labiaplasty surgery increase blamed on pornography', *The Guardian*, 27 February, <http://www.guardian.co.uk/lifeandstyle/2011/feb/27/ labiaplasty-surgery-labia-vagina-pornography> (accessed 29 February 2012).

Della Porta, Donatella and Mario Diani (1999) *Social Movements: An introduction*. Oxford: Blackwell.

Denfield, Rene (1996) *The New Victorians: A young woman's challenge to the old feminist order*. New York NY: Warner Books.

Department of Work and Pensions (2008) 'Consultation document: accepting and advertising employer vacancies from within the adult entertainment industry by Jobcentre Plus', December, <http://www.dwp.gov.uk/docs/adult-entertainment-jobs-consultation.pdf> (accessed 25 February 2009).

—— (2010) 'Grayling: we'll stop sex jobs being advertised in job centres', 2 August, <http:// www.dwp.gov.uk/newsroom/press-releases/2010/aug-2010/dwp101-10-020810. shtml> (accessed 2 August 2010).

de Sade, Marquis (1785) *The 120 Days of Sodom*, translated by Richard Seaver and Austryn Wainhouse, published electronically by Supervert.com, <http://supervert. com/elibrary/marquis_de_sade/> (accessed 8 July 2012).

Diani, Mario (2007) 'Networks and Participation' in D. A. Snow, S. Soule and H. Kriesi (eds), *The Blackwell Companion to Social Movements*. Oxford: Blackwell, pp. 339–59.

Dines, Gail (1998a) 'Dirty business: *Playboy* magazine and the mainstreaming of pornography' in G. Dines, R. Jensen and A. Russo (eds), *Pornography: The production and consumption of inequality*. London: Routledge, pp. 37–64.

—— (1998b) 'Living in two worlds: an activist in the academy' in G. Dines, R. Jensen and A. Russo (eds), *Pornography: The production and consumption of inequality*. London: Routledge, pp. 163–6.

—— (2009) 'From Stepford wives to Stepford sluts: how media constructs femininity', *Rain and Thunder* 44 (Media Issue).

—— (2010) *Pornland: How porn has hijacked our sexuality*. Boston MA: Beacon Press.

—— (2011a) 'Stop porn culture' in M. Tankard Reist and A. Bray (eds), *Big Porn Inc: Exposing the harms of the global pornography industry*. Melbourne: Spinifex Press, pp. 266–7.

—— (2011b) 'Exposing the myth of free porn' in ABC – Religion and Ethics, 21 December, <http://www.abc.net.au/religion/articles/2011/12/21/3396048.htm> (accessed 29 February 2012).

Dines, Gail, Robert Jensen and Ann Russo (eds) (1998) *Pornography: The production and consumption of inequality*. London: Routledge.

Dines, Gail, Linda Thompson and Rebecca Whisnant, with Karen Boyle (2010) 'Arresting images: anti-pornography slide shows, activism and the academy' in K. Boyle (ed.), *Everyday Pornography*. London: Routledge, pp. 17–33.

Donnerstein, E., D. Linz and S. Penrod (1987) *The Question of Pornography: Research findings and policy implications*. London: Collier Macmillan.

Duggan, Lisa (1988) 'Censorship in the name of feminism' in G. Chester and J. Dickey (eds), *Feminism and Censorship: The current debate*. Bridport, Dorset: Prism Press, pp. 76–86.

Duggan, Lisa and Nan D. Hunter (1995) *Sex Wars: Sexual dissent and political culture*. New York NY: Routledge.

Duggan, Lisa, Nan D. Hunter and Carole S. Vance (1988) 'False promises: feminist antipornography legislation in the US' in G. Chester and J. Dickey (eds), *Feminism and Censorship: The current debate*. Bridport, Dorset: Prism Press.

Duits, Linda and Liesbet van Zoonen (2006) 'Headscarves and porno-chic: disciplining girls' bodies in the European multicultural society', *European Journal of Women's Studies* 13 (2): 103–17.

—— (2007) 'Who's afraid of female agency? A rejoinder to Gill', *European Journal of Women's Studies* 14 (2): 161–70.

Duke, Diane and Peter Phinney (2011) 'Anti-piracy action programme: content piracy is rampant – find out what you can do about it', seminar held at Xbiz EU 2011: International Digital Media Conference, London, 22–24 September.

Duncan, Lauren E. (1999) 'Motivation for collective action: group consciousness as mediator of personality, life experiences and women's rights activism', *Political Psychology* 20: 611–35.

Durham, M. Gigi (2008) *The Lolita Effect: The media sexualization of young girls and what we can do about it*. Woodstock NY: The Overlook Press.

Dutta, Kunal (2011) 'British soldiers in Afghanistan show "war snuff movies"', *The Independent*, 25 September, <http://www.independent.co.uk/news/uk/home-news/british-soldiers-in-afghanistan-shown-war-snuff-movies-2360511.html (accessed 29 February 2012).

Dworkin, Andrea (1974) *Woman Hating*. New York NY: Dutton.

—— ([1979] 1981) *Pornography: Men possessing women*. London: Women's Press.

—— (1983) *Right-wing Women*. New York NY: Perigee Books.

—— (1985) 'Against the male flood: censorship, pornography and equality' in A. Dworkin (1988), *Letters from a War Zone*. London: Secker and Warburg.

—— (1988) *Letters from a War Zone*. London: Secker and Warburg.

—— (1990) 'Dworkin on Dworkin', interview with Elizabeth Braeman and Carol Cox, *Trouble and Strife* 19 (summer): 203–17.

Echols, Alice (1989) *Daring to Be Bad: Radical feminism in America 1967–1975*. Minneapolis MN: Minnesota University Press.

Edwards, Bob and John D. McCarthy (2007) 'Resources and social movement mobilisation' in D. A. Snow, S. Soule and H. Kriesi (eds), *The Blackwell Companion to Social Movements*. Oxford: Blackwell, pp. 116–52.

End Violence Against Women (no date) 'The facts', <http://www.endviolenceagainst women.org.uk/pages/the_facts.html> (accessed 29 February 2012).

Engle, Vanessa (Director) (2007) *Lefties: Angry Wimmin*. London: BBC4, October 2007, <http://www.bbc.co.uk/bbcfour/documentaries/features/lefties2.shtml> (accessed 14 March 2009).

—— (2010a) *Women: Libbers*. London: BBC4, 8 March.

—— (2010b) *Women: Mothers*. London: BBC4, 15 March.

—— (2010c) *Women: Activists*. London: BBC4, 22 March.

Epstein, Barbara (2001) 'What happened to the women's movement?' *Monthly Review* 53 (1) (May).

—— (2003) 'The decline of the women's movement' in J. Goodwin and J. M. Jasper (eds),

The Social Movements Reader: Cases and concepts. Oxford: Blackwell, pp. 328–34.

Eschle, Catherine and Bice Maiguashca (2007) 'Rethinking globalised resistance: feminist activism and critical theorising in international relations', *British Journal of Politics and International Relations (BJPIR)* 9: 284–301.

Evans, Adrienne, Sarah Riley and Avi Shankar (2010) 'Technologies of sexiness: theorizing women's engagement in the sexualization of culture', *Feminism and Psychology* 20 (February): 114–31.

Evans, Sara (1979) *Personal Politics: The roots of women's liberation in the civil rights movement and the new left.* New York NY: Alfred Knopf.

—— (2007) 'Women's consciousness and the southern black movement' in E. Hoshino Altbach, *From Feminism to Liberation.* Piscataway NJ: Transaction Publishers, pp. 13–27.

Everywoman (1988) *Pornography and Sexual Violence: Evidence of the links.* London: Everywoman Press.

Faludi, Susan (1991) *Backlash: The undeclared war against women.* London: Chatto and Windus.

Farley, Melissa (2011) 'Pornography is infinite prostitution' in M. Tankard Reist and A. Bray (eds), *Big Porn Inc: Exposing the harms of the global pornography industry.* Melbourne: Spinifex Press, pp. 150–9.

Fawcett Society (2007) 'Fawcett Society briefing on rape', <http://www.fawcettsociety.org. uk/index.asp?PageID=814> (accessed 15 January 2008).

—— (2009) 'Just below the surface: gender stereotyping, the silent barrier to equality in the modern workplace?',<http://www.fawcett society.org.uk/index.asp?PageID=879> (accessed 11 February 2010).

Ferreday, Debra (2008) 'Showing the girl: the new burlesque', *Feminist Theory* 9: 47–65.

Findlen, Barbara (1995) *Listen Up: Voices from the next feminist generation.* Seattle WA: Seal Press.

Firestone, Shulamith (1970) *The Dialectic of Sex: The case for feminist revolution.* New York NY: William *Morrow.*

Flood, Michael (2010) 'Young men using pornography' in K. Boyle (ed.), *Everyday Pornography.* London: Routledge, pp. 164–78.

Forna, Aminatta (1992) 'Pornography and racism: sexualizing oppression and inciting hatred' in C. Itzin (ed.), *Pornography: Women, violence and civil liberties.* Oxford: Oxford University Press.

Freeman, Jo (1971) 'The women's liberation movement: its origins, structures and ideas', <http://www.jofreeman.com/feminism/liberationmov.htm> (accessed 10 June 2012).

—— (1975a) 'The politics of women's liberation', <http://www.jofreeman.com/books/pwl. htm#TOC> (accessed 10 June 2012).

—— (ed.) (1975b) *Women: A feminist perspective,* <http://www.jofreeman.com/books/ women1.htm#Contents> (accessed 10 June 2012).

—— (2003) 'The women's movement' in J. Goodwin and J. M. Jasper (eds), *The Social Movements Reader: Cases and concepts.* Oxford: Blackwell. pp. 22–31.

Freire, Paulo (1973) *Education for Critical Consciousness.* New York NY: Continuum Publishing Company.

French, Marilyn (1992) *The War against Women.* London: Penguin.

Friedan, Betty (1963) *The Feminine Mystique.* New York NY: W. W. Norton and Co.

—— (1966) 'NOW Statement of Purpose', <http://www.now.org/history/purpos66.html> (accessed 20 December 2011).

Frye, Marilyn (1983a) *The Politics of Reality: Essays in feminist theory.* Berkeley CA: Crossing Press.

—— (1983b) 'Oppression' in *The Politics of Reality: Essays in feminist theory.* Berkeley CA: Crossing Press, pp. 1–16.

—— (1983c) 'A note on anger' in *The Politics of Reality: Essays in feminist theory.* Berkeley, CA: Crossing Press, pp. 84–94.

BIBLIOGRAPHY

—— (1983d) 'Some reflections on separatism and power' in *The Politics of Reality: Essays in feminist theory.* Berkeley, CA: Crossing Press, pp. 95–109.

Funnell, Nina (2011) 'Sexting and peer-to-peer porn' in M. Tankard Reist and A. Bray (eds), *Big Porn Inc: Exposing the harms of the global pornography industry.* Melbourne: Spinifex Press, pp. 34–40.

Gallego, Aina (2007) *Inequality in Political Participation: Contemporary patterns in European countries.* Irvine CA: Center for the Study of Democracy, University of California, <http://escholarship.org/uc/item/3545w14v> (accessed 25 July 2010).

Galtung, Johan (1990) 'Cultural violence', *Journal of Peace Research* 27 (3): 291–305.

Gamson, William A. (2007) 'Bystanders, public opinion and the media' in D. A. Snow, S. Soule and H. Kriesi (eds), *The Blackwell Companion to Social Movements.* Oxford: Blackwell, pp. 342–61.

Gelb, Joyce (1986) 'Feminism in Britain: politics without power?' in D. Dahlerup (ed.), *The New Women's Movement.* London: Sage, pp. 103–22.

Genz, Stéphanie (2009) *Postfemininities in Popular Culture.* Basingstoke: Palgrave Macmillan.

George, Sue (1988) 'Censorship and hypocrisy: some issues surrounding pornography that feminism has ignored' in G. Chester and J. Dickey (eds), *Feminism and Censorship: The current debate.* Bridport, Dorset: Prism Press.

George, Susan (1999) 'A short history of neoliberalism', paper delivered at conference on 'Economic Sovereignty in a Globalising World', Bangkok, 24–26 March.

Gill, Rosalind (2003) 'From sexual objectification to sexual subjectification: the resexualisation of women's bodies in the media', *Feminist Media Studies* 3 (1): 99–106.

—— (2007a) 'Critical respect: the difficulties and dilemmas of agency and "choice" for feminism: a reply to Duits and van Zoonen', *European Journal of Women's Studies* 14 (1): 69–80.

—— (2007b) *Gender and the Media.* Cambridge: Polity Press.

—— (2008) 'Empowerment/sexism: figuring female sexual agency in contemporary advertising', *Feminism and Psychology* 18 (1): 35–60.

—— (2009a) 'Beyond the "sexualization of culture" thesis: an intersectional analysis of "sixpacks", "midriffs" and "hot lesbians" in advertising', *Sexualities* 12 (2): 137–60.

—— (2009b) 'Supersexualize me! Advertising and the midriffs' in F. Attwood (ed.), *Mainstreaming Sex: The sexualisation of culture.* London: I. B. Tauris, pp. 93–110.

Gillies, Val and Yvonne Roberts (2010) 'Including and excluding: exploring gendered and racialised constructions of risk and vulnerability in the classroom', paper presented at the conference on 'Diversity and Social Inclusion', London South Bank University. 18 March.

Gilligan, Carol (1987) 'Woman's place in man's life cycle' in Sandra Harding (ed.), *Feminism and Methodology.* Milton Keynes: Open University Press, pp. 57–73.

Gillis, Stacey, Gillian Howie and Rebecca Munford (eds) (2007) *Third Wave Feminism: A critical exploration.* Basingstoke: Palgrave Macmillan.

Girlguiding UK/ Mental Health Foundation (2008) 'A generation under stress?', report, <http://www.mentalhealth.org.uk/publications/?entryid5=62067> (accessed 5 July 2010).

Giugni, Marco (2007) 'Personal and biographical consequences' in D. A. Snow, S. Soule and H. Kriesi (eds), *The Blackwell Companion to Social Movements.* Oxford: Blackwell. pp. 489–507.

Goffman, Erving (1974). *Frame Analysis: An essay on the organisation of experience.* New York NY: Harper Colophon.

Goodwin, Jeff and James M. Jasper (eds) (2003) *The Social Movements Reader: Cases and concepts.* Oxford: Blackwell.

Goodwin, Jeff, James M. Jasper and Francesca Polletta (2007) 'Emotional dimensions of social movements' in D. A. Snow, S. Soule and H. Kriesi (eds), *The Blackwell Companion to Social Movements.* Oxford: Blackwell, pp. 413–32.

Gorna, Robin (1993) 'Delightful visions: from anti-porn to eroticizing safer sex' in L. Segal and M. McIntosh (eds), *Sex Exposed: Sexuality and the pornography debate*. New Brunswick NJ: Rutgers University Press.

Gornick, Vivian (2000) 'Consciousness' in B. A. Crow (ed.), *Radical Feminism: A documentary reader*. New York NY: New York University Press, pp. 287–300.

Gossett, Jennifer Lynn and Sarah Byrne (2002) '"Click here": a content analysis of internet rape sites', *Gender and Society* 16 (5): 689–709.

Greer, Germaine ([1970] 1993) *The Female Eunuch*. London: Flamingo.

—— (2000) *The Whole Woman*. London: Anchor.

Griffin, Gabriele (ed.) (1995) *Feminist Activism in the 1990s*. London: Taylor and Francis.

—— (ed.) (2005a) *Doing Women's Studies: Employment opportunities, personal impacts and social consequences*. London: Zed Books.

—— (2005b) 'The institutionalisation of Women's Studies in Europe' in G. Griffin (ed.), *Doing Women's Studies: Employment opportunities, personal impacts and social consequences*. London: Zed Books, pp. 89–110.

Griffin, G., E. Blimlinger and T. Gerstenauer (2003) *The Institutionalization of Women's Studies in Europe: Findings from an EU-funded research project on women's studies and women's employment*. Brussels: European Commission.

Griffin, Susan (1981) *Pornography and Silence: Culture's revenge against women*. London: The Women's Press.

—— (1984) *Woman and Nature: The roaring inside her*. London: The Women's Press.

Guardian (2006) 'The legacy of Jane Longhurst', *The Guardian*, 1 July 2006, <http://www.guardian.co.uk/uk/2006/sep/01/ukcrime.gender> (accessed 8 July 2012).

Guinness, Molly (2011) 'Force-fed and beaten – life for women in jail', *The Independent*, 18 December, <http://www.independent.co.uk/news/world/politics/forcefed-and-beaten--life-for-women-in-jail-6278849.html> (accessed 29 February 2012).

Hanisch, Carol ([1969] 2006) 'The personal is political', <http://www.carolhanisch.org/CHwritings/PIP.html> (accessed 29 February 2012).

Hanmer, Jalna and Mary Maynard (eds) (1987) *Women, Violence and Social Control*. London: Macmillan.

Haraway, Donna (1991) 'Situated knowledges: the science question in feminism and the privilege of partial perspective' in *Simians, Cyborgs, and Women: The reinvention of nature*. New York NY: Routledge, pp. 183–201.

Harding, Sandra (ed.) (1987) *Feminism and Methodology*. Milton Keynes: Open University Press.

—— (2003) 'How standpoint methodology informs philosophy of social science', paper presented at the Women's Studies Symposium, University College Cork, 4 April.

Hardy, Simon (2008) 'The pornography of reality', *Sexualities* 11 (1/2): 60–4.

—— (2009) 'The new pornographies: representation or reality?' in F. Attwood (ed.), *Mainstreaming Sex: The sexualisation of culture*. London: I. B. Tauris, pp. 3–19.

Harne, Lynne and Elaine Miller (eds) (1996) *All the Rage: Reasserting radical lesbian feminism*. London: The Women's Press.

Harper, Catherine and Joan Skinner (2003) Presentation for the Scottish Women Against Pornography (SWAP) at the conference on 'Sexual Violence: Issues and Responses Across Europe', Rape Crisis Network Europe, Dublin, 3 October.

Harris, A. (2004) *Future Girl: Young women in the twenty-first century*. London: Routledge.

Hartsock, Nancy (1987) 'The feminist standpoint: developing the ground for a specifically feminist historical materialism' in Sandra Harding (ed.), *Feminism and Methodology*. Milton Keynes: Open University Press, pp. 157–80.

Hatton, Erin and Mary Nell Trautner (2011) 'Equal opportunity objectification? The sexualization of men and women on the cover of *Rolling Stone*', *Sexuality and Culture* 15 (3): 256–78.

Henry, Astrid (2004) *Not My Mother's Sister: Intergenerational conflict and thirdwave feminism*. Bloomington IN: Indiana University Press.

Hercus, Cheryl (1999) 'Identity, emotion, and feminist collective action', *Gender and Society* 13 (1) (February): 34–55.

Herzog, Eleanor (2012) 'There is no homogeneous "stripper tragedy"', *The Independent*, 17 January, <http://blogs.independent.co.uk/2012/01/17/there-is-no-homogen eous-%E2%80%9Cstripper-tragedy%E2%80%9D/> (accessed 29 February 212).

Heywood, Leslie and Jennifer Drake (eds) (1997) *Third Wave Agenda: Being feminist, doing feminism.* Minneapolis MN: University of Minnesota Press.

Hill Collins, Patricia (1989) 'The social construction of black feminist thought', *Signs* 14 (4): 745–73.

HMSO (1959) *Obscene Publications Act* (1959). London: Her Majesty's Stationery Office.

Hochschild, Arlie Russell (1975) 'The sociology of feeling and emotion: selected possibilities' in M. Millman and R. Moss Kanter (eds), *Another Voice.* Garden City NY: Anchor Books.

Hoff Sommers, Christine (1995) *Who Stole Feminism? How women have betrayed women.* New York NY: Touchstone.

Holland, Samantha and Feona Attwood (2009) 'Keeping fit in six inch heels: the mainstreaming of pole dancing' in F. Attwood (ed.), *Mainstreaming Sex: The sexualization of Western culture.* London: I. B. Tauris, pp. 165–81.

Holland, Janet, Caroline Ramazanoglu, Sue Sharpe and Rachel Thompson (1998) *The Male in the Head: Young people, heterosexuality and power.* London: Tufnell Press.

Hollibaugh, Amber (with Deirdre English and Gayle Rubin) (1987) 'Talking sex: a conversation on sexuality and feminism' in *Feminist Review* (ed.), *Sexuality: A reader.* London: Virago, pp. 63–81.

Holyoak, Rose (2008) '"Good-enough" feminists? A case study of activism in one third-wave feminist group'. Unpublished BA dissertation, University of Derby.

hooks, bell (1982) *Ain't I a Woman: Black women and feminism.* Boston MA: South End Press.

—— (1995) *Killing Rage: Ending racism.* New York NY: H. Holt and Co.

—— (1998) 'Selling hot pussy: representations of black female sexuality in the cultural marketplace' in R. Weitz (ed.), *The Politics of Women's Bodies: Sexuality, appearance, and behaviour.* Oxford: Oxford University Press.

Horvath, Miranda, Peter Hegarty, Suzannah Tyler and Sophie Mansfield (2011) '"Lights on at the end of the party": are lads' mags mainstreaming dangerous sexism?' *British Journal of Psychology*, article first published online (early view), Wiley Online, 13 December 2011.

Humm, Maggie (ed.) (1992) *Feminisms: A reader.* Hemel Hempstead: Harvester Wheatsheaf.

Hunt, Scott and Robert Benford (2007) 'Collective identity, solidarity and commitment' in D. A. Snow, S. Soule and H. Kriesi (eds), *The Blackwell Companion to Social Movements.* Oxford: Blackwell, pp. 433–58.

Hur, M. H. (2006) 'Empowerment in terms of theoretical perspectives: exploring a typology of the process and components across disciplines', *Journal of Community Psychology*, 34: 523–40.

Itzin, Catherine (1988) 'Sex and censorship: the political implications' in G. Chester and J. Dickey, *Feminism and Censorship: The current debate.* Bridport, Dorset: Prism Press.

—— (1992a) *Pornography: Women, violence and civil liberties.* Oxford: Oxford University Press.

—— (1992b) 'Legislating against pornography without censorship' in C. Itzin (ed.), *Pornography: Women, violence and civil liberties.* Oxford: Oxford University Press, pp. 401–34.

Jarayatne, T. E. and A. Stewart (1991) 'Quantitative and qualitative methods in social science: current feminist issues and practical strategies' in M. M. Fonow and J. A. Cook (eds), *Beyond Methodology: Feminist scholarship as lived research.* Bloomington, IN: Indiana University Press.

Jasper, James M. (1997) *The Art of Moral Protest*. Chicago IL: University of Chicago Press.
—— (2003) 'The emotions of protest' in J. Goodwin and J. M. Jasper (eds), *The Social Movements Reader: Cases and concepts*. Oxford: Blackwell, pp. 153–62.
Jeffreys, Sheila (1988) 'The censoring of revolutionary feminism' in G. Chester and J. Dickey, *Feminism and censorship: The current debate*. Bridport, Dorset: Prism Press, pp. 133–49.
—— (1990) *Anticlimax*. London: Women's Press.
—— (1993) *The Lesbian Heresy*. London: The Women's Press.
—— (1994) 'The queer disappearance of lesbian sexuality in the academy', *Women's Studies International Forum* 17 (5): 459–72.
—— (1996) 'How orgasm politics has hijacked the women's movement' in *On the Issues*, Spring, <http://www.ontheissuesmagazine.com/1996spring/s96orgasm.php> (accessed 29 February 2012).
—— (2005) *Beauty and Misogyny: Harmful cultural practices in the West*. London: Routledge.
—— (2009) *The Industrial Vagina: The political economy of the global sex trade*. Routledge: London.
Jensen, Robert (1998) 'Introduction: pornographic dodges and distortions' in G. Dines, R. Jensen and A. Russo (eds), *Pornography: The production and consumption of inequality*. London: Routledge, pp. 1–8.
—— (2004a) 'Cruel to be hard: men and pornography', *Sexual Assault Report* (January/February): 33–48.
—— (2004b) 'Pornography and sexual violence', National Electronic Network on Violence against Women (VAWnet) Applied Research Forum (July), available online from National Resource Centre on Domestic Violence, <http://www.vawnet.org/summary.php?doc_id=418&find_type=web_desc_AR>.
—— (2007) *Getting Off: Pornography and the end of masculinity*. New York NY: South End Press.
—— (2010) 'Pornography is what the end of the world looks like' in K. Boyle (ed.), *Everyday Pornography*. London: Routledge, pp. 105–13.
Jensen, Robert and Gail Dines (1998) 'The content of mass-marketed pornography' in G. Dines, R. Jensen and A. Russo (eds), *Pornography: The production and consumption of inequality*. London: Routledge, pp. 65–100.
Johnson, Jennifer (2010) 'To catch a curious clicker: a social network analysis of the online pornography industry' in K. Boyle (ed.), *Everyday Pornography*. London: Routledge, pp. 147–63.
—— (2011) 'The Janus face of the online pornography industry', presentation to the conference on 'Challenging Porn Culture', London, 3 December 2011.
Johnson, Hank and Bert Klandermans (eds) (1995) *Social Movements and Culture*. London: University College London (UCL) Press.
Jones, Beverly and Judith Brown (1968) 'Towards a female liberation movement', pamphlet, Boston MA: New England Free Press.
Juffer, J. (1998) *At Home with Pornography: Women, sexuality, and everyday life*. New York NY: New York University Press.
Kappeler, Susanne (1986) *The Pornography of Representation*. Oxford: Polity Press.
Karp, Marcelle and Debbie Stoller (1999) *The BUST Guide to the New Girl Order*. London: Penguin.
Katyachild, Maria, Sheila Jeffreys, Sandra McNeill, Jan Winterlake and Anon (1985) 'Pornography' in S. McNeill and d. rhodes, *Women against Violence against Women*. London: Onlywomen Press.
Keith, Lierre (2011a) 'We are disturbing the war against women! A history of the feminist anti-pornography movement', presentation at the Stop Porn Culture Conference, Wheelock College, Boston, 29 June.
—— (2011b) 'Liberals and radicals' in A. McBay, L. Keith and D. Jensen, *Deep Green*

Resistance: Strategy to save the planet. New York NY: Seven Stories Press, pp. 61–111.

Kelly, Liz (1988a) *Surviving Sexual Violence*. Minneapolis MN: University of Minnesota Press.

—— (1988b) 'The US ordinances: censorship or radical law reform' in G. Chester and J. Dickey (eds), *Feminism and Censorship: The current debate*. Bridport, Dorset: Prism Press.

Kelly, Liz, Linda Regan and Sheila Burton (1994) 'Researching women's lives or studying women's oppression? Reflections on what constitutes feminist research' in M. Maynard and J. Purvis (eds), *Researching Women's Lives from a Feminist Perspective*. London: Taylor and Francis.

—— (1995) 'Defending the indefensible? Quantitative methods and feminist research' in J. Holland and M. Blair (eds), *Debates and Issues in Feminist Research and Pedagogy*. Clevedon: Multilingual Matters/Open University.

Kemp, Sandra and Judith Squires (1997) *Feminisms*. Oxford: Oxford University Press.

Kendrick, Walter (1997) *The Secret Museum: Pornography in modern culture*. Berkeley and Los Angeles CA: University of California Press.

Kimmel, Michael (2008) *Guyland: The perilous world where boys become men*. New York NY: HarperCollins.

King, Mary (1987) *Freedom Song: A personal story of the civil rights movement*. New York NY: Morrow.

Kinser, Amber E. (2004) 'Negotiating spaces for/through third-wave feminism', *National Women's Studies Association Journal* 16 (3) (Autumn): 124–53.

Kitzinger, Celia and Rachel Perkins (1993) *Changing our Minds: Lesbian feminism and psychology*. London: Onlywomen Press.

Klandermans, Bert (2003) 'Disengaging from movements' in J. Goodwin and J. M. Jasper (eds), *The Social Movements Reader: Cases and concepts*. Oxford. Blackwell.

Klar, Malter and Tim Kasser (2009) 'Some benefits of being an activist: measuring activism and its role in psychological well-being', *Political Psychology* 30 (5): 755–77.

Koedt, Anne (1968) *The Myth of the Vaginal Orgasm*. Adelaide: Women's Liberation Movement.

Koopmans, Ruud (2007) 'Protest in time and space: the evolution of waves of contention' in D. A. Snow, S. Soule and H. Kriesi (eds), *The Blackwell Companion to Social Movements*. Oxford: Blackwell, pp. 19–46.

Kriesi, Hanspeter (2007) 'Political context and opportunity' in D. A. Snow, S. Soule and H. Kriesi (eds), *The Blackwell Companion to Social Movements*. Oxford: Blackwell, pp. 67–90.

Lai, Alexis (2011) 'Report: Ryanair considers serving in-flight porn', CNN, 10 November, <http://business.blogs.cnn.com/2011/11/10/report-ryanair-considers-serving-in-flight-porn/> (accessed 29 February 2012).

Lakhani, Nina (2008) 'Farewell to "predictable, tiresome and dreary" women's studies', *The Independent*, 23 March, <http://www.independent.co.uk/news/education/education-news/farewell-to-predictable-tiresome-and-dreary-womens-studies-799631.html> (accessed 8 August 2010).

Langton, Rae (1995) 'Sexual solipsism', *Philosophical Topics* 23 (2): 181–219.

—— (1997) 'Love and solipsism' in R. E. Lamb (ed.), *Love Analysed*. Boulder CO: Westview Press, pp. 123–52.

—— (1999) 'Pornography: a liberal's unfinished business', *Canadian Journal of Law and Jurisprudence* 12 (1): 109–33.

—— (2009) *Sexual Solipsism: Philosophical essays on pornography and objectification*. Oxford: Oxford University Press.

Langton, Rae and Caroline West (1999) 'Scorekeeping in a pornographic language game', <http://web.mit.edu/langton/www/pubs/Scorekeeping.pdf> (accessed 8 August 2012).

Lawrence, D. H. ([1928] 1960) *Lady Chatterley's Lover*. Penguin: Harmondsworth.

Leahy, Michael (2008) *Porn Nation: Conquering America's #1 addiction*. Chicago IL: Northfield Publishing.

Lederer, Laura (ed.) (1980) *Take Back the Night: Women on pornography*. New York NY: William and Morrow.

Leeds Revolutionary Feminist Group (1981) *Political Lesbianism: The case against heterosexuality*. London: Onlywomen Press.

Leidholt, Dorchen and Janice Raymond (eds) (1990) *The Sexual Liberals and the Attack on Feminism*. Oxford: Pergamon Press.

Lennox, Annie (2011) Panel address to *Women of the World* Festival, Southbank Centre, London, 11–13 March.

Letherby, Gayle (2003) *Feminist Research in Theory and Practice*. Buckingham: Open University Press.

Levin, Diane E. and Jean Kilbourne (2008) *So Sexy, So Soon: The new sexualized childhood and what parents can do to protect their kids*. New York NY: Ballantine.

Levy, Ariel (2005) *Female Chauvinist Pigs: Women and the rise of raunch culture*. New York NY: Simon and Schuster.

Liberman, Rachel (2009) 'Defining feminist pornography as an extension of the Third Wave', paper presented at conference on 'Porn Cultures: Regulation, Political Economy, Technology', Leeds, 15–16 June.

Lister, David (2009) 'So why the rape joke, Ricky?' *The Independent*, 29 August, <http://www.independent.co.uk/opinion/columnists/david-lister/david-lister-so-why-the-rape-joke-ricky-1778987.html> (accessed 3 September 2009).

Logan, Brian (2009) 'The new offenders of standup comedy', *The Guardian*, 27 July, <http://www.guardian.co.uk/stage/2009/jul/27/comedy-standup-new-offenders> (accessed 3 September 2009).

Long, Julia (2011) 'OBJECT! The re-emergence of feminist anti-pornography activism'. Unpublished doctoral thesis, London South Bank University.

Longford Committee (1971) *Inquiry and Report on Pornography*. London: Coronet.

Lorde, Audre (1984a) *Sister Outsider*. Berkeley CA: The Crossing Press.

—— (1984b) 'The transformation of silence into language and action' in A. Lorde, *Sister Outsider*. Berkeley CA: The Crossing Press, pp. 40–4.

—— (1984c) 'Uses of the erotic' in A. Lorde, *Sister Outsider*. Berkeley CA: The Crossing Press, pp. 53–9.

—— (1984d) 'The master's tools will never dismantle the master's house' in A. Lorde, *Sister Outsider*. Berkeley CA: The Crossing Press, pp. 110–13.

—— (1984e) 'Age, race, sex and class: women redefining difference' in A. Lorde, *Sister Outsider*. Berkeley CA: The Crossing Press, pp. 114–23.

—— (1988) *A Burst of Light: Essays*. New York NY: Firebrand Books.

Lovenduski, Joni and Vicki Randall (1993) *Contemporary Feminist Politics: Women and power in Britain*. Oxford: Oxford University Press.

MacKinnon, Catharine A. (1989) *Toward a Feminist Theory of the State*. Cambridge MA: Harvard University Press.

—— (1993) 'Feminism, Marxism, method and the state: toward feminist jurisprudence', *Signs* 8 (4): 635–58.

—— (1994) *Only Words*. London: Harper Collins.

Maddison, Stephen (2009) '"Choke on it, bitch!": porn studies, extreme gonzo and the mainstreaming of hardcore' in F. Attwood (ed.), *Mainstreaming Sex: The sexualisation of culture*. London: I. B. Tauris, pp. 37–55.

Maiguashca, Bice (2006) 'Making feminist sense of the "anti-globalisation movement": some reflections on methodology and method', *Global Society* 20 (2): 115–36.

Malamuth, N. and B. Spinner (1980) 'A longitudinal content analysis of sexual violence in the best-selling erotic magazines', *The Journal of Sex Research* 16: 226–37.

Maltz, Wendy and Larry Maltz (2008) *The Porn Trap: The essential guide to overcoming problems caused by pornography*. New York NY: Harper.

BIBLIOGRAPHY

Marshall, Penny (Director) (2009) *Online Damage: Porn in the twenty-first century*, Radio 4, 13 January.

Martinson, Jane (2012) 'Annie Lennox: "The world has become more sexualised"', The Guardian, 5 March 2012, <http://www.guardian.co.uk/lifeandstyle/2012/mar/05/annie-lennox-world-more-sexualised> (accessed 8 July 2012).

Marx Ferree, Myra and Carol McClurg Mueller (2007) 'Feminism and the women's movement: a global perspective' in D. A. Snow, S. Soule and H. Kriesi (eds), *The Blackwell Companion to Social Movements*. Oxford: Blackwell, pp. 576–607.

Mason, Jennifer ([1996] 2002) *Qualitative Researching*. London: Sage.

Mason, Rowena (2011) 'Miss Venezuela crowned Miss World 2011, but 200 protest outside', *The Telegraph*, 7 November 2011, <http://www.telegraph.co.uk/news/uknews/8873423/Miss-Venezuela-crowned-Miss-World-2011-but-200-protest-outside.html> (accessed 8 July 2012).

Maynard, Mary (1994) 'Methods, practice and epistemology: the debate about feminism and research' in M. Maynard and J. Purvis (eds), *Researching Women's Lives from a Feminist Perspective*. London: Taylor and Francis.

McAdam, Doug (1982) *Political Process and the Development of Black Insurgency*. Chicago IL: University of Chicago Press.

—— (1988) *Freedom Summer*. New York NY: Oxford University Press.

—— (1989) 'The biographical consequences of activism', *American Sociological Review* 54 (5): 744–60.

—— (1994) 'Culture and social movements' in E. Laraña, H. Johnson and J. Gusfield (eds), *New Social Movements*. Philadelphia, PA: Temple University Press, pp. 36–57.

—— (2003) 'Recruits to civil rights activism' in J. Goodwin and J. M. Jasper (eds), *The Social Movements Reader: Cases and concepts*. Oxford: Blackwell, pp. 55–63.

McCabe, Janice, Emily Fairchild, Liz Grauerholz, Bernice A. Pescosolido and Daniel Tope (2011) 'Gender in twentieth-century children's books: patterns of disparity in titles and central characters', *Gender and Society* 25 (2): 197–226.

McElroy, Wendy (1995) *XXX: A Woman's Right to Pornography*. New York NY: St Martin's Press.

McGlynn, Clare (2010) 'Marginalizing feminism? Debating extreme pornography laws in public and policy discourse' in K. Boyle (ed.), *Everyday Pornography*. London: Routledge, pp. 190–202.

McGlynn, Clare, Erica Rackley and Nicole Westmarland (eds) (2007) 'Positions on the politics of porn: a debate on government plans to criminalise the possession of extreme pornography', report, Durham University, Durham.

McGrady, Mike and Linda Lovelace (1980) *Ordeal: An autobiography by Linda Lovelace*. New York NY: Citadel Press.

McIntosh, Mary (1993) 'Liberalism and the contradictions of sexual politics' in L. Segal and M. McIntosh (eds), *Sex Exposed: Sexuality and the pornography debate*. New Brunswick NJ: Rutgers University Press, pp. 155–68.

McKee, Alan (2009) 'Does pornography damage young people?', paper presented at conference on 'Porn Cultures: Regulation, Political Economy, Technology', Leeds, 15–16 June.

McLellan, Betty (2010) *Unspeakable: A feminist ethics of speech*. Townsville, Australia: OtherWise Publications.

—— (2011) 'Pornography as free speech: but is it fair?' in M. Tankard Reist and A. Bray (eds), *Big Porn Inc: Exposing the harms of the global pornography industry*. Melbourne: Spinifex Press, pp. 249–56.

McLune, Jennifer (2006) 'Celie's revenge: hip-hop's betrayal of black women', *Said It* 4 (1), <http://saidit.org/archives/jan06/article4.html> (accessed 29 February 2012).

McNair, Brian (1996) *Mediated Sex: Pornography and postmodern culture*. London and New York NY: Hodder Arnold.

—— (2002) *Striptease Culture: Sex, media and the democratisation of desire*. London: Routledge.

231

—— (2009) 'From porn chic to porn fear: the return of the repressed?' in F. Attwood (ed.), *Mainstreaming Sex: The sexualisation of Western culture*. London: I. B. Tauris, pp. 55–73.

McNeill, Sandra (1985) Commentary on contribution in S. McNeill and d. rhodes, *Women against Violence against Women*. London: Onlywomen Press.

McNeill, S. and d. rhodes (1985) *Women against Violence against Women*. London: Onlywomen Press.

McRobbie, Angela (2009) *The Aftermath of Feminism*. London: Sage.

Melucci, Alberto (1988) 'Getting involved: identity and mobilization in social movements', *Research in Social Movements, Conflicts and Change* 1: 329–48.

—— (1989). *Nomads of the Present: Social movements and individual needs in contemporary society*. London: Hutchinson.

Merck, Mandy (1993) 'From Minneapolis to Westminster' in L. Segal and M. McIntosh (eds), *Sex Exposed: Sexuality and the pornography debate*. New Brunswick NJ: Rutgers University Press.

Merskin, Debra (2004) 'Reviving Lolita? A media literacy examination of sexual portrayals of girls in fashion advertising', *American Behavioral Scientist* 48 (1) (September): 119–29.

Mesure, Susie (2009) 'The march of the new feminists', *The Independent*, 29 March, <http://www.independent.co.uk/news/uk/home-news/the-march-of-the-new-feminists-1830514.html> (accessed 29 March 2009).

Millett, Kate (1970) *Sexual Politics*. London: Virago.

Miriam, Kathy (2005) 'Stopping the traffic in women: power, agency and abolition in feminist debates over sex-trafficking', *Journal of Social Philosophy* 36 (1): 1–17.

Mitchell, Juliet (1966) *Women: The longest revolution*. Boston MA: New England Free Press.

Modleski, Tania (1991) *Feminism without Women: Culture and criticism in a 'post-feminist' age*. New York NY: Routledge.

Mohanty, Chandra Talpade (1992) 'Feminist encounters: locating the politics of experience' in M. Barrett and A. Phillips (eds), *Destabilising Theory: Contemporary feminist debates*. Stanford CA: Stanford University Press, pp. 74–92.

Monbiot, George (2011) 'This bastardised 'libertarianism' makes freedom an instrument of oppression', *The Guardian*, 19 December 2011, <http://www.guardian.co.uk/commentisfree/2011/dec/19/bastardised-libertarianism-makes-freedom-oppression> (accessed 8 July 2012).

Moore, Wendy (1988) 'There should be a law against it . . . shouldn't there?' in G. Chester and J. Dickey (eds), *Feminism and Censorship: The current debate*. Bridport, Dorset: Prism Press, pp. 140–50.

Morgan, Robin (ed.) (1970) *Sisterhood is Powerful: An anthology of writings from the women's liberation movement*. New York NY: Vintage Press.

—— (1974) 'Theory and practice: pornography and rape' in R. Morgan, *Going Too Far: The personal chronicle of a feminist* (1977). New York NY: Random House.

Mott, Rebecca (2012) 'Being made a porn-doll', <http://rmott62.wordpress.com/2012/03/12/being-made-a-porn-doll/> (accessed 12 March 2012).

Munford, Rebecca (2009) 'BUST-ing the third wave: barbies, blow jobs and girlie feminism' in F. Attwood (ed.) (2009) *Mainstreaming Sex: The sexualisation of culture*. London: I. B. Tauris, pp. 183–98.

Murray, Andrew (2009) 'New extreme porn law will be "impossible to enforce"', <http://www2.lse.ac.uk/researchAndExpertise/researchHighlights/Law/new ExtremePornLaw.aspx> (accessed 29 February 2012).

Nagy Hesse-Biber, Sharlene (2007) 'The practice of feminist in-depth interviewing' in S. Nagy Hesse-Biber and P. L. Leavy (eds), *Feminist Research Practice*. Thousand Oaks CA: Sage, pp. 111–48.

Nagy Hesse-Biber, Sharlene and Patricia Lina Leavy (eds) (2007) *Feminist Research*

BIBLIOGRAPHY

Practice. Thousand Oaks CA: Sage.

Nakasatomi, Hiroshi (2011) 'When rape becomes a game: *RapeLay* and the pornification of crime' in M. Tankard Reist and A. Bray (eds), *Big Porn Inc: Exposing the harms of the global pornography industry.* Melbourne: Spinifex Press, pp. 167–70.

Naples, Nancy (2003) *Feminism and Method: Ethnography, discourse analysis and activist research.* New York NY: Routledge.

Naples, Nancy and Manisha Desai (eds) (2002) *Women's Activism and Globalisation: Linking local struggle and transnational politics.* New York NY: Routledge.

National Union of Teachers (2007) *Growing Up in a Material World: Charter on commercialisation.* London: Ruskin Press.

Norden, Barbara (1990) 'Campaign against pornography', *Feminist Review* 35 (Summer).

Norris, Sian (2008) 'Let's make some noise', *The Guardian*, 26 November 2008.

Northern Rock Foundation (2010) 'Sexual exploitation in the north east: prevalence and practice', report, Newcastle, 20 January.

NSPCC (National Society for the Prevention of Cruelty to Children) (2008) 'Response to the impact of the commercial world on children's wellbeing', <http://www.nspcc.net/Inform/policyandpublicaffairs/consultations/2008/ImpactOfTheCommercialWorld_wdf58611.pdf> (accessed 23 July 2010).

Nussbaum, Martha (1995) 'Objectification', *Philosophy and Public Affairs* 24 (4): 249–91.

Oakley, Ann (1981) 'Interviewing women: a contradiction in terms' in H. Roberts (ed.) *Doing Feminist Research.* London: Routledge and Kegan Paul.

—— (2000) *Experiments in Knowing: Gender and method in the social sciences.* New York NY: New Press.

Oakley, Ann and Juliet Mitchell (eds) (1997) *Who's Afraid of Feminism? Seeing through the backlash.* London: Hamish Hamilton.

Oberschall, Anthony (1973) *Social Conflict and Social Movements.* Englewood Cliffs NJ: Prentice-Hall.

OBJECT (2008) 'A Growing Tide update: the need to reform licensing of lapdancing clubs', <http://www.object.org.uk/files/A%20Growing%20Tide%20Update%20Dec%202008.pdf> (accessed 11 June 2009).

—— (2009) 'Joining up the dots: Why urgent action is needed to tackle the sexualisation of women and girls in the media and popular culture', <http://www.object.org.uk/files/Joining%20up%20the%20dots%284%29.pdf> (accessed 8 July 2012).

O'Hara, Jennie and Hazel Kent (2010) 'A (brief) feminist critique of Object' (statement from Riveters Collective, University of Manchester Student Union), 'Young Feminism' PhD Seminar, University of Manchester, 11 May.

Olsen, Tillie (1978) *Silences.* New York NY: Delacorte.

Olson, Mancur (1971) *The Logic of Collective Action.* Cambridge MA: Harvard University Press.

O'Reilly, Karen (2005) *Ethnographic Methods.* Oxford. Routledge.

Orbach, Susie (2009) *Bodies.* London: Profile Books.

—— (2010) 'The new feminists: still fighting', *The Observer*, 15 August.

Ortner, Sherry B. (1995) 'Resistance and the problem of ethnographic refusal', *Comparative Studies in Society and History* 37 (1): 173–93.

Ozimek, John (2008) '"Extreme porn" law could criminalise millions', 25 April, <http://www.theregister.co.uk/2008/04/25/justice_bill_extreme_pron/> (accessed 29 February 2012).

Paasonen, Susanna (2007) 'Strange bedfellows: pornography, affect and feminist reading', *Feminist Theory* 8 (1): 43–57.

Paasonen, Susanna, Kaarina Nikunen and Laura Saarenmaa (eds) (2007) *Pornification: Sex and sexuality in media culture.* Oxford: Berg.

Paglia, Camille (1993) *Sex, Art and American Culture.* London. Viking.

Palmer, Sue (2006) *Toxic Childhood: How modern life is damaging our children and what we can do about it.* London: Orion.

Papadopoulos, Linda (2010) 'Sexualisation of young people', government review, Home Office, London.

Parmar, Pratibha (1988) 'Rage and desire: confronting pornography' in G. Chester and J. Dickey (eds), *Feminism and Censorship: The current debate*. Bridport, Dorset: Prism Press.

Parvez, Fareen Z. (2006) 'The labor of pleasure: how perceptions of emotional labor impact women's enjoyment of pornography', *Gender and Society* 20 (5): 605–31.

Patterson, Zabet (2004) 'Going on-line: consuming pornography in the digital era' in L. Williams (ed.), *Porn Studies*. Durham NC: Duke University Press, pp. 105–23.

Paul, Pamela (2005) *Pornified: How pornography is transforming our lives, our relationships and our families*. New York NY: Times Books.

Pelling, Rowan (director) (2008) *The Crisis on the Top Shelf*. BBC Radio 4, 4 November.

Phillips, Anne (1998) *Feminism and Politics*. Oxford: Oxford University Press.

Picker, Miguel and Chyng Sun (directors) (2008) *The Price of Pleasure: Pornography, sexuality and relationships*. DVD, Open Lens Media.

Pizzorno, Alessandro (1978) 'Political exchange and collective identity in industrial conflict' in C. Crouch and A. Pizzorno (eds), *The Resurgence of Class Conflict in Western Europe*. New York NY: Holmes and Meier, pp. 277–98.

Plunkett, John (2012) 'Sherlock's nude "dominatrix" says she found role "empowering"', *The Guardian*, 10 January, <http://www.guardian.co.uk/media/2012/jan/10/sherlock-nude-dominatrix> (accessed 29 February 2012).

Polletta, Francesca and James M. Jasper (2001) 'Collective identity and social movements', *Annual Review of Sociology* 27: 283–305.

Power, Nina (2009) *One-Dimensional Woman*. Ropley: Zero Books.

Press Association (2004) 'A failed musician with a taste for violence', 4 February, <http://www.guardian.co.uk/uk/2004/feb/04/ukcrime1?INTCMP=ILCNETTXT3487> (accessed 29 February 2012).

—— (2006) 'The legacy of Jane Longhurst', 1 September, <http://www.guardian.co.uk/uk/2006/sep/01/ukcrime.gender?INTCMP=SRCH> (accessed 29 February 2012).

Pritchard, Jane (2010) 'The sex work debate', *International Socialism* 125 (Winter): 161–82.

Radicalesbians (1971) 'The woman-identified woman' in Anne Koedt (ed.), *Notes from the Third Year*. New York NY: New York Radical Feminists.

Rake, Katherine (2008) 'Stop lap dancing clubs opening', address to public meeting, Fawcett Society and OBJECT, London, 4 November.

Randolph, Sherie M. (2011) 'The lasting legacy of Florynce Kennedy, black feminist fighter', *Solidarity*, <http://www.solidarity-us.org/node/3272> (accessed 29 February 2012).

Raphaely, Vanessa (28 March 2011) 'Want to sell it? Pornify it!', 28 March, <http://hurricanevanessa.com/sometimes-ads-confuse-me/> (accessed 29 February 2012).

Raven, Charlotte (2010) 'How "new feminism" went wrong', *The Guardian*, 6 March, <http://www.guardian.co.uk/books/2010/mar/06/charlotte-raven-feminism-madonna-price> (accessed 26 July 2010).

Reay, Diane (1995) 'Feminist research: the fallacy of easy access', *Women's Studies International Forum* 18 (2): 205–13.

Redden, Guy (2001) 'Networking dissent: the Internet and the anti-globalisation movement', *Mots Pluriel* 18, Queensland.

Redfern, Catherine and Kristin Aune (2010) *Reclaiming the F-Word: The new feminist movement*. London: Zed Books.

Rees, Jeska (2007) 'All the rage: revolutionary feminism in England, 1977–1983'. Unpublished doctoral thesis, University of Western Australia.

Reeves, Carole and Rachel Wingfield (1996) 'Serious porn, serious protest' in L. Harne and E. Miller (eds), *All the Rage: Reasserting radical lesbian feminism*. London: Women's Press.

Reger, Jo (2002) 'More than one feminism: organizational structure and the construction of collective identity' in D. S. Meyer, N. Whittier and B. Robnett (eds), *Social Movements: Identity, culture and the state*. New York NY: Oxford University Press, pp. 171–84.

Reinharz, Shulamit (1985) 'Feminist distrust: problems of context and content in sociological work' in D. Berg and K. Smith (eds), *The Self in Social Inquiry*. Thousand Oaks CA: Sage Publications, pp. 153–72.

—— (1992) *Feminist Methods in Social Research*. Oxford: Oxford University Press.

Rich, Adrienne (1980) *On Lies, Secrets and Silence: Selected prose 1966–1978*. London: Virago.

Richter, Douglas, Allan Henning, Mark Harrison, Yuval Kijel and Marc Jarrett (2011) 'Cams and dating: piracy-proof profits – learn what live and interactive adult entertainment can do for your business', seminar held at Xbiz EU 2011: International Digital Media Conference, London, 22–24 September.

Rogers, Simon (2012) 'UK plastic surgery statistics: breasts up, stomachs in', *The Guardian*, 30 January, <http://www.guardian.co.uk/news/datablog/2012/jan/30/plastic-surgery-statistics-uk> (accessed 29 February 2012).

Rogers, Simon and Sophia Vanco (2011) 'US plastic surgery statistics: breasts up, chins down', *The Guardian*, 27 February, <http://www.guardian.co.uk/news/datablog/2011/jul/22/plastic-surgery-medicine> (accessed 29 February 2012).

Rogg Korsvik, Trine and Ane Stø, (2011) *The Nordic Approach*. Copenhagen: Feminist Group Ottar.

Roiphe, Katie (1994) *The Morning After: Sex, fear, and feminism*. London: Hamish Hamilton.

Roseneil, Sasha (1995) *Disarming Patriarchy: Feminism and political action at Greenham*. Buckingham: Open University Press.

Ross, Tim (2012) 'Top Totty beer deemed far too fruity for House of Commons bar', *The Telegraph*, 2 February.

Rothman, Emily (2011) 'Study of Boston clinic users suggests teen group sex could be emerging public health concern', The Insider, Boston University School of Public Health, 16 December, <http://sph.bu.edu/insider/Recent-News/group-sex-among-adolescents-an-emerging-public-health-concern.html> (accessed 29 February 2012).

Rowbotham, Sheila (1972) 'The beginnings of women's liberation in Britain' in W. Michelene (ed.), *The Body Politic: Writings from the women's liberation movement in Britain, 1969–72*. London: Stage One, pp. 91–102.

—— (1989) *The Past before Us: Feminism in action since the 1960s*. Pandora Press: London.

Rubin, Gayle (1984) 'Thinking sex: notes for a radical theory of the politics of sexuality' in C. Vance (ed.), *Pleasure and Danger*. New York NY: Routledge and Kegan Paul, pp. 267–319.

—— (1993) 'Misguided, dangerous and wrong: an analysis of anti-pornography politics' in A. Assiter and A. Carol (eds), *Bad Girls and Dirty Pictures*. London: Pluto Press, pp. 18–40.

Russell, Diana E. H. (1998) *Dangerous Relationships: Pornography, misogyny and rape*. London: Sage.

Russo, Ann (1998) 'Feminists confront pornography's subordinating practices' in G. Dines, R. Jensen and A. Russo (eds), *Pornography: The production and consumption of inequality*. London: Routledge, pp. 9–36.

Ryan, Barbara (1992) *Feminism and the Women's Movement: Dynamics of change in social movement ideology and activism*. New York NY: Routledge.

Ryan-Flood, Róisín and Rosalind Gill (eds) (2009) *Secrecy and Silence in the Research Process: Feminist reflections*. London: Routledge.

Samuels, Tim (2009) *Hardcore Profits*, BBC2 programme, 30 and 31 August.

Saner, Emine (2009) 'I felt completely violated', *The Guardian*, 25 February.

Sarracino, Carmine and Kevin M. Scott (2008) *The Porning of America: The rise of porn culture, what it means, and where we go from here.* Boston MA: Beacon Press.

Say No/Unite to End Violence against Women (no date) 'Violence against women – facts and figures', <http://saynotoviolence.org/issue/facts-and-figures> (accessed 29 February 2012).

Scharff, Christine M. (2010) 'Young women's negotiations of heterosexual conventions: theorizing sexuality in constructions of "the feminist"', *Sociology* 44 (5): 827–42.

Scottish Government (2000) 'National strategy to address domestic abuse in Scotland', <http://www.scotland.gov.uk/Publications/2003/04/17059> (accessed 25 July 2010).

—— (2009) 'Safer lives, changed lives: a shared approach to tackling violence against women in Scotland', <http://www.scotland.gov.uk/Publications/2009/06/02153519/0> (accessed 25 July 2010).

Segal, Lynne (1993a) 'Does pornography cause violence? The search for evidence' in P. Church Gibson and R. Gibson (eds), *Dirty Looks: Women, pornography, power.* London: British Film Institute, pp. 5–21.

—— (1993b) 'Sweet sorrows, painful pleasures: pornography and the perils of heterosexual desire' in L. Segal and M. McIntosh (eds), *Sex Exposed: Sexuality and the pornography debate.* New Brunswick NJ: Rutgers University Press, pp. 65–91.

—— (2004) 'Only the literal: the contradictions of anti-pornography feminism' in P. Church Gibson (ed.), *More Dirty Looks: Gender, pornography and power.* London: British Film Institute, pp. 59–70.

Segal, Lynn and Mary McIntosh (1993) *Sex Exposed: Sexuality and the pornography debate.* New Brunswick NJ: Rutgers University Press.

Sere, Adrienne (2004) 'Sex and feminism: who is being silenced?' in C. Stark and R. Whisnant (eds), *Not for Sale: Feminists resisting prostitution and pornography.* Melbourne: Spinifex, pp. 278–91.

Sherr Klein, Bonnie (Director) (1981) *Not a Love Story: A film about pornography.* National Film Board of Canada.

Short, Clare (1991) *Dear Clare – This is what women feel about page 3.* London: Hutchinson Radius.

—— (1991) Introduction to *Dear Clare – This is what women feel about page 3*, <http://www.clareshort.co.uk/node/12> (accessed 29 Ferruary 2012).

—— (2004) 'My day in *The Sun* and other page 3 stories', <http://www.independent.co.uk/news/uk/politics/clare-short-my-day-in-the-sun-and-other-page-3-stories-535382.html> (accessed 25 March 2009).

Smelser, N. (1962) *Theory of Collective Behaviour.* London: Routledge and Kegan Paul.

Smith, Clarissa (2007) *One for the Girls! The pleasures and practices of reading women's porn.* London: Intellect.

—— (2007) 'Designed for pleasure: style, indulgence and accessorized sex', *European Journal of Cultural Studies* 10 (2): 167–84.

—— (2009) 'Pleasing intensities: masochism and affective pleasures in porn fictions' in F. Attwood (ed.) (2009) *Mainstreaming Sex: The sexualisation of culture.* London: I. B. Tauris, pp. 19–37.

Snow, David A. (2007) 'Framing processes, ideology, and discursive fields' in D. A. Snow, S. Soule and H. Kriesi (eds), *The Blackwell Companion to Social Movements.* Oxford: Blackwell, pp. 380–412.

Snow, David A., Sarah Soule and Hanspeter Kriesi (eds) (2007) *The Blackwell Companion to Social Movements.* Oxford: Blackwell.

Sorensen, Anette Dina (2003) 'Pornography and gender in mass culture' in *NIKK Magasin 3: The power of gender.* Oslo: Nordic Institute for Women's Studies and Gender Research, pp. 34–6.

Spradley, James (1979) *The Ethnographic Interview.* New York NY: Holt, Rinehart and Winston.

Sprinkle, Annie and Scarlot Harlot (1999) *Annie Sprinkle's Herstory of Porn: From reel to real, 1999* (DVD).

BIBLIOGRAPHY

Stabile, Michael (2012) 'End of the porn golden age' in *Salon*, 3 March <http://life. salon.com/2012/03/03/life_after_the_golden_age_of_porn/singleton/> (accessed 29 February 2012).

Stack, S., I. Wasserman and R. Kern (2004) 'Adult social bonds and use of internet pornography', *Social Science Quarterly* 85 (1): 75–88.

Stark, Christine and Rebecca Whisnant (eds) (2004) *Not for Sale: Feminists resisting prostitution and pornography*. Melbourne: Spinifex.

Stoltenberg, John (2004) 'Pornography and international human rights' in C. Stark and R. Whisnant (eds) (2004) *Not for Sale: Feminists resisting prostitution and pornography*. Melbourne: Spinifex.

Stop Porn Culture (no date) 'Pornography statistics and studies', <http://stoppornculture. org/stats-and-studies/> (accessed 24 May 2009).

Straayer, Chris (1993) 'The seduction of boundaries: feminist fluidity in Annie Sprinkle's art/education/sex' in P. Church Gibson and R. Gibson (eds), *Dirty Looks: Women, pornography, power*. London: British Film Institute, pp. 156–75.

Strossen, Nadine (1995) *Defending Pornography: Free speech, sex and the fight for women's rights*. New York NY: New York University Press.

Tankard Reist, Melinda (ed.) (2009) *Getting Real: Challenging the sexualisation of girls*. Melbourne: Spinifex.

Tankard Reist, Melinda and Abigail Bray (2011) *Big Porn Inc: Exposing the harms of the global pornography industry*. Melbourne: Spinifex Press.

Tarrow, Sydney (1998) *Power in Movement: Social movements, collective action and politics*. Cambridge. Cambridge University Press.

Tasker, Yvonne and Diane Negra (eds) (2007) *Interrogating Postfeminism: Gender and the politics of popular culture*. Durham NC: Duke University Press.

Taylor, Verta (1989) 'Social movement continuity: the women's movement in abeyance', *American Sociological Review* 54 (5): 761–75.

—— (1998) 'Feminist methodology in social movements research', *Qualitative Sociology* 21 (4): 357–79.

—— (1999) 'Gender and social movements: gender processes in women's self-help movements', *Gender and Society* 13 (1): 8–33.

Taylor, Verta and Leila J. Rupp (1993) 'Women's culture and lesbian feminist activism: a reconsideration of cultural feminism', *Signs: Journal of Women in Culture and Society* 19: 32–61.

Taylor, Verta and Nella van Dyke (2007) '"Get up, stand up": tactical repertoires of social movements' in D. A. Snow, S. Soule and H. Kriesi (eds), *The Blackwell Companion to Social Movements*. Oxford: Blackwell, pp. 262–93.

Taylor, Verta and Nancy Whittier (1995) 'Analytical approaches to social movement culture: the culture of the women's movement' in Johnston and Klandermans (eds), *Social Movements and Culture*. Minneapolis MN: University of Minnesota Press, pp. 163–87.

Thomas, Jan E. (1999) '"Everything about us is feminist": the significance of ideology in organisational change', *Gender and Society* 13 (1): 101–19.

Thompson, Linda (2011) 'Misuse of women's images' in 'Rape Crisis Scotland and Women's Support Project News Issue 8' (Spring), <http://www.rapecrisisscotland. org.uk/workspace/publications/Rape_Crisis_News_8.pdf> (accessed 29 February 2012).

Tilly, Charles (1978) *From Mobilization to Revolution*. Reading MA: Addison-Wesley.

—— (1995) *Popular Contention in Great Britain, 1758–1834*. Boulder CO: Paradigm Publishers.

Time Magazine (1970). 'Nation: Women on the march', 7 September.

Tolman, Deborah L. (1998) 'Daring to desire: culture and the bodies of adolescent girls', in R. Weitz (ed.), *The Politics of Women's Bodies: Sexuality, appearance and behaviour*. Oxford: Oxford University Press.

Toynbee, Polly (1981) 'The Williams Committee worked hard. We giggled, and even blushed a bit. Who wouldn't? But now does anyone really care what we decided?', *The Guardian*, 30 October, p. 9.

—— (2008) 'Girlification is destroying all the hope we felt in 1968', *The Guardian*, 15 April, <http://www.guardian.co.uk/society/2008/apr/15/equality.gender> (accessed 8 July 2012).

Turner, Janice (2009a) 'When feminism went nuts', *The Sunday Times*, 5 August, <http://women.timesonline.co.uk/tol/life_and_style/women/article6739270.ece> (accessed 5 August 2009).

—— (2009b) 'It's time to challenge casual sexism', *The Sunday Times*, 28 September, <http://women.timesonline.co.uk/tol/life_and_style/women/article6849600.ece> (accessed 28 September 2009).

—— (2009c) 'The pantechnicon of porn hits a roadblock', *The Sunday Times*, 21 November, <http://www.timesonline.co.uk/tol/comment/columnists/janice_turner/article6926112.ece> (accessed 21 November 2009).

Tyler, Meagan (2010) '"Now that's pornography!": Violence and domination in adult video news' in K. Boyle (ed.), *Everyday Pornography*. London: Routledge.

—— (2011a) *Selling Sex Short: The pornographic and sexological construction of women's sexuality in the West*. Newcastle: Cambridge Scholars.

—— (2011b) 'A new anti-porn feminism?', paper presented at 'The Futures of Feminism: New Directions in Feminist, Women's and Gender Studies', Annual Feminist and Women's Studies Association (FWSA) Conference, 5–7 July 2011, Brunel University.

UK Ministry of Justice (2009) Information Policy Division, Circular No. 2009/01, 'Possession of extreme pornographic images and increase in the maximum sentence for offences under the Obscene Publications Act 1959: implementation of Sections 63–67 and Section 71 of the Criminal Justice and Immigration Act 2008', 19 January.

UN (2010) 'The world's women 2010: trends and statistics', <http://unstats.un.org/unsd/demographic/products/Worldswomen/WW_full%20report_BW.pdf> (accessed 29 February 2012).

Urwin, Rosamund (2011) 'March of the new feminists', 8 June, <http://www.thisislondon.co.uk/news/march-of-the-new-feminists-6409290.html> (accessed 29 February 2012).

van Aelst, Peter and Stefaan Walgrave (2001) 'Who is that wo(man) in the street? From the normalisation of protest to the normalisation of the protestor', *European Journal of Political Research* 39 (4): 461–86.

van Heeswijk, Anna (2011) 'OBJECT: challenging 'sex-object culture' in M. Tankard Reist and A. Bray (eds), *Big Porn Inc: Exposing the harms of the global pornography industry*. Melbourne: Spinifex Press, pp. 274–80.

Vance, Carole (ed.) (1984) *Pleasure and Danger*. New York NY: Routledge and Kegan Paul.

Viner, Katharine (2002) 'While we were shopping...', *The Guardian*, 5 June, <http://www.guardian.co.uk/world/2002/jun/05/gender.katharineviner> (accessed 1 July 2008).

Walby, Sylvia (1990) *Theorizing Patriarchy*. Oxford: Blackwell.

Walch, J. (1999) *In the Net: An internet guide for activists*. London: Zed Books.

Walker, Alice (1983) *In Search of Our Mothers' Gardens: Womanist prose*. New York NY: Harcourt Brace Jovanovich.

Walker, Rebecca (ed.) (1995) *To Be Real: Telling the truth and changing the face of feminism*. London: Anchor Books.

Walter, Natasha (1998) *The New Feminism*. London.

—— (2010) *Living Dolls: The return of sexism*. London: Virago.

Waters, Melanie (2007) 'Sexing it up? Women, pornography and third wave feminism' in S. Gillis, G. Howie and R. Munford (eds), *Third Wave Feminism: A critical exploration*. Basingstoke: Palgrave Macmillan, pp. 250–65.

Weir, Angela and Elizabeth Wilson (1984) 'The British women's movement', *New Left Review*, 148.

Whelehan, Imelda (1995) *Modern Feminist Thought.* Edinburgh: Edinburgh University Press.

—— (2000) *Overloaded: Popular culture and the future of feminism.* London: Women's Press.

—— (2007) 'Foreword' in S. Gillis, G. Howie and R. Munford (eds), *Third Wave Feminism: A critical exploration* (second edition). Basingstoke: Palgrave Macmillan.

Whillock, Rita Kirk (1995) 'The use of hate as a stratagem for achieving political and social goals' in R. K. Whillock and D. Slayden (eds), *Hate Speech.* Thousand Oaks, CA: Sage, pp. 28–54.

Whisnant, Rebecca (2001) 'Beyond multiple choice', <http://www.saidit.org/archives/mar01/article1.html> (accessed 15 May 2010).

—— (2004) 'Confronting pornography – some conceptual basics' in C. Stark and R. Whisnant (eds), *Not for Sale: Feminists resisting prostitution and pornography.* Melbourne: Spinifex.

—— (2007) 'Not your father's playboy, not your mother's feminist movement', paper given at conference on 'Pornography and Pop Culture: Re-framing Theory, Re-thinking Activism', Boston, 24 March 2007.

—— (2009) 'It's easy out there for a pimp', paper given at the conference on 'Challenging Demand', Women's Support Project, Glasgow, 4–5 March, 2009.

—— (2010) 'From Jekyll to Hyde: the grooming of male pornography consumers' in K. Boyle (ed.), *Everyday Pornography.* London: Routledge, pp. 114–33.

Whitehead, Kally and Tim Kurz (2009) '"Empowerment" and the pole: a discursive investigation of the reinvention of pole dancing as a recreational activity', *Feminism and Psychology* 19 (2): 224–44.

Whittier, Nancy (1995) *Feminist Generation: The persistence of the radical.* Philadelphia PA: Temple University Press.

—— (2003) 'Sustaining commitment among radical feminists' in J. Goodwin and J. M. Jasper (eds), *The Social Movements Reader: Cases and concepts.* Oxford: Blackwell, pp. 103–15.

Williams Committee (1979) *Inquiry into Obscenity and Film Censorship.* London: Home Office.

Williams, Linda (1999) *Hardcore: Power, pleasure and the frenzy of the 'visible',* expanded edition. Berkeley CA: University of California Press.

—— (ed.) (2004) *Porn Studies.* Durham NC: Duke University Press.

Wilson, E. (1993) 'Feminist fundamentalism: the shifting politics of sex and censorship' in L. Segal and M. McIntosh (eds), *Sex Exposed: Sexuality and the pornography debate.* New Brunswick NJ: Rutgers University Press.

Wilson-Kovacs, Dana (2009) 'Some texts do it better: women, sexually explicit texts and the everyday' in F. Attwood (ed.), *Mainstreaming Sex: The sexualisation of culture.* London: I. B. Tauris, pp. 147–64.

Wolf, Naomi (1991) *The Beauty Myth: How images of beauty are used against women.* London: Vintage.

—— (1993) *Fire with Fire.* London: Chatto and Windus.

Woodward, Kath and Sophie Woodward (2009) *Why Feminism Matters: Feminism lost and found.* Hampshire: Palgrave.

XBIZ EU Event Schedule (2011) <http://www.xbizeu.com/schedule.php> (accessed 29 February 2012).

Zurbriggen, E. L. *et al.* (2007) 'Report of the APA task force on the sexualization of girls', American Psychological Association, Washington, <http://www.apa.org/pi/women/programs/girls/report-full.pdf> (accessed 4 April 2008).

INDEX

knowledge transfer, intergenerational,
151
Kramer, Henry, 124

labiaplasty(ies), 117, increase in, 2
'lads' mags', 1-2, 5, 44, 51, 59, 78, 118, 151;
campaigns against, 152, 177
Lady Chatterly's Lover, Penguin Books
trial, 57
Langton, Rae, 79
lap-dancing clubs, 118, 136, 151; increase
of, 2; regulatory re-licensing demand,
158-9, 168-9, 173; stunts against, 170;
women from, 172
Lee jeans, advertisment, 122
Leeds, sex-shop arsonists, 28
Lennox, Annie, 187
'Let Girls Be Girls' campaign', 'Mumsnet',
126
Lévêque, Sandrine, 169
liberalism, language of, 176; liberal social
theory, 62-4
libertarianism, 93
London: 'Angry Women', 28; anti-porn
actions, 153
London AntiPorn Group, 1970s, 188, 212
London Feminist Network, 137, 147, 150,
155, 159, 167, 184, 187, 194
London Revolutionary Feminist Anti-
Pornography Conference, 25-6
Longford Inquiry, 57
Longhurst, Liz, 174
Lorde, Audre, 47, 215
love, 'moralistic' smear, 214
Lovelace, Linda, 21

MacKay, Finn, 137, 150
MacKinnon, Catharine, 4, 33, 36-7, 58-60,
91, 94; *see also*, Dworkin-MacKinnon
Ordinance
Madeley, Chloe, 98
Madeley, Richard, 98
Mahon, Alice, 40
Maiguascha, Bice, 195
Mailer, Norman, 15
male demand, reality of erased, 83
male domination: replication potential,
190; structure of, 71; subjectivity, 78-9
male gaze, 77, 99, 100
'male in the head', 86
male violence, 16; media representations,
20; revolutionary feminist focus on,
26; second wave focus, 18; service for
victims of, 69; WLM agenda against,
22
Manwin, company, 114

Maran, Josie, 122
market, male-dominated, 92
Marks and Spencers, campaign against,
151
marriage, conservative ideal of, 61
Marxism, UK feminism, 15
masculinity: construction of, 130;
hegemonic, 165
Max Factor *Self-Defense*, campaign
against, 20
McGlynn, Clare, 176
McNair, Brian, 111-12, 117, 131, 133-4
McNeill, Sandra, 155
McRobbie, Angela, 51-2, 200
media: gender biases, 135; misreporting
potential, 172
men, anti-porn involvement, 187
menstruation, taboos, 124
Millett, Kate, 14
Million Women Rise marches, 147, 167,
171, 184-5, 187, 191
Minaj, Nicki, 2
Minneapolis, 33; hearings, 40; ordinance,
35-6
minority groups, 89
Miriam, Kathy, 44-5, 102
Miss America beauty pageant, 1968, 17
Miss World contest, London 1970, 17
Miss World contest, 2011 protest, 184-5,
198
Mitchell, Juliet, 15
Mitchell, Sharon, 113
mobile phone companies, 97; 3G, 116
mobilisation, 'incubatary' stages, 149
Monbiot, George, 93
moral panic, 62
moralism, language of, 176
Mordan, Rebecca, 154
Morgan, Robin, 19
Mormino, Maria, 195
Mott, Rebecca, 154, 186
Mowlam, Mo
MPs, UK Conservative, 38
multiplicity, uncritical celebration of, 201
Mumsnet, 129
Murdoch, Rupert, Labour Party
Courtship, 49
Murray, Pauli, 14
music, 171; videos, 117
MySpace, 116
Myth of the Vaginal Orgasm, The, 17

National Council for Civil Liberties, 39
National Organisation of Women
(NOW), USA, 13-14

INDEX